A Guide to
Charter Schools

Research and Practical
Advice for Educators

Edited by Myron S. Kayes
and Robert Maranto

ROWMAN & LITTLEFIELD EDUCATION
Lanham • *New York* • *Toronto* • *Oxford*

Published in the United States of America
by Rowman & Littlefield Education
A Division of Rowman & Littlefield Publishers, Inc.
A wholly owned subsidiary of The Rowman & Littlefield Publishing Group, Inc.
4501 Forbes Boulevard, Suite 200, Lanham, Maryland 20706
www.rowmaneducation.com

PO Box 317
Oxford
OX2 9RU, UK

British Library Cataloguing in Publication Information Available

Library of Congress Cataloging-in-Publication Data

A guide to charter schools : research and practical advice for educators / edited by
Myron S. Kayes and Robert Maranto.
     p. cm.
Includes bibliographical references and index.
ISBN 1-57886-404-6 (cloth : alk. paper) — ISBN 1-57886-405-4 (pbk. : alk. paper)
ISBN 978-1-57886-404-1   ISBN 978-1-57886-405-8
1. Charter schools—United States. 2. Educational change—United States. 3.
School improvement programs—United States.   I. Kayes, Myron S., 1947–   II.
Maranto, Robert, 1958–
LB2806.36.G847 2006
371.01—dc22   2005037699

Contents

List of Figures and Tables

FIGURES

v

TABLES

1

Charter Schools and School Reform: What We Know and Where We'll Go

Robert Maranto, Myron S. ("Mike" or "M. S.") Kayes, and April Gresham Maranto

Before the charter school law, I was going to quit teaching and open a bookstore. The [school] district would never let me have this kind of program.

—A former district school teacher
who now runs two successful charter schools.

The district schools are a big cruise ship . . . they offer a little of everything for everybody, but you have to go with the cruise and you can't go off on your own, and they can't turn around very easily. The charters are little sailboats. They don't offer as many things, but if you decide to change course and check out an island, you can do it. You are more on your own.

—A former district school administrator
who now consults for charter schools.

REINVENTING PUBLIC EDUCATION

From a mere notion of education reformers in the 1980s, charter schools have become the most dynamic and potentially most revolutionary contemporary school reform (Hassel, 1999). The first charter school opened in Minnesota in 1991. As of January 2005, an estimated 3,400 charter schools educate over 800,000 students in 38 states and the District of Columbia; thus, charters serve more than five times the number of students currently using

1

public and private voucher systems (Center for Education Reform, 2005). As of this writing, only ten states have no charter law.

What are charter schools? Charter schools are public schools which receive a charter contract from a public authority to operate for a specified period of time, to provide students a particular educational program and achieve specified results, often as measured by standardized tests. Supported by President George W. Bush, former President Clinton, and Senator John Kerry, charter schools combine the best of public and private sector education. Like other public schools, charters are approved by public authorities, cannot discriminate in admissions, must offer special education, and must abide by public testing and financial accountability requirements. Yet charter schools "reinvent" public education, since like private schools, charters have substantial autonomy over their personnel, curricula, and schedules. Charter teachers and administrators are usually "at-will" employees rather than tenured civil servants. Charters often offer unusual curricula (such as Montessori or Spaulding Phonics) and nonstandard schedules (i.e., extended days, year-round, etc.).

Further, charters are market-based schools: parents *choose* to send their children to charter schools rather than being assigned to a school based on attendance boundaries. Charters thus face market accountability: if parents pull out their children, some school staff lose their jobs. If too many parents leave, the school closes. Charters are also held accountable to public authorities, which can close schools which fail to meet the goals specified in their charters. The "charter bargain" offers schools autonomy in exchange for academic results (Finn et al. 2000; Gill et al. 2001; Maranto 2001, 2003; Milliman et al. 2004; Murphy and Shiffman, 2002; Nathan, 1996).

While charter schools often have a difficult first year and about 6 percent of those opened have closed, research shows that most charter schools succeed. Charter parents, students, and teachers rate their schools far more favorably than do parents in traditional public schools. Charter parents and students who transferred from traditional public schools also grade the charters more favorably, often by 50 percent margins! In aggregate, charters do not have higher test scores than traditional public schools; yet three of the four studies of student academic growth ("value added") find that charters do a bit better than traditional public schools, even while spending less. Charters frequently use innovative educational programs and personnel practices. Indeed, in fieldwork, Robert Maranto has identified more than thirty innovations introduced or developed by individual charter operators. Further, charters are apparently no more segregated than traditional public schools (Finn et al. 2000; Gill et al. 2001; Maranto 2001, 2003; Milliman et al. 2004; Murphy and Shiffman, 2002; Nathan, 1996). Finally, there is growing evidence that district schools improve in response to the market pressures exerted by charter schools, particularly where state funds follow parental enrollment decisions (Hess et al. 2001; Maranto et al. 2001).

Perhaps most importantly, since they gain funding based on the number of parents who *choose* to enroll their children, charter schools are parent-centered. Traditional public schools, all too often, are not (McDermott 1999). While charters must find a willing market niche and please those parents, conventional public schools need only please elected officials, organized interests, and regulators. One of the editors of this book was reminded of this recently, when he sought to visit a traditional public school in his district. After leaving three messages at the principal's office during business hours over a three-week period, none of which were returned, he finally had a brief phone conversation with a principal's assistant:

Parent: "Hi, I'm Bob Maranto. I'm a parent who lives in ___ Elementary's attendance zone. My son will be old enough for kindergarten next fall. He's actually right on the edge so he could go next fall or the following fall, and I was wondering if I could come visit the school sometime."

School Official: "We don't have any visiting this year. We're doing construction and a lot of things are going on, but the first two weeks of March for Kindergarten registration you can come in the school. It will be advertised in the paper and TV."

Parent: "Could I watch a class in session?"

School Official: "No, even when there's no construction you could not watch a class."

Parent: "Well, could I meet my son's teacher?"

School Official: "No, the teachers are busy teaching all day and then they go home."

While this school district spends more than $20,000 per child annually, even that was apparently not enough for its "public" schools to be open to *the public*. Rather, the school has customer service worthy of the department of motor vehicles. A charter school with similar practices would soon close for lack of parents.

While some fear that charter schools work as a right-wing attack on public education (e.g., Wells 2002, and see Kayes in the final chapter of this book), Republican-leaning states, in fact, have no more charter schools per capita, nor stronger charter laws. Indeed, states more apt to vote for Democratic presidential candidates actually have more charter school campuses and stronger charter laws. States with lower National Assessment of Education Progress (NAEP) scores have more charter schools, mainly since troubled policy makers may try charters in response to district school failure. Similarly, states with greater numbers of African American and Hispanic students have more charters. Finally, and perhaps most importantly, states with larger numbers of smaller school districts have fewer charter schools. This may reflect Maranto's Law: *whoever runs the local school district hates charter schools, and whoever does not run the local school district loves charter schools.* Thus, in Republican rural Virginia, charters are championed by countercultural parents who vote Democratic (or Green), in moderate Colorado suburbs they are backed by saved Christians who vote Republican, and everywhere charters are loved by disempowered ethnic minorities. In states with many small school districts, like Pennsylvania, New Hampshire, and Nebraska, district officials know and cultivate relationships with local businesses and political leaders, who view the local public schools as "their" schools and fight efforts to pass and implement strong charter laws. And even if a charter law does pass, local notables may use zoning decisions or "persuasion" to keep charters out. (One businesswoman we know insists that no one in her small town who relies on government contracts has the guts to help a charter.) In contrast, where school districts are very large, district leaders may lose touch with local business elites and political activists, and thus cannot protect themselves from charter inroads (Schmidt et al., 2003).

WHAT FOLLOWS

Over a decade into the charter movement, social scientists have produced a robust academic literature on charter schools, most notably Chester E. Finn, et al.'s *Charter Schools in Action,* Joseph Murphy and Catherine Dunn Shiffman's *Understanding and Assessing the Charter School Movement,* and Brian P. Gill, et al.'s *Rhetoric Versus Reality: What We Know and What We Need to Know About Vouchers and Charter Schools,* discussed in chapter 9 below. While useful, these works are geared to academics, not to busy charter school operators, state policy makers, school board members, and interested parents. There are now in excess of 800,000 students and more than one million parents, friends, educators, and others intimately participating in the charter school movement. Indeed, books for this audience, along with charter operators, administrators, and teachers simply do not exist. Yet these educational stakeholders both want and need information in an understandable form to help them face the challenges of running, working in, or using a charter. Accordingly, the edited volume which follows offers a user-friendly review of existing writings, plus some new pieces, on charters and how to make them work better, by bringing together the best of the *National Charter School Clearinghouse Review* (NCSCR), the first academic journal on charter schools, which had as its mission "bringing useful ideas, humor, and non-boring scholarship" to the charter school community.

SCHOOL REFORMS PAST:
TEACHER ABUSE AND WHY WE NEED CHARTER SCHOOLS

In the first section, we discuss school reforms present and past, explaining the need for charter schools. In chapter 2, charter authorizer Liane Zimney reviews Tyack and Cuban's *Tinkering Toward Utopia*, summarizing the various education reform movements of the past hundred years and arguing that the "next big thing in American education" will be the small schools movement. Zimney follows with a brief description of Oakland's Small Autonomous Schools Policy. She maintains that small schools will succeed because the change is comprehensible and welcome to teachers and laypeople, is linked to "goals of achieving excellence and equity," has demonstrated results that outweigh difficulties of change, has political support from powerful sponsors, and can be easily replicated.

In chapter 3, *Big City Schools Are Not in Kansas: Why It's Impossible to Save City Schools Without School Choice*, Robert Maranto summarizes a recent multiyear NSF research program searching for successful, long-lasting reforms in big city schools—and coming up empty. Maranto describes why cities seem unable to reform their schools. Essentially, big city schools find it impossible to agree on a reform path (and on superintendents to implement that path) for the required decade or so. School choice, in contrast, offers a way out of policy stalemate. Similarly, in chapter 4, American Enterprise Institute scholar Frederick M. Hess describes *The Spinning Wheels: The Politics of Urban School Reform*, summarizing his award-winning book of the same title. Hess examines the paradoxically damaging nature of education's constant waves of reform and recommends reform grounded in a stable, supportive community environment. He notes the usefulness of choice-based and standards-based reforms in assuaging a need for immediate visible improvement.

While the first chapters discuss the macro politics of education reform, later chapters examine the real world inside conventional public schools. In chapter 5, Robert Maranto steps up to the plate with *R-E-S-P-E-C-T: Teacher Abuse and How to Stop It*. Reviewing some of the most credible works on school management, Richard Ingersoll's *Who Controls Teachers' Work?* and Normal Dale Norris's *Perspectives on the Mistreatment of American Education*, Maranto argues that the bureaucratic practices of traditional public schools discourage collaboration and alienate or drive out the most capable teachers. While Ingersoll and Norris describe the disease, Edward J. Dirkswager's *Teachers as Owners* offers the cure. Describing the Edvisions cooperative, Dirkswager (and Maranto) argue for treating teachers as autonomous professionals free to make their own decisions, but also held accountable for results, just like doctors and accountants.

However teachers are treated, do more of them make a difference? In chapter 6, *Smaller Classes or Better Teachers*, former UCLA dean Lewis C. Solmon and scholar Kimberly Firetag Agam review the education literature on class size and teacher quality. They report that while class size has little impact on student performance, teacher quality has tremendous import. Unfortunately, efforts to lower class size often result in hiring larger numbers of lower quality teachers. The authors propose merit pay for more effective teachers, a personnel policy more compatible with charters rather than district schools. Yet Solmon and Agam acknowledge that traditional merit pay programs have failed since they discouraged collaboration. Accordingly, they propose using the Teacher Advancement Program (TAP) developed by the Milken Family Foundation and show that this program, by combining individual and school-level incentives, has succeeded where other merit pay plans fail.

Chapter 7 also tackles the alleged teacher shortage. In *Why Certified Teachers Aren't in the Classroom*, Morrison Institute researcher Rebecca Gau and Western Michigan University professor Louann Bierlein Palmer survey inactive but certified teachers in Arizona, showing that most leave for personal reasons, though pay and school climate also matter. Thus, we could easily end the "teacher shortage" by improving either teacher pay or school climate. Charter schools have the greatest potential to do the latter. Also tackling teacher certification, chapter 8, *Where's the Alternative? Identifying, Training, and Certifying* by Amy Ashley and Mike Kayes, advocates alternative certification. The authors propose that alternative certification find some way to incorporate interpersonal connectivity, verbal ability, and creative thinking, while discussing current alternative certification programs such as NBPTS and ABCTE.

CURING THE DISEASE: THE RESEARCH ON CHARTER SCHOOLS

While the first section discusses reforms of public education, our middle chapters describe the research on charter schools. In chapter 9, teasingly titled *Revenge of the (Nerdy) Professors: Scholarly Research on Charter Schools and Why It Matters*, Robert Maranto summarizes the state of charter school research. As noted above, most studies show that charter schools succeed, yet as in any research, the findings one gets depend on the questions one asks. If one asks whether charters—at least charters more than two years old—work better than nearby district schools, the answer seems to be yes. If, on the other hand, one asks whether *all* charters work well, or whether charters have brought the sort of revolution that some supporters promised, the answers are less positive. Among all the recent charter works, Maranto argues that the Rand Foundation's *Rhetoric Versus Reality: What We Know and What We Need to Know about Vouchers and Charter Schools* offers the most complete, most readable, and most honest assessment of school choice generally and charter schools in particular.

In chapter 10, *Personnel Policy in Traditional Public, Charter, and Private Schools*, University of Missouri economist Michael Podgursky reports preliminary results comparing personnel policies in traditional public, private, and charter schools from a major new national survey conducted by the U.S. Department of Education. He finds that charters take advantage of the relaxed regulations to create more innovative, flexible personnel policies in terms of setting teacher salaries, not requiring certification, eschewing collective bargaining agreements, using merit pay, and dismissing poor performers. Thus, they resemble private schools much more than traditional public schools, and offer considerable potential to improve public education.

In chapter 11, *The Future of Chartered Schools—The Supply Side*, Progressive Policy Institute scholar Bryan C. Hassel describes the unique challenges facing the current charter movement. Charters' maverick style and small, independent status make possible their creative approaches, which characterize the movement. Yet many charters must scale up and expand their unique innovations to other schools and sites to prevent the movement from being an evolutionary dead end. Hassel analyzes and compares the abilities of EMOs (Educational Management Organizations), leadership development, and foundation-supported school expansion programs in enabling chartered schools to take this next step in expansion. Finally, he calls for institutions to fill the critical gap of helping chartered schools select and monitor their vital support services (e.g., legal, accounting, etc.) and points out the need for greater scope, intensity, and diversity of services.

While the small size of most charters offers many advantages, it can also make it difficult for charters to adapt to the accountability demands of the No Child Left Behind Act. In chapter 12, *Charter School Accountability Issues—Pragmatic or Practical*, university charter educator Heather Boyer offers a participant observer case study of a Texas charter school, examining its difficulties with rules and regulations based on charter accountability. The school's small size and nontraditional population hamper its ability to meet accountability measures designed for larger and more conventional public schools.

Among other things, No Child Left Behind requires that every public school student have a qualified, though not necessarily certified, teacher. In most states, charter schools are already partly exempted from traditional teacher certification requirements. Research suggests that this may in fact offer an advantage to charters. In chapter 13, *Teacher Quality Leadership from Public Charter Schools*, Michael Poliakoff, the creator of the American Board for Certification of Teacher Excellence project, reviews the literature on teacher quality, certification, and alternative certification, finding no link between certification and student learning. Thus, charters potentially can use their freedom from conventional certification requirements to recruit well-qualified nontraditional educators.

Do charters founded by different entities differ? For example, for-profit operators may be less effective or more elitist than not-for-profits, as Miron and Nelson (2002) suggest. In chapter 14, *Charter School Operators and Charter School Operations*, Teachers College (Columbia University) political scientist Jeff Henig and his collaborators summarize results from a survey of charter operators to see if those founded by businesses differ from those founded by parents or educators. The authors find relatively few differences, though for-profit operators are slightly more likely to develop larger schools and more likely to focus on elementary grades, perhaps since these offer the best possibility for profits.

PERSONAL REFLECTIONS: TIPS AND HORROR STORIES FROM CHARTER OPERATORS AND CHARTER CONSULTANTS

While previous chapters cover school reforms and charter reforms generally and thus appeal to general readers and students of public schooling, the final section provides tips and stories by and for charter operators and consultants—the real world of charter education.

Most notably, as Joe Nathan (1996) reported nearly a decade ago, new charters typically have a tough time. In chapter 15, *How the Best Laid Schemes Go Astray: The Agony and (Occasional) Ecstasy of Charter Start-ups*, Robert Maranto reviews some of the most prominent works about new charter schools. Journalist Jonathan Schorr's *Hard Lessons* describes the horrid first year of two inner city Oakland charters, while education professor Patty Yancey's *Parents Founding Charter Schools* explains the difficulties faced by parents going into education. In contrast, charter educator James Nehring's *Upstart Startup* describes a successful Massachusetts charter, a part of the Coalition of Essential Schools. Taken together, these works give basic lessons about the difficulties of starting charter schools: start early, hire carefully, make use of education professionals, and most important, assure that all parents and teachers agree on the school mission long before the first day of classes, and if possible, before the first staff are hired.

While most charters are new schools, more than a tenth have "converted," having previously operated either as private schools or as conventional public schools. In chapter 16, *Whose Idea Was This Anyway? The Challenging Metamorphosis from Private to Charter*, Montessori School of Flagstaff operator Jim Spencer humorously describes how he converted his private school to a charter school. Going public gave Spencer's schools more resources to develop better education, but also brought paperwork, oversight, and resentment from traditional public schools. It also meant an end to exclusive admissions. Still, Spencer would do it all over again since "the pioneers tend to get all the arrows, but they also get to be the first to cross the Rockies and see the Pacific."

In chapter 17, *If You Build It, They Will Come*, financial adviser John Buck offers an amusing but informative informal discussion of facilities management that tells operators how to get the loan to buy or build a facility, whether to buy one or build one, where to go for money, and how to decide what you want before actually trying to obtain a facility. Buck does the impossible by making facilities fun. This is a must-read for charter operators, especially those planning to expand. Similarly, in chapter 18, *Measurement: The Key to Charter School Marketing*, Mackinac Center for Public Policy analyst Brian L. Carpenter explains the necessity of marketing one's school to ensure viability. He explains key marketing principles, including how to create a favorable impression in the minds of prospective students/parents. Most importantly, he explains the importance of measurement, which can be broken down into data collection, analysis, creativity, and evaluation. In other words, know your audience, your target population, catchment area data, and all internal data about your school's performance before you design creative pieces to draw students in. Finally, evaluate whether or not your creative pieces are working better than no advertising.

All schools need more money, but charter schools, which lack bonding authority and typically get about a quarter less than traditional public schools, are in special need. To remedy this, in chapter 19, *When Charter Schools Have a Distinct Advantage over Districts: Show Me the (Grant) Money*, Amy Ashley and Mike Kayes examine educational philanthropy. They conclude that charter schools, being smaller and more community-oriented, are better able to win both corporate and foundation grants than their public district counterparts. They offer tips about how to do so.

Every educator possesses horror stories, but because they are new, different, and often hated by establishment educators, charter operators almost certainly have more than their share. Accordingly, chapter 20 offers three horror stories, told to Robert Maranto by three charter operators, with the names changed to protect the guilty. In *Death by Process or Special Ed Blackmail*, a "special education" student with a highly idiosyncratic diagnosis held up a school for an unusual amount of accommodation, demands waived once monetary payment was offered. Think open racism is a thing of the past? Think again. In *What Do You Want to Work with Those F—in' N—s For?*, a charter operator buys a site for his mainly African American school in a mainly white neighborhood. Local officials refuse to approve the necessary permits—until the charter operator threatens to register his parents to vote in the next election! Finally, *Why the Ed Business is Like No Business* describes how a state's first cyber charter was first approved and then dismantled by jealous state regulatory officials reacting to local district complaints of losing students (and dollars). State regulators found that they could end the school by failing to enforce regulations requiring that traditional school districts pay the money they owed the cyber charter. This is a tale of egos and money, with education only rarely mattering to state and local "educators."

Finally, in chapter 21, *Charting the Future*, the editors debate the future of charter schools in particular, and school choice in general, as a sort of he said/he said forum. Mike Kayes fears that the charter movement is being hijacked by conservatives who are hostile to public schools generally. Further, he fears that vouchers, in particular, threaten to erode our traditional separation of church and state. Finally, Kayes laments that charters have shown less academic success than he, and many other supporters, had predicted. Robert Maranto, in contrast, sees charters and vouchers as positive developments, which help kids and parents by making public education more public and by somewhat improving academic performance. Such trends as more intensive child-raising and the enhancement of individual choice make increased school choice a near certainty. Charters, moreover, might be more apt to take off than vouchers for a variety of institutional and ideological reasons. Yet challenges remain. Just as past reform movements such as civil service reform, the women's movement, and the civil rights movement took decades to advance against powerful counter ideas and entrenched interests, charter schools might be more likely to help our grandchildren than our children.

REFERENCES

Center for Education Reform. 2005. Charter School Highlights and Statistics, accessed at http://edreform.com/pubs/chglance.htm on April 28, 2005.

Finn, Chester E., Bruno V. Manno, and Gregg Vanourek. 2000. *Charter Schools in Action*. Princeton: Princeton University Press.

Gill, Brian P., P. Michael Timpane, Karen E. Ross, and Dominic J. Brewer. 2001. *Rhetoric Versus Reality: What We Know and What We Need to Know about Vouchers and Charter Schools*. Santa Monica: Rand Education.

Hassel, Bryan C. 1999. *The Charter School Challenge*. Washington: Brookings Institution.

Hess, F., R. Maranto, and S. Milliman. 2001. "Coping with Competition: The Impact of Charter Schooling on Public School Outreach in Arizona," *Policy Studies Journal*, 29 (3): 388–404.

Maranto, R. 2003. "Lobbying in Disguise: The American Federation of Teachers 'Studies' Charter Schools," *Education Next*, 3, no. 1 (winter): 79–84; accessible at www.educationnext.org/20031/79.html.

Maranto, R., S. R. Milliman, F. Hess, and A. W. Gresham, eds. 2001. *School Choice in the Real World: Lessons from Arizona Charter Schools*. Boulder: Westview.

Maranto, R. (2001). "The Death of One Best Way: Charter Schools as Reinventing Government." In *School Choice in the Real World: Lessons from Arizona Charter Schools*, ed. R. Maranto, S. Milliman, F. Hess, and A. Gresham, 39–57. Boulder: Westview.

McDermott, Kathryn. 1999. *Controlling Public Education: Localism versus Equity*. Lawrence: University Press of Kansas.

Milliman, S., R. Maranto, and A. Gresham. 2004. "Does School Choice Segregate or Integrate Public Schools? Arizona Charter Schools as a Test Case," *Journal of Public Management and Social Policy*, 8, no. 2: 1–22.

Miron, Gary, and Christopher Nelson. 2002. *What's Public about Charter Schools?* Thousand Oaks: Corwin Press.

Murphy, Joseph, and Catherine Dunn Shiffman. 2002. *Understanding and Assessing the Charter School Movement.* New York: Teachers College Press.

Nathan, Joe. 1996. *Charter Schools.* San Francisco: Jossey-Bass.

B. D. Schmidt, Robert Maranto, and M. S. Kayes. 2003. "Charter Schools, Not of the Party, But of the People: A Quick and Dirty Analysis," *NCSC Review* 2: 1–7, accessed at www.nationalcharterschoolclearinghouse.net/NCSCReview/Edition Two.pdf.

Wells, Amy Stuart, ed. 2002. *Where Charter School Policy Fails.* New York: Teachers College Press.

2

Book Review: *Tinkering Toward Utopia: A Century of Public School Reform*

Liane Zimny

I beseech you to treasure up in your hearts these my parting words: Be ashamed to die until you have won some victory for Humanity.

—Horace Mann (in an address to the graduating class of Antioch College, June 1859, two months before his death). Horace Mann was the first secretary of the Massachusetts Board of Education, the nation's first state Board of Education and president of Antioch College, and is also known as "the Father of American Education."

PART I

Why Is Education Tough to Reform?

Education reforms share much in common with dieting: Both are easy to launch, hard to sustain, and subject to interpretation and adaptation during implementation. Both are likely to achieve varied results depending on the individuals and unique circumstances involved. Both are subject to faddish enthusiasms for easy quick fixes that may demonstrate some initial success, but not healthy, sustained improvement.

Both education reform and dieting are most likely to be successful when the implementers are not only internally motivated, but also supported by the life systems around them. Implementation is likely to continue when the essential changes are easy to understand and implement and do not require dramatic changes from known behaviors. Both are most likely to achieve and maintain their long-term desired outcomes when undertaken as a long-term sustained effort to implement changes that feel fun, offer variety, and generate high self-esteem and energy in the implementers.

Which Reforms Have Had the Most Impact over Time?

The reforms that have had the most impact over time are the reforms that reflect a deep understanding of how humans behave in relationship to each other and to their institutions. David Tyack and Larry Cuban isolate the main institution and the key people in education reform when they emphasize the need for "a sophisticated understanding of *the school as an institution* [and] insight into *the culture of teachers* [emphasis added]" (Tyack and Cuban 1995, 113). Throughout *Tinkering Toward Utopia,* Tyack and Cuban identify specific factors that enhance the impact of educational reforms:

- Propitious timing.
- Political support from powerful sponsors.
- Freezing reforms into regulations and laws.
- Interlocking reforms with other systems.
- Linking reforms to broader social movements.
- Clearly demonstrable advantages that outweigh the burdens of implementing change.
- Easy replication (Tyack and Cuban 1995, 107–8)

The presence of these factors has helped assure the continuing impact of Horace Mann's reforms from the first half of the nineteenth century, for example. Of these factors, interlocking reforms with other systems and linking reforms to broader social movements were the most critical to the endurance of his reforms. Education reforms have the most impact when they promote philosophies that are in harmony with a broad array of values in other institutions. Education reformers may succeed at the front of a wave of change, but they will not endure if they remain disconnected from other political, economic, social, or religious values.

Mann led efforts to standardize the offering of American education in the 1830s and 1840s as a means of securing the Protestant republican ideals of a literate, moral citizenry (Tyack and Cuban 1995, 1, 2, 141). Mann's selection as the first secretary of education to the nation's first state Board of Education (in Massachusetts) was the result of propitious (and probably political) circumstances. Mann was a senator at that time and voted in favor of establishing the new board, but he was not the primary promoter of the concept.

As the secretary of education, Mann linked his reforms to broader social movements in a dozen annual reports on "the integral relationship between education, freedom, and republican government." Mann believed that the primary goal of school was to promote the social harmony that he believed would result if schools were available and equal for rich and poor alike. Poverty would decline as education tapped natural abilities and led to greater economic prosperity. He also expected a more broadly educated populace would be less likely to engage in crime, violence, or fraud. Mann wanted a system of public common schools that would be a "wellspring" of freedom and a "ladder of opportunity" (Cremin 1957, 8).

Mann's desire to create a system of education that would foster a critical-thinking populace had the powerful political support of Daniel Webster, notable orator, lawyer, and U.S. senator from Massachusetts, who entreated, "Make them intelligent, and they will be vigilant—give them the means of detecting wrong, and they will apply the remedy."

Mann froze his reforms into regulations and laws and interlocked them with other systems. He persuaded the Massachusetts legislature to establish a six-month minimum school year in 1839 (Filler 1965, 15). He also reinvigorated a Massachusetts law establishing high schools and stimulated the creation of fifty new high schools during his twelve-year tenure (Cremin 1957, 21). These schools, and others that would follow, would need qualified teachers. To provide for this need, Mann led a movement to set up teacher institutions (called normal schools) throughout the state. The normal schools provided prospective teachers with a laboratory for learning, using model classrooms as a place to practice their skills. The emphasis was on common everyday learning, rather than on the classical studies being taught at colleges. Graduates of Massachusetts normal schools easily disseminated their pedagogy as they took positions in other states. Thus the normal schools, and the common schools where they taught, became interlocking institutions.

Swiss education reformer Johann Heinrich Pestalozzi's philosophy of pedagogical methods, inspired by Jean-Jacques Rousseau, was gaining popularity in the United States and Europe. This approach became the dominant pedagogy in teacher education at the Massachusetts normal schools. Rousseau's approach stressed directing the child in the unfolding of one's latent powers and emphasized the harmonious development of the individual's faculties into a complete personality. This was far different from the rote memorization and strict discipline paradigm that had previously dominated schools in the United States and Europe.

In order to implement Rousseau's teaching approach, schools could not rely on four months of schooling (between farming responsibilities) provided by whichever young, single woman would accept the low status and low pay of this position for a short time until marrying. Pestalozzi believed there was a unified science of education that could be learned and practiced. Teacher training, he thought, should include a broad liberal education followed by a period of research and professional training.

This approach was widely adopted throughout the United States and Europe and continues to be the standard practice today. As normal schools expanded, their graduates readily replicated their knowledge and pedagogic philosophy in the schools where they taught. As "teaching" evolved into a profession whose members shared a common philosophy, ethical code, training experience, and body of knowledge, "teachers" became a new social institution and, thus, an important force to be considered in any subsequent educational reform movement.

At the turn of the twentieth century, our nation's leadership elite sought ways to absorb another tidal wave of immigrants from other countries, many who were fleeing famine and oppression in their homelands, and to cope with the flood of people migrating from our farms in search of greater opportunities. While adults found employment in newly emerging factory-model workplaces that efficiently produced interchangeable products, public education began to implement a similar production model to produce uniformly educated students. In *Tinkering Toward Utopia*, Tyack and Cuban discuss at length how "scientific management" and the "social efficiency model" supported the adoption and persistence of certain institutional trends. The trends included higher percentages of and a greater diversity of students enrolling in and graduating from high school, larger and more elaborate curricula, an expanding range of course offerings, and increasing per-pupil expenditures. These twentieth-century trends persist for reasons that parallel the bulleted factors (above) that supported Mann's success a century earlier (Tyack and Cuban 1995, 47–54).

PART II

What Will Be "The Next Big Thing" In American Education?

The next big thing in American education will actually be small—the small schools movement. This movement qualifies as an education reform, by Tyack and Cuban's definition, because it is a planned effort to change schools in order to correct perceived social and educational problems (1995, 4). The educational leaders of New York City, Chicago, and Oakland, California, have been in the forefront of implementing this movement that is taking root nationwide.

Growing support for the small schools movement represents a steady turning away from the "bigger is better" (or at least more cost effective) theory that dominated the mid–twentieth century in the United States. The books, theories, and practices of notables such as Ted Sizer and Deborah Meier have helped articulate what, why, and how small schools benefit students and teachers. Organizations such as the Small Schools Organization (headquartered in Chicago), the Coalition for Essential Schools, the Bay Area Coalition for Essential Schools, the Bay Area Coalition for Equitable Schools, the Center for Education Reform, and the Center for Collaborative Education lend their voices to promote the benefits of small schools.

Research demonstrates that small schools produce more equitable outcomes. They decrease traditionally large achievement gaps between white and nonwhite students (Lee and Smith 1995; Friedkin and Necochea 1988), and between those of higher and lower socioeconomic status (Lee and Bryk 1989; Lee and Smith 1995; Lee, Smith, and Croniger 1995). At-risk students in smaller learning environments are more likely to meet graduation requirements, have higher attendance rates, and engage in fewer risk-taking behaviors (Kemple and Snipes 2000). Test scores for poor children increase as school size decreases (Howley and Bickel 2000). Smaller schools reduce the negative effect of poverty on school performance by as much as 70 percent (Howley and Bickel 2000).

Small schools have a demonstrably better chance of improving outcomes for poor children and students of color. Urban parents are demanding choice, in particular the option of sending their children to new small, autonomous schools with high expectations in their own neighborhoods. In Oakland, we believe that this is the single most effective strategy for dramatically improving student outcomes in urban schools (Gordon, 2001).

The Oakland Small Schools Initiative (SSI) is a community-based reform led by Oakland parents and teachers. This effort intends to systematically transform the design and culture of the Oakland Unified School District (OUSD) and its schools to dramatically improve the educational experiences and outcomes of students and their families. Initial emphasis is on relieving large, overcrowded schools in neighborhoods primarily serving racial and ethnic minorities and lower-income students and on improving the quality of their learning environment. Three organizations, Bay Area Coalition for Equitable Schools (BayCES), OUSD, and Oakland Community Organizations (OCO), work in alliance to implement this initiative.

On May 24, 2000, the Oakland School Board unanimously passed a New Small Autonomous Schools Policy, drafted by the Bay Area Coalition of Schools (BayCES) in collaboration with educators and community members working through the Oakland Community Organizations (OCO). The policy allows for the creation of ten new small autonomous schools during the first three years. These schools are each granted charterlike autonomies in exchange for increased accountability, while operating within the District's support system and benefiting from its economies of scale. Oakland established the maximum enrollments for small schools at the mid-range of researchers' definitions, as follows: K–5 = 250; K–8 = 400; K–12 = 500; 6–8 = 400; 6–12 = 500; and 9–12 = 400.

The nation's small schools movement is likely to have a dramatic and sustained impact on education over time for the following reasons:

Interlocking Reforms with Other Systems

The small schools movement does not presume that the present system is in ashes. Rather, it strives to create environments in which teachers can be more effective. The small schools philosophy does not assume that teachers have been incompetent or lazy. It does not blame these institutional reform implementers for the present system failures. The structural change (not precisely an "add-on") to smaller learning communities can be implemented without disturbing standard operating procedures at school sites and without demanding fundamental changes in teachers' behaviors. The change to small schools is readily understood by laypeople, school boards, and legislators (Tyack and Cuban 1995, 57).

Linking Reforms to Broader Social Movements

Participants in the small schools movement consistently link their efforts to goals of achieving excellence and equity. Small schools are not promoted as the quick-fix silver bullet solution to all of society's ills, or even to the challenges facing the nation's education system. Supporters of the movement consistently try to manage expectations (and forestall disillusionment) by emphasizing that being small does not guarantee a high-quality school. However, the characteristics of effective schools occur more often and more readily in a small school. In a small school, it is more likely that the following conditions that support effective schooling will occur:

- Everyone will be seen as a meaningful individual (probably wearing several "hats"), not hidden behind a role.
- Each student will be known by many adults who all take responsibility for the student's progress.
- Staff members will understand and share a common vision.
- The school will be more maneuverable and flexible than a larger institution in order to meet its goals (www.bayces.org/small schools/index.htm).

Clearly Demonstrable Advantages that Outweigh the Burdens of Implementing Change

A growing body of research (see the late Kathleen Cotton's overview in *New Small Learning Communities: Findings from Recent Literature*, December 2001, available online at www.nwrel.org/scpd/sirs/nslc.pdf) supports the hypothesis that smaller schools achieve better results. Research is demonstrating that small schools have the following benefits:

- Higher student achievement, especially among students facing more socioeconomic challenges.
- Improved student attendance rates (generally a precondition to academic achievement) and higher graduation rates (sometimes phrased "lower dropout rates").
- Greater student visibility (a function of both the smaller absolute number of students to be known by teachers, staff, and other students, and the greater percentage of students with an opportunity to participate in leadership roles and extracurricular activities when the total school population is smaller).
- Increased teacher satisfaction (arising from increased teacher visibility, more supportive professional relationships, closer ties to students, and higher student achievement that smaller school structures foster).
- Greater cost effectiveness (when calculated on a cost-per-graduate basis, rather than a cost-per-warehoused student basis).

Although several implementation controversies still engage the small schools movement, proponents are taking care to build a solid base of support on clear evidence of benefit. Supporters introduce models to revise the public notion of what a "real school" ought to be by recalling images of schools in the recent past—the early-to-middle twentieth century—rather than directly challenging current trends, in order to implement the small school reform at a pace that does not exceed the pedagogic speed limit for change (Tyack and Cuban 1995, 57).

Entire districts are not asked to overthrow existing school designs and faculty assignments. Instead, a few model schools are established in a community, with plans to add more small schools or to gradually break up large schools. Oakland, for example, opened five new small autonomous schools (NSAS) in 2001. Two more opened in 2002. Another two are approved to open, but are seeking facility space. The superintendent coaches the NSAS. An executive director coaches a cluster of traditional schools that happen to already be small. His mission is to help them adopt the autonomy and accountability features of the NSAS models. The district has a charter schools coordinator (the author) working directly with Oakland's thirteen independent charter schools, all of which are small enough to meet the model's size criterion, but which do not all meet the quality education goals of the small schools movement.

The District is also discussing other small autonomous school models with school design teams that may fill additional places on the continuum between traditional schools and independent charter schools. District leaders want all Oakland parents to be able to choose a small, high quality public school for their children to attend in Oakland. District and community leaders estimate that meeting this demand will require the creation or redesign of at least forty small, high quality public schools.

Propitious Timing

The small schools movement has patiently developed demonstration small schools and conducted research studies. Now it has data-based research to demonstrate how small schools address the national horror over student violence at large middle class schools like Columbine High School, growing demand for parental choice, and the federal government's demand that all schools help all students perform academically—leaving no child behind. The movement benefits precisely because it has been willing to make progress slowly and build allies in many sectors.

Political Support from Powerful Sponsors

According to Parent Power!—an electronic newsletter published by the Center for Education Reform ("Why We Need Small Schools," October 1999, Vol. 1, Issue 5)—everyone from Hillary Clinton to George W. Bush is calling for smaller, more personal, more responsive learning places, and for kids to have stronger ties to adults (http://edreform.com/parentpower/99oct/99oct2.htm).

Because the small schools movement calls for systemic reforms that will enhance the teaching and learning environment, it is generally supported by large and powerful constituencies of teachers, counselors, their unions, and parents. This reform effort currently benefits from strong financial support from nonprofit public benefit foundations such as the Bill & Melinda Gates Foundation, the Annie E. Casey Foundation, and the Annenberg Foundation.

In some communities, principals and their unions may object to the reform if they feel their opportunities for salaries and prestige will be reduced because they will serve smaller populations. Some parents may fear their children will unduly suffer from reduced course offerings or fewer extracurricular opportunities at smaller schools with smaller overall budgets. The small schools movement must explicitly address these concerns in order to maintain the support of these constituencies in local communities.

Freezing Reforms into Regulations and Laws

This is the next area that the small schools movement needs to address. Small classroom sizes for K–3 and ninth grade students became the norm when California law provided a financial incentive for keeping these class sizes small. (It also had the unintended outcome of further worsening teacher shortages.) State legislation that provides a financial incentive for keeping school enrollments small would be welcomed, especially by fiscally challenged urban districts. Meanwhile, OUSD, for example, adopted the Small Schools Initiative policy that encourages the creation of small schools, but no OUSD policy prohibits the creation, consolidation, or continuation of large schools.

As OUSD implements its Small Schools Initiative, it discovers that many policies must be reviewed and revised to implement the initiative. At a tipping point of approximately forty small autonomous schools, the different service and monitoring demands that small autonomous schools place on central systems are expected to generate an irresistible need for internal system changes. After District central office systems are redesigned to serve small autonomous schools, then that institutionalized change will become positive inertia to forestall the District's backsliding into former service relationships.

Easy Replication

The concept of small autonomous schools is easy to envision. What community members, school leaders, and district staff in Oakland discovered, however, was there is no guarantee that we are all sharing the same understanding. What is important is for all partners in Oakland's Small Schools Initiative (or similar coalitions in communities throughout the small schools movement) to stay the course. Clarifications and compromises will occur over time. Oakland was initially inspired by small schools in New York, Boston, and Chicago. Now our small schools offer another variation on that theme. Each community adapts the concept to fit local conditions, and each school adapts the model to serve its own students, parents, and teachers.

PART III

Epilogue—February 2005

The text above, written in November 2002, urged all partners in Oakland's Small Schools Initiative to "stay the course." But fiscal and political storm clouds would soon jeopardize that itinerary. As reported by Dean E. Murphy in the *New York Times* ("Dream Ends for Oakland School Chief as State Takes Over" 6/7/2003).

> On [Monday,] June 2, 2003, Gov. Gray Davis approved a $100 million emergency [revolving] loan for Oakland, the biggest school bailout in California history. The state also appointed an administrator, Randolph E. Ward, who will begin

running the 48,000-student district on June 16. Mr. Chaconas was told by state officials that he no longer had a job. By Tuesday he was officially a nonentity.

In addition, the governor stripped the District's Board of Education of its decision-making authority, reducing this elected body to a mere advisory organization. Analysis of the merit or folly of the state's actions, the accuracy or exaggeration of the reported District deficit, the layers of political factors that affected outcomes, and the community's response could provide a rich source of discussion for another article on the politics of education reform. For our purpose, we will only consider the effect of this change on Oakland's Small Schools Initiative.

Many leaders of new small autonomous schools feared the new state administrator would end support for their programs by slashing their budgets, eliminating their curricular autonomy, forcing them to achieve economies of scale by growing large, or calling for teacher layoffs that would gut their staff of new (untenured) recruits. Several schools contemplated converting to charter schools to retain their autonomy. A few even filed charter petitions, but none were approved by the state administrator, so they continued as before, and waited.

Standardized test score results released that August showed that student performance at Oakland's small autonomous schools continued to exceed student performance at other District schools. Long waiting lists demonstrated parents' enthusiasm for this learning approach. A few months after Dr. Ward's arrival, while addressing a gathering, he acknowledged the fear that many had, a fear that he might throw out the small schools concept, one of the things that was working at the District. "Now, wouldn't that have been the dumbest thing to do?" he chided. People in the room chuckled at his candor, because all too often, that "dumb thing" is exactly what a new leader does.

Media reports are currently describing two sets of schools that are the current focus of Dr. Ward's reform attention and a variety of possible reform approaches (e.g., nonprofit or for-profit charters, charter management organizations, contract schools, designing new District schools, or training new administrators).

Thirteen Elementary Schools in NCLB Program Improvement Year 4

A request for letters of interest (RFLOI) recently asked internal or external individuals, groups, collaborations, nonprofits, and for-profits to describe things they have an interest in doing to improve the academic performance of students currently attending thirteen District elementary schools in No Child Left Behind (NCLB) Program Improvement Year 4.

Although some of these schools have shown improvement and achievement in some academic categories, Program Improvement Year 4 status means that things the District has tried for the past six years have not been sufficiently successful to place them on track for achieving NCLB goals by 2014.

Last year, none of these elementary schools achieved both of the California NCLB benchmark goals of

- 13.6 percent of students proficient or advanced in English language arts (ELA), school-wide and by each subgroup; and
- 16.0 percent of students proficient or advanced in math, school-wide and by each subgroup.

In 2005, as California strives toward NCLB's 2014 goal of 100 percent proficiency, the goals for all schools will increase to

- 24.4 percent proficient or advanced ELA, school-wide and by each subgroup; and
- 26.0 percent proficient or advanced math, school-wide and by each subgroup.

Since the District has not been able to create the conditions to enable these thirteen elementary schools to meet their targets for six years, and we do not anticipate a windfall of new resources, the RFLOI sought new partners, new perspectives, and new possibilities.

The RFLOI attempted to cast a wide net, inviting responses from those who believe they may have the total solution for all thirteen schools, a solution for one or a few of the schools, or an essential support for one or more schools. However, the RFLOI also transparently expressed some preferences (e.g., small learning environments, school site autonomy, charters interested in leasing employees from the District) that the District would be inclined to favor.

Respondents were asked to reply based on one of three categories:

Category 1 would include responses from single charter developers, charter management organizations, or contract schools with solutions for one, some, or all of the schools that might be implemented in 2005–2006. This category would include new governance through a school conversion or creation of a new school.

Category 2 respondents would propose to implement a new school design using the New School Design Group (NSDG) approach, opening in 2006 or in 2007. This process would require a bridge solution for students during the intervening year(s).

Category 3 was the catch-all category. With this category, the District invited other creative responses, including responses from individuals not interested in leading or managing schools themselves. In effect, this

category asked "What else is possible? What else should we consider?" like
the child on Santa's lap that ends her list with "and bring me lots and lots
of surprises."

Fifty-one individuals and groups responded to the RFLOI, including eight
interested in applying a charter school or contract school solution to one or
more of the thirteen schools, eleven interested in the school redesign
process that has incubated small autonomous schools in the District, and
thirty-two interested in supporting one or more of the schools' reform efforts
with various services. These last ranged from an individual with education
experience offering to volunteer at one school, to various organizations
whose mission is to support particular aspects of school operation, to an organization prepared to help any group create and implement charters. Based
on what LOI responses reveal to be possible and feasible, the District will
create detailed requests for proposals.

Seven Additional Underperforming Low Enrollment Schools

Seven additional school programs will be closed because of poor academic performance (measured by three academic strands of review), declining enrollment, or both. These seven schools include all grade levels (elementary, middle, and high schools). For some the closure concludes a
multiyear plan in which no new students were added as current students
proceeded toward matriculation. In some cases, a newly designed school is
already operating on the campus or at a temporary site and is scheduled to
grow into the space vacated by closing programs. Fremont-In-Transition, for
example, was created for Fremont High School students who did not wish to
choose any of the new small autonomous schools that opened on that campus last year. Thus juniors and seniors were allowed to graduate, but no
younger students were admitted. The School of Social Justice is still officially
on the books, but it had no students this year.

Two School Design Paths that Might Apply to Either Set of Schools

The New Schools Development Group (NSDG) is the successor program implementing what began as Oakland's New Small Autonomous
Schools Initiative. The NSDG application process is on its website
(www.nsdg.net). This program is a possible source of school designs with
strong leaders to serve students who would otherwise have attended one
of the seven closing education programs. The NSDG program might also
be part of an individual or group's response to the RFLOI (category 2) for
the thirteen elementary schools in Program Improvement Year 4. NSDG
does the following:

- supports the development of new school leaders for newly designed schools in partnership with New Leaders for New Schools (www.nlns.org); and
- helps experienced, credentialed school leaders design new schools.

In both cases, leaders work with a team of teachers, parents, students, community members, and other partners to design schools that will open a year later. Applicant leaders may be linked to a school design team after applying, or may already be part of a school design team. To date, the New School Design Group has only fostered the development of District schools, not charter schools.

Where Do Charter Schools Fit as a Means of School Reform in Oakland?

The District seriously regards its responsibility to evaluate new and monitor existing charter schools, and to implement reforms within the district when charter school best practices are applicable. Although OUSD views charter schools as one component of educational reform, and appreciates that well-managed charters can offer additional sources of quality public education for every child in Oakland, the District recognizes that the legal and fiscal relationship between authorizing districts and charter schools in California is fraught with turbulence. As a consequence, we seek ways to bridge the troubled waters that can divide our interests.

All charter applicants must conform to the application requirements defined in California's Charter School Law (CA Ed Code Section 47600 *et seq.*). The District will continue to authorize and monitor standard, independent charter schools arising from motivated individuals, from grassroots communities, from inspired teachers, and from charter management organizations.

In addition, the District has launched a concept it calls "internal charters." These are charters with a special, closer-than-standard, cooperative relationship with the District. The nature of that relationship can vary, charter school by charter school, and is defined in a contract (letter of agreement) that supplements the charter. Internal charter special arrangements might involve use of district facilities, leasing of district employees, access to professional development, or various service arrangements.

The RFLOI for the thirteen Program Improvement Year 4 schools invited charter school solutions and described the District's particular interest in internal charter arrangements with certain features. OUSD has authorized nineteen charter schools that operate today, including one internal charter; three more charters have approval to open in 2005–2006, including another internal charter, and additional proposals are under consideration. All but one of the District's charter schools are small schools (the exception being a six-hundred-student independent study program). About 9 percent of

Oakland's public school population is enrolled in a charter school. OUSD is the largest charter authorizer in Northern California.

The Prognosis for Small Schools in Oakland, California

Tyack and Cuban tell us that school reforms are sustained when key conditions are met: interlocking reforms with other systems; linking reforms to broader social movements; clearly demonstrating advantages that outweigh the burdens of implementing change; propitious timing; political support from powerful sponsors; freezing reforms into regulations and laws; and easy replication. Oakland's small schools initiative has been successful in each of these regards, even capitalizing on disruptive change in governance as an opportunity to catalyze reform.

Twenty new small schools operate in Oakland today. Six will open in September 2005, and more are incubating. The District continues to replicate the success factors for these schools district-wide. In 2005–2006, all District schools will have a substantial amount of fiscal autonomy at their school sites as OUSD implements results-based budgeting. Site budgets will be funded based on student attendance. School principals will control purchasing choices at their schools and have substantial authority in position development decisions. The District is replacing attendance area boundaries with attendance zones that offer families more choice. All graduating eighth graders have the opportunity to select from thirty-three high school programs throughout the District. Schools with poor academic performance records are encouraged and supported in redesign efforts from which they emerge as small schools with well-prepared leaders and staff who share an educational vision and are prepared to implement proven curricula. The District's overall goal is to provide quality public schools to all families, and small schools have become both flagships and squadrons in our fleet of public schools to fulfill that plan.

REFERENCES

Brown University. "Horace Mann, Class of 1819." www.brown.edu/webmaster/about/history/mann.shtml.

Bickel, R. and C. Howley. 2000. "The influence of scale on school performance: A multi-level extension of the Matthew principle." Education Policy Analysis Archives, 8(22). http://olam.ed.asu.edu/epaa/v8nss/.

Center for Education Reform. 1999. "Why We Need Small Schools." *Parent Power* 1: 5 (October).

Cheek, Karen. "The Normal School." www.nd.edu/~rbarger/www7/normal.html.

Cotton, Kathleen. December 2001. New small learning communities: Findings from recent literature. Available online at www.nwrel.org/scpd/sirs/nslc.pdf.

Cremin, Lawrence A. 1957. *The Republic and the School: Horace Mann on the Education of Free Men*. New York: Teachers College.

Friedkin, N. and J. Necochea. 1988. "School system size and performance: A contingency perspective." Educational Evaluation and Policy Analysis, 10(3), 237–249.

Filler, Louis. 1965. *Horace Mann on the Crisis in Education*. Ohio: Antioch Press.

Gordon, Mark. 2001. "What's Good About Small Schools?" Unpublished article.

Howley, C. and R. Bickel. 2000, 6-03-02. "Reducing effects of poverty on achievement: A four state study." *American School Board Journal*. Available: http://www.asbj.com/2000/04/0400beforetheboard.html [2002, 6-03-02].

"Johann Heinrich Pestalozzi." The Columbia Encyclopedia, sixth edition. 2001. www.bartleby.com/65/pe/Pestaloz.html.

Kemple, James J. and Jason Snipes. 2000. "Career academies: Impacts on students' engagement and performance in high school." Eleven-page paper published by MDRC.

King, Pam Mason. "Horace Mann." www.nd.edu/~rbarger/www7/mann.html.

Lee, V. E. and A. S. Bryk. 1989. "A multilevel model of the social distribution of high school achievement." Sociology of Education, 62, 172–192.

Lee, V. E. and J. B. Smith. 1995. "Effects of high school restructuring and size on early gains in achievement and engagement." Sociology of Education, 68(4), 241–270.

Lee, V. E., J. B. Smith, and R. G. Croninger. Fall 1995. "Another look at high school restructuring: More evidence that it improves student achievement, and more insight into why." *Issues in Restructuring Schools*, 7, 1-10.

Murphy, Dean E. 2003. "Dream ends for Oakland school chief as state takes over." *New York Times*, June 7.

Parent Power! 1999. "Why we need small schools." Vol. 1, issue 5 (October 1999), http://edreform.com/parentpower/99oct/99oct2.htm.

Tyack, David and Larry Cuban. 1995. *Tinkering Toward Utopia: A Century of Public School Reform*. Harvard University Press.

3

Big City Schools Are Not in Kansas: Can We Improve City Schools Without School Choice? Not in Your Lifetime!

Robert Maranto

Critics of school choice argue that we don't really need choice because we know how to improve schools without school choice. After all, public schools are public institutions governed by our democracy, by the school boards, state legislatures, governors, congresses and presidents we all vote for, and all too often by the judges they select. If we can just unite business, labor, our local school board, the state legislature, the governor, Congress, and the president, and spend lots of money to do what we all know works—whatever that is—then surely we can all improve our public schools for all our children. We really don't need to allow parents to make their own choices. Indeed that would be bad, for it would not improve all our schools in the same way that we all know they need to be improved.

And if it takes a long time for the schools to improve, well, democracy was not meant to move capriciously. So what if maybe your grandchildren rather than your children get a good education? At least you'll have the satisfaction of knowing that the improvements took place for everyone in an open, democratic process.

Give me a break!

One of the more insightful, but still off-base examples in this line of work comes in the form of a series published by the University Press of Kansas, one of the top scholarly presses in public policy. The numerous authors make up part of an NSF-funded, multiyear study of school reform in Atlanta, Baltimore, Boston, Denver, Detroit, Houston, Los Angeles, Pittsburgh, St. Louis, San Francisco, and Washington, D.C. The authors, skilled political scientists, interviewed 516 elites in their 11 cities, and almost in spite of the oddness of their approach, they offer real wisdom about inner-city education reform. While *Black Social Capital* is a fascinating (and equally depressing) case study of failed school reform in Baltimore, *City Schools and City Politics* offers fairly interesting case studies of three cities, and *Building Civic Capacity* dryly (but also perceptively) summarizes the lessons from all eleven cities.

The authors' basic thesis is what political scientists refer to as "regime theory." Where key economic and political elites develop close relationships, forming a "regime" of elites, and work together to improve education, then real improvements might occur. This is almost a parody of the "why can't we all get along" view of political processes: you can't fight city hall, but maybe if you are lucky city hall will fight for you.

And one thing all the authors agree, and amply document, is the need for fighting. As they show all too well, big city schools do not perform very well, largely since their clientele is poor and uneducated. Spending the same, and often less than nearby suburbs, inner-city systems have a tough job educating the children of underclass and blue-collar parents. Big city schools struggle with crime, racial divisions, and teachers unions and entrenched bureaucracies that more often hinder than help learning.

Further, there is something to regime theory. In some cities elites are more united and idealistic than in other cities. Where elites from different sectors unite, stay united for long periods of time, focus on education, make good choices about what policies to pursue, and most important, choose a talented and long-serving school superintendent, even against overwhelming odds, school reform is possible. Possible, but not bloody likely. In only one of the eleven cities studied, Pittsburgh, do elites come together for a long period of time with a united and well-led school board, a cooperative teachers' union, and a wise and politically skilled superintendent. In the 1980s, Pittsburgh, under Superintendent Richard Wallace, developed a regime of constant student testing and constant teacher training that drove test scores to national norms. Unfortunately, by the 1990s personal jealousies, racial divisions, budget cuts, and community annoyance at elite leadership (domination?) led to a gradual unraveling. What the political system giveth, that system also taketh away. And that was the best case.

More typical is the Baltimore case ably chronicled in *Black Social Capital*. Here, Marion Orr shows that persistent mistrust stemming from past racial injustice kept black leaders and white businesspeople from uniting behind privatization, or any other reform agenda. Opponents to school reform had merely to play the race card and wait for white contractors to make mistakes to see reform abandoned.

And anyway, as the authors find, even elites rarely agree on how to improve schools—there is no such thing as "what we all know will work." Policy disagreement and policy making involving numerous institutions leads to what the authors of *Building Civic Capacity* admit is "disjointed and unfocused change as the system rushes from one magic bullet to the next" (141). Ultimately, the authors do a good job diagnosing the failures of the political governance of education, but for ideological reasons cannot get over their disdain for parental choice. Parents must patiently wait for the whole political system to get its act together, rather having the choices to take matters into their own hands.

Yet some political scientists are more open to change. Reviewing the literature and presenting very engaging (and at times funny) case studies of four Connecticut school systems struggling under desegregation court orders and attendant legislative mandates, *Controlling Public Education: Localism versus Equity* by Kathryn McDermott offers a good diagnosis of the problems of public education, and an insightful (if politically unlikely) set of solutions. This is a great book about the politics of education. Read it. McDermott explains how and why school systems freeze out serious parent involvement, why school boards are so seldom effective, and how and why white suburban parents block integration even when it's the law. But she doesn't stop there. She also offers possible solutions. For integrationist liberals, McDermott wants to abolish traditional local school districts, to equalize funding, and to enshrine racial and class integration as one of the key goals of public education. But for pro-marketeers, McDermott proposes to make schools autonomous, incentive-driven, and (within certain restrictions to ensure integration) choice-based. She also wants to measure results, in order to bring a regime of both rising standards and social equity. Indeed, she sees standards and choice as key to making socioeconomic integration work.

Of course politically, this won't sell. The school board is the first step for many an aspiring state legislator. State legislatures will not abolish school boards, however ineffective they are. Nor will school district offices and superintendents go gentle into that good night. The education establishment does not wish parental choice, and well-off suburbs scarcely want financial equity, not to mention integration. And yet McDermott's case is compelling . . . if only all of us would get together and . . . well, we won't. But maybe, with a few charter schools here and a few interdistrict choices there, we can help at least some city kids escape bad places, until someday we do all come together and McDermott's revolution comes about.

REFERENCES

McDermott, Kathryn. 1999. *Controlling Public Education: Localism versus Equity.* Lawrence: University Press of Kansas.

Orr, Marion. 1999. *Black Social Capital: the Politics of School Reform in Baltimore, 1986–1998.* Lawrence: University Press of Kansas.

Portz, John, Lana Stein, and Robin R. Jones. 1999. *City Schools and City Politics: Institutions and Leadership in Pittsburgh, Boston, and St. Louis.* Lawrence: University Press of Kansas.

Stone, Clarence N., Jeffrey R. Henig, Bryan D. Jones, and Carol Pierannunzi. 2001. *Building Civic Capacity: The Politics of Reforming Urban Schools.* Lawrence: University Press of Kansas.

4

The Spinning Wheels
of Urban School Reform

Frederick M. Hess

A few years ago I wrote a book entitled *Spinning Wheels: The Politics of Urban School Reform*. The volume caused something of a stir and contributed to a broader effort to focus reform efforts on the causes—rather than merely the symptoms—of urban school failure. For those in the charter school movement seeking to more fully understand the trouble with the status quo and how to avoid the pitfalls therein, it might be worth revisiting the thrust of that argument. On a brighter note, larger changes in accountability and choice may be starting to help address the plight of urban school systems.

Critiques of urban schooling almost invariably end with calls for more change and new "solutions." Critics call for new curricula, different pedagogy, longer school days, altered classroom schedules, smaller classes or schools, refined professional development, and so on. Advocates of each proposal traditionally suggest that nothing more radical is necessary. They suggest that all we need to do is listen to the education professors and the consultants and adopt the right combination of these measures (although there is the problem that the professors and consultants settle upon new solutions almost as fast as districts catch on to the old ones).

These critiques have dominated the discourse and lent urgency to calls for reform in the two decades since the 1983 report *A Nation at Risk* scathingly critiqued the nation's schools. An ensuing cacophony of reform has produced a lot of activity but little real change in urban schooling. Why? Advocates of reform, ranging from proponents of massive restructuring to those arguing for a particular pedagogy or curriculum, often contend that there has been too little school reform or that school systems are largely static. This claim is refuted by the record. My 1999 book reported on reform activity in fifty-seven urban school districts. I found that the typical urban district had launched at least twelve significant initiatives in a three-year span—that's a new reform every three months! No similar study has been conducted recently, so it is possible that the rate has slowed since—though that's not the way most veteran observers of urban districts would be likely to bet.

With most urban districts continuing to flounder amidst shocking dropout rates and poor test scores, both observation and achievement data suggest that few of these efforts have yielded the desired results. Why? The problem is the nature of the reform enterprise itself. Most of these reforms are an alluring distraction that has actually aggravated the plight of urban school districts.

Not only is the frenetic embrace of reform counterproductive, but the incentives that promote reform also make the failure of individual reforms almost inevitable. Policy makers are driven by professional and community pressures to consistently embrace dramatic-sounding changes, while trying to avoid provoking conflict. The result is the embrace of a series of toothless reforms in a fruitless search for the silver bullet. Crucially, these efforts rarely attempt to change the way adults are assigned to schools, how they are compensated, their job security, or anything that really matters, because such changes create controversy and complicate the superintendent's life.

For too long, reform has been largely a symbolic effort to reassure impatient communities. Reform is visible evidence that mediocrity is not tolerated and that improvement is around the corner. The result is that districts recycle initiatives, constantly modify previous initiatives, and adopt innovative reform A to replace practice B even as another district is adopting B as an innovative reform to replace practice A. The amount, pace, and nature of reform efforts are inimical to effective change and responsible governance. These reforms do not—and are not designed to—significantly alter the nature of schooling, but do frustrate, confuse, and finally alienate teachers.

While I am *not* suggesting that educators or policy makers engage in any of this behavior out of venal motives, a state of constant reform is the status quo in urban school systems. It has hindered school performance by distracting faculty from the core functions of teaching and learning. Evidence on the performance of parochial and high-performing schools suggests that the best schools are characterized by focus, and develop expertise in specific approaches. School improvement requires time, focus, and the commitment of core personnel. This requires that the leadership focus on selected efforts and then nurture those efforts in the schools. As Richard Elmore first observed more than a decade ago, "Really good schools . . . often aren't very innovative; indeed, their main strength often seems to be that they persist in, and develop increasingly deep understandings of, well-developed theories of teaching and learning" (1991, 38).

The consistent failure of reforms to deliver promised improvement has done little to reduce the appeal of reform. Reformers argue that the disappointing results of reform simply indicate that the right solutions have not yet been used or that reforms were not given a fair trial. These critiques are valid. It is true that districts do not select the optimal reforms, nor do they nurture or properly implement reforms, but this is a distraction from the more fundamental problem. Reformers presume that the troubled state of urban education is due to current practice and that reforms will improve schooling, a belief that is shared by urban residents and professional educators impatient for progress. As Roland Barth observed in 1991, "Urban schools are seen as so helpless, so hopeless, so broken that it seems there's little to lose by giving them a good hard kick. To use a dated metaphor, it's like kicking a broken radio. Perhaps the tube filaments will align by chance in a different way, and the radio will work. In any case, since it's already broken, what is there to lose?" (124).

The law of averages ensures that some policy initiatives somewhere are bound to appear successful, regardless of their real promise. Those reforms that appear successful are anointed. Researchers who pursue them receive funding, consultants who preach them win work, and district policy makers often seize upon them in the hope that this reform will be the one that works. District leaders who don't jump on the bandwagon risk being criticized by their communities as uncommitted or unprofessional. The belief that innovation will eventually bring improvement is not unique to education—researchers often presume that more innovation is the mark of a good organization. The problem is that quick fixes have distracted attention from performance and have undermined organizational coherence.

The cruel paradox is that the same impulses which compel education policy makers to adopt reform also ensure that they will do so under conditions which make large-scale success highly unlikely. Problems with urban school reform are symptomatic of larger problems. Until the larger constraints are addressed, reforms—no matter how well designed—are likely to prove futile, waste resources, and foster faculty frustration.

WHY THEY DO WHAT THEY DO

Getting urban schools unstuck requires a shift in emphasis—away from the pursuit of the curricular or pedagogical "silver bullet" that will *really* work—and toward an understanding of why urban school systems engage in reform and why nearly every reform produces disappointing results. Insufficient attention to the structure within which school reform is pursued has crippled efforts to understand the failure of school reform.

Urban school systems are governed by professional superintendents subject to intense pressures from the amateur boards that supervise them. Vulnerable board members, accountable for mediocre urban schools but with little power to generate short-term solutions, rely on the superintendent's professional judgment to provide forward direction. This increases the pressure upon the superintendent to produce visible and impressive results. In this high-stakes situation, if things go poorly, the board is able to help the system off to a fresh start by replacing a disappointing superintendent with one who inspires community confidence. Board members who fail to use the superintendent in this fashion court political risk and may be pushed out by impatient community members who want evidence that things will improve quickly.

The evidence shows that urban superintendents are rarely in place long enough to make a significant difference, the typical tenure being three years or less. As Theodore Kowalski has argued, "The idea that one individual can successfully transform a complex organization by imposing his or her vision in a relatively short period of time is simply myopic" (1995, 152). Given the superintendent's short tenure, the visibility of his or her position, the lack of effective short-term control over classroom performance in urban districts, and the difficulties in assessing the impact of new leadership on district outcomes in just a two- or three-year period, superintendents do not have the opportunity to prove their value via substantive long-term leadership.

Fundamentally, the problems with reform are rooted in the fact that urban administrators are encouraged to concentrate on proposing change—rather than results—because it is visible activity by which they are judged. Unable to accurately assess the performance of the district leadership, due to rapid leadership turnover, the multiple social and economic difficulties impeding urban school performance, and the challenge of linking a leader's efforts to short-term performance fluctuations in a large system, communities demand evidence that the district leaders will make matters better. The result is that community and district leaders have incentives to focus upon inputs—visible effort to improve schooling—rather than long-term performance.

For a long time, this dynamic has been dramatically compounded by the lack of clear, reliable, or agreed-upon measures of student performance. In the world of No Child Left Behind and increasingly sophisticated state accountability systems, however, this obstacle is slowly dissipating.

The public expects that superintendents should rapidly demonstrate that better times are coming and community support is crucial to any improvement effort. District leaders are much more likely to be effective if they enjoy business support, parental cooperation, the active participation of community organizations, and the backing of municipal officials. The surest way to earn this kind of support is to cultivate a community reputation as a promising innovator. Superintendents who initiate reforms are feted in the local media, praised by the mayor and local business community, and offered a honeymoon in which to reshape troubled school systems. Superintendents are propelled into proactivity—if only as a tactic to rally resources and support. Superintendents who focus on the long term and fail to propose quick fixes will be handicapped by a lack of support and resources. Superintendents who proceed in a controlled, deliberate, incremental fashion will find their effectiveness hobbled by a lack of community prestige. In short, *current arrangements create a situation in which pursuing significant change in a responsible manner undermines the district's ability to secure the resources and community trust necessary to enact significant change.*

The urban superintendent faces a dilemma. Focusing on selected initiatives enhances the likelihood of producing significant change, but attracts relatively little notice and makes it unlikely the superintendent will be able to finish the job he or she set out to do. On the other hand, by initiating a great deal of activity and leaving his or her successors to worry about results, the superintendent can set a district upon the "right path" and can trust others to finish the job. Additionally, the proactive superintendent benefits because he or she is positioned to take credit for apparent successes, while the managerial successor is often seen as a mere technician. Obviously, most superintendents will choose to be initiators, and there will be a lack of implementers to finish their handiwork. *Whether or not the schools are viewed as improving, professional and political realities reward those superintendents who are seen as proactive.*

Those reformers perceived as successful are offered a series of increasingly prestigious positions atop larger and larger districts, and find doors into government, consulting, and academia opened to them. Acclaimed reformers are sought after by more prestigious districts, increasing their influence and visibility. Aspiring superintendents learn to emulate these success stories while less active superintendents are selected out. This Darwinian process serves to ensure that hyper-reformers are encouraged and rewarded.

Aware of their short expected tenure, superintendents have strong incentives to rapidly establish their reputations as effective leaders by emphasizing input, even at the expense of careful program design, oversight, and implementation. Emphasizing follow-through is often professionally self-defeating in the high-turnover world of the urban superintendency, because professional status accrues to those who initiate programs. Carrying on a predecessor's innovations is a caretaker role which does little to establish a strong reputation, so new superintendents are compelled to launch their own reforms.

LOOKING AHEAD

Reform—rather than being the remedy to what ails urban schools—has generally been a distraction and a hindrance. Reform is an expensive endeavor, requiring time, money, and energy and imposing significant opportunity costs on urban school systems. A series of partial reform efforts can serve to undermine the school-level stability, focus, consistency, enthusiasm, trust, and commitment that are the keys to effective schooling.

The irony of school reform is that the sheer amount of activity impedes the ability of schools to improve in meaningful ways. Meaningful reform requires time, energy, commitment, and focus. The infatuation with new reforms ensures that only the rare measure is seen through to the end. The churning of policy distracts administrators, teachers, and community members from fostering faculty commitment and expertise—the real keys to school improvement. Dramatic top-down reforms, which tend to be hobbled by vague conceptions of how teaching and learning will improve, rarely foster this commitment. Rapid leadership turnover and the constant search for new solutions cause commitments to the initiatives of former superintendents to dry up and programs to be abandoned. The result is that faculty and administrators become disillusioned and increasingly resist further change. The problem has not been that "nothing ever changes," but that "everything changes."

In effect, policy churn punishes teachers who throw themselves into reform efforts, even though these very teachers are likely to be among the more effective teachers in a school system. The disinterested and unmotivated teachers who are the targets of most reform activity safely ride out the successive waves of reform behind the closed doors of their classrooms. Those teachers who invest their energy, disrupt their classrooms, and sacrifice their time find their efforts wasted if reforms dissipate. Because each regime tends to initiate new reforms, within a few years this entire process starts again. Veteran teachers quickly learn to close their classroom doors and simply wait for each reform push to recede (often getting labeled as "burnouts" in the process), ensuring that each subsequent wave of reform is largely manned by newer teachers who lack institutional memory.

The inability of urban districts to make reforms work says little about the intrinsic merit of individual initiatives or the efforts of those who have designed them. On the other hand, the well-intentioned promises and programs produced by the professional reform community have aggravated the perverse incentives driving short-term district leadership and policy churn. By continuously promising newer and better mousetraps, reformers increase the pressure to pursue new initiatives, while encouraging the public to hold unrealistic expectations. Rather than look to reformers and consultants who promote "new and improved" remedies for educational problems, educational leaders need to provide focused, consistent, stable leadership that cultivates expertise and community.

The spread of accountability-based and choice-based reform have also helped to address these challenges. By using achievement measures or market forces to gauge performance and increase accountability, these reforms help assuage the anxieties that feed the demand for visible change. Accountability systems change the way in which superintendents are measured, so that visible reform is no longer so palatable if unaccompanied by results. Meanwhile, it becomes easier to justify a slow and deliberate leadership style if results testify to real improvement.

Choice-based reform creates the possibility for market-based and contractual accountability while decentralizing management and removing school governance from the sporadic and erratic oversight of the urban community. Instead, it delivers this authority to a smaller school community of interested parties. It is far easier for this small community to assess school performance in a straightforward way, reducing the incentive for school officials to engage in high-profile reforms of uncertain value.

In short, while urban schools continue to suffer from arrangements that tempt leaders to chase one shallow reform after another, the larger environment is starting to change in ways that appear likely to help address this problem. It is vital, however, that charter operators and authorizers take care not to invite the pathologies of urban school reform into their sector and their schools as they move into urban communities.

REFERENCES

Barth, R. S. 1991. "Restructuring Schools: Some Questions for Teachers and Principals." *Phi Delta Kappan* 73 (October): 123–28.

Elmore, R. F. 1991. *Innovation in Education Policy.* Prepared for the Conference on Fundamental Questions of Innovation at Duke University, Durham, NC.

Kowalski, T. 1995. *Keepers of the Flame: Contemporary Urban Superintendents.* Thousand Oaks, CA: Corwin Press.

5

R-E-S-P-E-C-T: Teacher Abuse and How to End It

Robert Maranto

As a college sophomore back in 1978, I decided against becoming a high school teacher when an education professor very condescendingly explained that I need not *understand* what I taught since "the curriculum people will tell you what to teach." This convinced me to spend six years in graduate school to become a college professor. Though I make less money than most high school teachers of comparable experience, as a professor I'm a respected professional. *I* decide what I teach and how I teach it.

Fast forward twenty years. Scott Milliman and I were playing with our data set of Arizona school districts to figure out where charter schools arise and where they don't. In other words, we wanted to know why teachers and parents desert traditional public schools. Much to our surprise, charter market share did not reflect poor district school test scores or "white flight." Rather, our survey showed that charters drew large numbers of students wherever district school teachers *disagreed* with the statement "I feel I'm treated as a valued employee." Fieldwork confirmed the results, as our team reported in "Small Districts in Big Trouble" (*Teachers College Record*, December 2001).

Wherever district school administrators treat their parents and teachers like children, those stakeholders leave for charter schools as soon as they get the chance. Essentially, the demand for charter schooling reflects the basic professionalism—or lack thereof—of district school administrators. Where district school "leaders" mislead to monopolize power, the better teachers and parents grow alienated. On the other hand, where principals and supers treat parents and teachers as partners, there is little need for charter schools. Unfortunately, good school leaders may be more exception than rule.

Our findings would come as no surprise to Richard Ingersoll, whose recently published *Who Controls Teachers' Work?* offers what may be the best treatment of how administrators micromanage their teachers, and what that costs education. A former public and private school teacher and now professor of education and sociology at the University of Pennsylvania, Ingersoll uses both fieldwork and surveys to show that *contrary to popular belief, school administrators really can manage their teachers. Unfortunately, they usually do so in ways which undermine education.*

Ingersoll starts by comparing two conflicting views of school management. Some education reformers believe that teachers have too much control over education and thus administrators need do more to "tighten the ship." In contrast, others see schools as too bureaucratic, with demoralized teachers having little or no power. Ingersoll goes beyond the contending parties, showing that "while the U.S. education system is relatively decentralized, schools themselves are not" (220)—principals are in charge. While teachers have considerable control in their classrooms, they have little or no influence over scheduling, budgets, personnel, and discipline, areas which principals dominate:

> The "perks" that principals typically control include the distribution of physical space; the determination of each faculty member's daily schedule, teaching assignment, and course load; the distribution of students to courses and teachers; the assignment of nonteaching duties; and the control of the portion of the budget devoted to such things as funding for field trips, projects, and professional development conferences. (126)

By determining who teaches "desirable" and "undesirable" kids, who teaches out of field, who does lunch duty, who gets the good rooms, and most important, whose disciplinary practices are backed and whose are undermined, principals punish and reward their teachers. They can use this power for good or ill, to reward good teaching or to encourage toadyism.

Principal power is not based on resources alone. Formal "evaluations" of teachers—class visits—are almost completely ineffective as measures of teaching effectiveness, but these highly subjective exercises do give administrators power over teachers. Though tenured teachers are practically impossible to fire, bad evaluations block upward mobility into administration, and in any event exert a psychological toll. As Ingersoll writes, in most schools "teachers have little control over who evaluates them, what criteria are used, and the method by which evaluations are carried out" (113). As informants at one school put it, administrators treat teachers as "tall children."

The proliferation of rules and regulations, often intended to "teacher proof" schools, may do more harm than good by undermining the "consent, goodwill, commitment, and cooperation of their employees":

Regulations often don't work well for irregular work. Unlike the example of automobile production, much of what teachers do cannot be routinized; that is, it can be difficult to codify and "freeze" the work of teachers into set routines, standard operating procedures, and measurable products. . . . The one size fits all approach to rules can deny teachers the flexibility they need to do their job effectively. For just these reasons, rules can generate resistance. (142)

Or as Anthony Downs wrote more than thirty years ago in *Inside Bureaucracy*, "the greater the effort made by a sovereign or top level official to control the behavior of subordinates officials, the greater the efforts made by those subordinates to evade or counteract such control."

Teachers are driven by a public service ethic. Yet when harassed by principals, parents, and often unwilling "clients," teachers too often give up. They become whiners who do just enough to get by. Ingersoll amends Lord Acton to argue that "Powerlessness corrupts. Absolute powerlessness corrupts absolutely" (210).

Yet the news is not all bad. In some schools teachers are treated as professionals. Ingersoll conducted fieldwork in four Philadelphia high schools: an inner city public school, a wealthy suburban public school, an urban Catholic school, and a Quaker school. In the Quaker school, faculty were actually accorded the respect due professionals. Nationally, survey research shows that teachers report more collegiality and more cooperation with fellow teachers, as well as better relations with their principals, in private schools and in small schools. Further, "schools that delegated more control to teachers had fewer problems among teachers and less conflict between teachers and administrators" (202). Schools with empowered teachers reported less trouble with student misbehavior and lower teacher turnover. Economist Richard Vedder makes the same point in a recent *Education Next* article. Private schools pay teachers less *money* than public schools, but make up for it by paying them greater *respect*.

Ingersoll wants principals to treat teachers with respect, giving them real power over school resources, student discipline, and hiring and evaluating peers. Only then will teachers have high morale and dedication. And only then will large numbers of bright, competent folks like Ingersoll (and me) want to teach in public schools.

Alas, this may prove too facile in at least two respects. First is the chicken and egg problem. Are the worst schools in trouble because they are rule-bound, or rule-bound because they are in trouble? Perhaps well-meaning administrators issue edicts to "tighten the ship" only where the ship is already sinking. (Of course, this does not mean that more rules can patch the hull.) And anyway, since teachers are not trained for empowerment, can they handle it? I doubt that the Quaker school Ingersoll studies hires certified teachers from our local education schools. Most likely, it recruits teachers from

Penn rather than Kutztown. Do the Kutztown grads that staff most schools
want empowerment? (A friend who teaches there is not so sure.)

Second, the rules of schools reflect deep social conflicts over the purposes
of public education, a point made most clearly by John Chubb and Terry
Moe in their landmark book *Politics, Markets, and America's Schools.* So
long as those both inside and outside a school building disagree as to its purpose, we can expect the contending parties to seek to codify their views
through endless regulations. That's democracy. The only way around it is to
allow teachers and parents to choose schools in line with their own values,
as in the charter school movement.

These issues aside, *Who Controls Teachers' Work?* is a great book, both interesting and important. Still, it may work better for academics than practitioners. I loved the extensive literature review, the mix of quantitative and
qualitative data, and Ingersoll's telling anecdotes about how battles over
control distract from teaching and learning. (Check out pages 213–15 on the
hat wars at an urban high school.) A busy practitioner, however, may have
trouble wading through it. Still, you could do worse than to order *Who Controls Teachers' Work?* for your library and read it in your abundant free time.

In *Perspectives on the Mistreatment of American Educators*, Norman Dale
Norris examines many of the same themes as Ingersoll less systematically,
but with more passion. Norris, a longtime Louisiana public school music
teacher now teaching education at Nichols State University and the University of Phoenix, has written an angry polemic in equal parts compelling and
exasperating. His insightful book has much to admire, and equally much
with which to argue.

Norris both defends and attacks public education, defending the autonomy and status of teachers while at the same time calling for greater professionalism within this very demanding profession. He properly bristles at the
phrase "just a teacher." Chiefly, Norris addresses four topics: schools of education, standards and testing, the battles between progressive and traditionalist educators, and most importantly, teacher abuse.

A good soldier true to his school, Norris defends education schools, perhaps more than they deserve. While admitting that EdDs come faster and
easier than PhDs, he points out that the former embody more real world experience than the latter. On weaker ground, he maintains that the field holds
a body of agreed-upon knowledge, an argument contradicted by his later
discussion of progressive education. Of teachers themselves, Norris correctly
carps that society demands too much. We do not blame the doctor if the can-
cer patient smokes: "it would be a very shallow assumption that any physi-
cian or team of physicians will actually cure the ills of every patient who
walks through the door" (25). Yet we do blame teachers when students fail.

Good-soldier Norris is right, but only up to a point. After all, only a hand-
ful of would-be doctors get into medical school and pass licensing exams,

compared to *most* would-be teachers. Further, while we do not blame doctors whose patients smoke, we *sue* doctors who remove the wrong lung. Yet my undergraduates cannot sue the high school teachers who never taught them about World War II, leaving me to do the academic corrective surgery.

Norris hates standardized testing, decrying curricular narrowing and game-playing which further erode teachers' autonomy. He sees standardized testing as another "quick fix" increasing cynicism rather than achievement: "every state that has attempted to implement a high stakes program has seen what is a grossly inflated and deceptive increase in scores that didn't last long" (131). The "most vile mistreatment of educators (and children) comes in the publication of test scores to compare schools against schools, districts against districts, and states against states." Since student achievement depends on social class, the tests "can't really tell us anything we don't already know" (137). Norris implies that you can't teach poor kids.

Here again, Norris is only part-right. The European and Asian schools we envy make much use of standardized testing. Done right, testing makes teachers' work easier by clarifying education goals, and more important, by getting students and teachers on the same team. Traditionally, American schools have let teachers set the standards. That sounds good, but in practice it gives students (and parents) incentives to lobby for low standards and punish teachers who set the bar too high, letting the inmates run the asylum. In contrast, standards set by external bodies put teachers and students on the same team: everyone works together to beat the test.

And contrary to Norris's views, standardized testing does in fact tell us things we did not already know. For example, NAEP scores show that Texas has had the most success narrowing the gaps between white and minority achievement: perhaps other states should adopt similar standards and accountability policies. Testing also tells us that some schools succeed teaching low-income students, meaning the rest of us should copy their methods.

Norris is on far stronger grounds in his outstanding discussion of the 150-year-old battle between traditionalist "teacher-centered" and progressive "student-centered" educators. While much of the "research" backing progressivism is bogus, progressive methods do have their place. Teacher-centered teaching works best for low-income kids, but middle-class kids do equally well in child-centered classrooms. Norris claims that school administrators and education school professors privately admit the need for more tradition. Indeed, Norris claims education schools teach child-centered methods largely "to ensure a high passing rate on the Praxis" (52). But who designed the Praxis? Perhaps the field of education really does not have body of knowledge, after all.

Norris is at his teacher-centered best bashing the teacher-abuse fostered by a whole industry of consultants and, though he prefers not to say it, by education professors. He describes the incredible demands placed upon educators who face abuse from students on the job and from parents after hours, combined with unrealistic expectations from psychologists:

> This PhD-level psychologist attended the next meeting where the child was on the agenda. She reported to us that she had designed a very elaborate plan of behavior modification whereby if the child went one hour without fighting or soiling himself, the teacher was to apply a blue sticker to the left hand. After three stickers (three hours—half the school day) the boy would get a red sticker on the right hand. After two red stickers (an entire school day) then a green sticker was placed on a chart on the wall. While the idea of this kind of structure and consistency was not inherently bad, it did create one additional thing for the poor teacher to maintain, practically to the neglect of all those children who did not fight or soil themselves. (35–36)

This became more interesting when the psychologist demanded that staff escort the child to the rest room to assure that he cleaned himself thoroughly. Obviously, we would never ask a psychologist for this kind of service.

In a story typical of Ingersoll, Norris chronicles degrading teaching evaluations. In his school, evaluators refused to show teachers the seventy-one-item evaluation instrument in advance:

> Teachers reported being denied credit for various indicators on the basis of papers being passed out after the lesson began (rather than at an appropriate point during the lesson) or not having clearly articulated the objective to the lesson (according to the evaluator). . . . Other teachers reported a loss of points over such matters as having worded an explanation in a manner that did not please the evaluator or the classroom seating not having pleased the evaluator, and so forth. (97)

Accused of not saying "closure" to mark a lesson's end, teachers said it multiple times to make sure it counted. This mechanical approach drove the passion from teaching. To his credit Norris struck back, taping his evaluation and thereby infuriating his tormenter:

> [She said] "I didn't appreciate you doing that. I'm only human, I can only see and observe so much. I can't compete with an audiotape that hears everything. This process is new and everyone is still learning." While I understood her concern, I was adamant in my position. If I was expected to teach "correctly," from the beginning, according to this new instrument, she should be held accountable to the same standard and likewise be expected to evaluate "correctly," from the beginning according to the instrument. (98)

As Ingersoll says, such "management" drives the talented away from teaching.

Agree with Norris or disagree with him, and I did plenty of both, he is an eclectic, learned, passionate educator who cares about teachers. In a field fraught with ideological orthodoxies of left and right, Norris is that rare educator who quotes with equal ease from reformers like Diane Ravitch and apologists like David Berliner. *Perspectives on the Mistreatment of American Educators* is one of the best books about some of the worst practices of traditional public schools. Implicitly, it is a charge for charter educators to do it better.

So far we have seen more fear than hope, but all is not lost. While Ingersoll and Norris diagnose the disease, Edward J. Dirkswager's *Teachers as Owners* provides a cure. Dirkswager, a longtime consultant and businessman associated with St. Paul's Center for Policy Studies, leads a team proposing to transform teachers from employees of large bureaucracies to practitioners in small firms or collectives, much as doctors or lawyers band together to form practices.

Dirkswager starts by pointing out that even though surveys show that most taxpayers want professionals—meaning teachers—to control education, 70 percent of teachers feel left out of the decision process. To become empowered, teachers must own the schools, or at least the education service providers. Through teacher professional partnerships (TPPs), teachers can take over the teaching business.

Of course, for many educators "business" is a bad word. Yet as with some medical practices, a teacher practice would focus more on service than money: teachers "need to understand that the most successful businesses are driven by a desire to provide excellent service, to meet and exceed the expectations" (25). In particular, TPPs would honor and enhance the status of teaching: administrators would now work for teachers, rather than the other way round. As Dirkswager writes, doctors or lawyers "hire administrators, if necessary, to run the administrative aspects of their business. In this way, they can spend their time using their expertise to its fullest extent" (2). Especially vitally, a TPP leader "is not the boss but first among equals, the *principal teacher*, who is also evaluated by his or her peers" (20).

The partnership makes personnel and resource decisions, but in return "if learning does not occur to the satisfaction of the clients, parents, and students, the practice cannot remain in business" (3). With rewards come risks, including possible TPP bankruptcy, or individual termination by one's peers if students do not learn. Naturally, this requires standards of learning, since you cannot judge peers honestly without objective, or at least agreed-upon, criteria for success. If you can't agree on what students should learn, how can you measure good teaching? Similarly, other ingredients of success are much the same as for any service business: intelligent and trustworthy leadership, strong cultures of openness, collaboration, and civility. These allow peer review to work.

In TPPs, teachers get more power over their careers, curricula, and resources. But what's in it for students? TPPs offer more cohesive schools with better teaching. As a wealth of scholarship shows, currently teachers have little incentive to change their practices even if it would help their students. Ownership and peer review (with peer pressure) could change this (75). After all, would I want a nonperforming lawyer to drag down my law firm?

TPPs put the people who know the most about the schools in charge—the teachers. TPPs might end teacher shortages (78), since research shows that smarter teachers are better teachers, and such people prefer life as owners than as mistreated drones.

Notably, many of the insights for the book come from the real world experiences of EdVisions, a Minnesota teachers' cooperative founded in 1994. EdVisions changed the whole dynamic of education:

> The teachers in schools run by the cooperative have chosen to pay themselves higher than average salaries, and the technology budget of the school has also been set higher than average. The learning programs are developed, implemented, and improved by the teachers. Teachers, students, and parents form close relationships geared toward learning. Each teacher is expected to develop and implement his or her own professional development plan. Evaluation is by peer review, and teachers who have failed to perform have been asked to leave. (3)

By 2001 EdVisions served eight schools under seven different sponsors. It pays a lower than usual percentage of the budget for salaries, yet still pays teachers above average salaries by deploying personnel more intelligently than the typical school district (and having no high-paid superintendent). It also has a large reserve fund.

After the first three chapters, *Teachers as Owners* is essentially a reference/how-to book, offering detailed road maps of how to structure partnerships and boards, how larger size complicates organization culture, how to judge contractors (a perennial problem for charter schools), developing standards, peer review planning, fringe benefits, unions, managing relations with sponsors, and so on. Such details are less inspiring, but no less vital in achieving Dirkswager's vision.

Of course, no vision is without problems. Just as there are better and worse medical practices, there will be good and bad TPPs. Will parents and school boards have the expertise to keep the former and fire the latter? And how could we keep TPPs from being as self-serving in peer review as college professors are? Or as hierarchical as law firms? Most likely, the lack of guaranteed contracts and the general culture of teaching will avoid these pitfalls, but only time will tell. More important, TPPs threaten the power of traditional education administrators and unions. How do we keep them from declaring war on TPPs?

Yet such small clouds should not rain on Dirkswager's parade. Whatever their potential problems, TPPs seem far better than traditional district schools, and indeed better than most existing charter schools, though many charters have elements of the TPP model already in place. *Teachers as Owners* offers much needed hope for reforming schools in ways that will empower teachers, and ultimately lead to innovations as yet un-dreamt of.

When I do fieldwork, in some schools I have minders while in others I can wander freely. In the latter schools, teachers say the same things no matter who is in the room. In the former, they are guarded. In the latter, teachers and principals admit problems while in the former they blame others for their failings. Fieldwork and teacher surveys indicate that charter school teachers are more empowered than their counterparts in district schools, but this does not mean that charters have no need for improvement. Indeed, some charters are as bad as anything described by Ingersoll or Norris. Hopefully, as our movement grows and matures, we will see more TPP type schools and fewer traditional bureaucracies. If not, then teachers and children will continue to suffer mistreatment.

REFERENCES

Chubb, John, and Terry Moe. 1990. *Politics, Markets, and America's Schools.* Washington, DC: Brookings Institution Press.

Dirkswager, Edward J., ed. 2002. *Teachers as Owners: A Key to Revitalizing Public Education.* Lanham: Scarecrow Press.

Downs, Anthony. 1967. *Inside Bureaucracy.* Prospect Heights: Waveland Press.

Hess, F., R. Maranto, and S. Milliman. 2001. "Small Districts in Big Trouble: How Four Arizona School Districts Coped With Charter Competition," *Teachers College Record.* 103, no. 6 (December): 1102–24.

Ingersoll, Richard M. 2003. *Who Controls Teachers' Work? Power and Accountability in America's Schools.* Cambridge: Harvard University Press.

Norris, Norman Dale. 2002. *Perspectives on the Mistreatment of American Educators: Throwing Water on a Drowning Man.* Lanham: Scarecrow Press.

Vedder, Richard. 2003. "Comparable Worth," *Education Next* 3, no. 3 (summer): 14–19.

6

Smaller Classes or Better Teachers?

Lewis C. Solmon and Kimberly Firetag Agam

The flat growth line of student achievement and the U.S. students' dismal ranking on international comparisons of student achievement have led to decades of flawed reforms intended to reverse these trends. That the U.S. Department of Education has designated 11,008 schools as "in need of improvement" underlines the failure of most reforms to date. Yet we are in danger of repeating our mistakes.

Class size reduction (CSR), a very popular reform among both teachers and parents, has been tried in California and other states, and passed in November 2002 as a ballot proposition in Florida. The reform that currently is giving CSR a run for its (substantial) money is teacher quality (TQ). There is almost universal agreement—rare in education policy debates—that teacher quality is the most important school-related input affecting student learning. In one large study, equally able fifth grade students who had weak teachers three years in a row scored at the twenty-ninth percentile, while those who had three consecutive years of strong teachers scored at the eighty-third percentile. The disagreement arises when trying to determine how to attract, motivate, and retain the best, the brightest, the most knowledgeable, and the most capable into the teaching profession.

We can learn from medical research as we ponder the choices policy makers face. A New York Times article ("Mixed Medical Messages," Sunday, August 25, 2002, Section 4) discussed the recent confusing messages coming from the medical profession, which are due to different interpretations of research. For example, mathematical correlations do not necessarily imply a cause-and-effect relationship. Moreover, even the "gold standard in epidemiology," randomized controlled clinical trials, are difficult to execute and expensive to complete, but they are essential because bad studies only lead to bad information, according to Dr. Kenneth Shine, the former president of the Institute of Medicine.

But Dr. Shine acknowledged that even the best-designed clinical trial can produce misleading data. "Science is imperfect and dependent on an accumulation of information," he said. "Rather than relying on a single study, we need to draw from the ever-increasing body of knowledge."

These are lessons that social scientists must heed well. They bemoan the fact that randomized experiments are difficult if not impossible to construct in education. They forget that correlation does not necessarily mean causation. And they often pick the studies that confirm their political views rather than draw from the ever-increasing body of knowledge as suggested by Dr. Shine.

Nowhere is this more evident than in the class size debates. Class size reduction has become a popular education reform; in the past five years, over $25 billion dollars has been pumped into programs to lower class size. The supposed benefits of CSR include more individual attention for students, fewer discipline problems, more manageable classrooms, and a better working environment; therefore, more student learning would take place. Despite inconclusive research about its effectiveness, billions of additional dollars are slated for spending on this endeavor, both to maintain already lowered class sizes and to establish additional smaller classes.

Between 1960 and 1995 the pupil/teacher ratios in the United States fell from 25.8 to 17.3 (Mishel and Rothstein 2002). However, despite this drop in class size there has been essentially no change in standardized NAEP test scores. Smaller classes have an intuitive appeal—almost all parents would prefer their kids be in smaller classes. But no one poses the choice of a class of thirty-seven with a truly inspiring, knowledgeable teacher, or one of twenty with an unprepared teacher who sought the job only because jobs in other fields were scarce.

Advocates of CSR point to Tennessee's Student Teacher Achievement Ratio (STAR) project to argue that smaller classes lead to greater student achievement, even though there have been enough criticisms of that experiment to make many thoughtful analysts wary of relying on it to determine public policy. STAR is one of the few randomized experiments in education, so those advocating CSR attach themselves to it uncritically.

Yet its conclusions are by no means beyond question. Attrition of below-average achieving students from small classes (20–30 percent of students left each year) could be one reason why the study reported that students in smaller classes had statistically significantly greater achievement. Although students were randomly assigned to large or small classes, teachers were not randomly assigned, nor were the schools randomly selected. What if the best teachers were rewarded by being assigned to smaller classes? Schools that are interested in reform usually have many reforms going on at the same time, so how do we know which one led to the greater achievement? Do certain other reforms interact better with small than large classes to produce greater student learning?

If randomized experiments are the "gold standard" in medicine, they are the "holy grail" in social sciences. They are so rare that when they are conducted, they are assumed to be the best evidence possible. However, to base policy on this single unreplicated study would be like observing remission of a disease in one patient in a clinical trial, ignoring side effects, and then putting the drug on the market. STAR classes ranged in size from twelve to seventeen to twenty-two to twenty-six. Thus part of the comparison is between classes of twelve and classes of twenty-six.

If reduction of that magnitude were to increase achievement, does that mean that a reduction from twenty-three to eighteen, as is being advocated for the lower grades in Florida, would have a similar effect? Not necessarily.

As suggested above for medical research, "rather than relying on a single study, we need to draw from the ever-increasing body of knowledge." The class size research began at least as long ago as the first decade of the last century. A study in 1909 categorized classes as less than forty students (small), forty to forty-nine students (medium), and fifty or more students (large)! So apparently in the olden days some kids were taught in classrooms with more students than even the poorest, least-concerned schools would allow today. Of course in those days most students wanted to learn and were able to do so, or they would have dropped out, or been kicked out. A recent paper by Edward Lazear argues that students who attend smaller classes learn more because they experience fewer student disruptions during class time (Lazear 1999). In earlier days the disruptors probably would not have been tolerated. So, smaller classes may be an expensive way to avoid having to discipline today's students.

There have been a number of "meta-analyses" that look at hundreds of studies and try to draw a consensus. Most of the included studies are correlational analyses where the authors infer causation from correlation. In 1979, a meta-analysis by Gene Glass and Mary Lee Smith found some benefits in smaller classes (Glass and Smith 1979). But more recently, Eric Hanushek's meta-analysis concluded just the opposite. Alan Krueger disputes Hanushek's conclusion based on technical issues, but Hanushek remains steadfast (Mishel and Rothstein 2002).[1] There is no general agreement on the value of CSR for student achievement.

Studies of other CSR initiatives have had mixed results. Analyses of California CSR programs found that no strong connection to student achievement can be inferred (Bohrnstedt and Stecher 2002) and that the program created a severe teacher shortage that compromised teacher quality, caused a classroom shortage, and hurt poorest schools the most. The biggest "side effect" of class size reduction is that it exacerbates the teacher quality problem—especially in the most troubled schools. There is a continuum of quality of teachers, with those at the top almost always choosing to teach in relatively high–socioeconomic status, suburban schools. Most effective teachers in urban settings would prefer suburban schools but there were no openings—until class size reduction kicked in. CSR opens teaching positions at high–socioeconomic status schools, exacerbating the flow of quality teachers from poor to rich areas, leaving an even less effective group in the inner cities, along with more openings. The California experience shows that an unintended consequence of CSR when a teacher shortage already exists is drastically decreased quality in new hires. Indeed, during the first year of CSR, teacher hiring in California rose 46 percent as 28,500 teachers were hired. Uncredentialed teachers rose from 1.8 percent to 13 percent of the teaching force.[2]

Some might point out that in the Los Angeles Unified School District, test scores have been rising somewhat in the grades affected by CSR. However, during the same period, bilingual education was abolished, phonics replaced the whole language method of teaching reading, direct instruction was begun, and a stronger accountability system was put in place, so it is not clear that the observed improvements should be credited to CSR.

Our conclusion is that by far, the most studies and the best studies come out on the side of CSR having few significant positive effects on student learning. At most one can conclude that CSR produces gains in the lowest grades, in the poorest schools, and in certain subjects. Thus programs like the Florida proposition aimed at reducing size of all classes in all schools, grades, and subjects are quite simply a waste of money. CSR will not work unless teachers change how they teach—a dreary lecture will have the same impact on a student whether there are eighteen or thirty-five kids in the room. The question is whether CSR motivates teachers to change how they teach, and whether many teachers are capable of doing things better even if they wanted to.

While the impact of CSR is uncertain, there is mounting evidence that teacher quality (TQ) is the single most important school-related factor in student achievement. The Secretary's Third Annual Report of Teacher Quality stresses that an important determinant of children's education is their teachers (CITE) and a recent report by The Teaching Commission highlights research that shows the difference a high quality teacher can make (The Teaching Commission 2004). A nonpartisan report prepared by the Office of Policy Research at the Florida Department of Education cites research that finds teacher quality and expenditures on professional development had a greater impact on student achievement than increased teacher salaries or lower pupil/teacher ratios did (Florida Department of Education 2002).

Low quality teachers have adverse effects on students in addition to smaller learning gains, creating additional costs to society by causing some students to be held back and thereby shortening their working life, or worse, not to reach their academic potential due to poor quality instruction.

The question is how to attract, motivate, and retain the best and the brightest into the teaching profession. Many things have been tried recently to attract new teachers including forgiving college loans, housing subsidies, public service announcements, new recruiting strategies, and even perks like health club memberships when signing on. But most of these efforts are small, isolated, not school-centered, poorly designed, or poorly implemented. They are not systemic changes, but rather, piecemeal efforts that often raise more problems than they solve. If better teachers are attracted into the same old profession, they will leave soon after they begin.

Of course, the most frequently urged solution to the teacher quality (and quantity) problem is to pay teachers more. According to the American Federation of Teachers, the $45,771 average teacher salary [in 2002–2003] fell short of wages of other white-collar occupations (American Federation of Teachers 2004). For example, according to the Bureau of Labor and Statistics, mid-level accountants earned an average $55,430, computer system analysts, $66,180, and attorneys, $107,800. Obviously these gaps are reduced once we adjust for days worked per year and fringe benefits, and allow for extra income that teachers can earn for ancillary jobs around the school like coaching the football or debate teams.

The salary solution is often manifested by the recommendation that "we bring our teacher salaries up to the national average." Fully thirty-six states have average salaries below the national average of $45,771. To reach that level, salaries in Ohio would have to rise by $250, and in South Dakota by $13,357. Overall, the thirty-six states would have to increase salaries by an average of $6,266 at a total incremental cost of $9 billion. Would a salary increase for all teachers drive the best talent into the teaching profession, motivate them, and keep them teaching for the long haul? We think not.

We should be eager to grant higher salaries to effective teachers—but do we want to give the same pay raises to the most effective, energetic, motivating, and up-to-date teachers as to the ineffective ones? And everyone—teachers, students, parents—knows which teachers fall into each category.

Many of our best and brightest do not choose teaching careers today, because of the terrible environment in most schools, because women have many more opportunities than in the past, and because of the low pay. The question—after "Can we afford this?"—is whether raises in the $5,000–6,000 range will draw those now considering much more lucrative careers as law, medicine, or business into teaching. We think they will not. Moreover, such across-the-board increases would do more to keep the least effective teachers in the profession because they have few alternative opportunities.

Salary variance (or range from high to low) rather than average salary is an important attraction to the best, the brightest, the most successful college graduates. The college grad who has won all the prizes, received all the academic and extramural awards, and is used to succeeding does not look at what the "average" person earns. She looks at what is earned by the best in the field because she is highly confident that she will be at the top of any profession she enters. She is willing to compete because she knows she will win. The average lawyer salary is irrelevant; she looks at what the all-star lawyers earn. She looks at the teaching profession and is appalled and repelled by a field where the least energetic, least knowledgeable, and least successful teacher earns the same as the one with the same years of experience and college credits who is always current in his subject, works from morning to late at night every day, and has the talent to make kids learn. In sum, there is no financial incentive for teachers to be more productive, that is, to get their students to learn more. If only the effective teachers get performance bonuses, these can be high enough to get noticed by top-notch potential teachers, both new grads and career changers.

There are many rebuttals to the above, all fallacious. First, it is claimed that teachers should not be in it for the money, rather they should love teaching and love their jobs. Many lawyers and doctors also love their jobs but that does not preclude them from earning excellent incomes, if they are successful. Then it is argued that surveys of teachers "prove" that teachers do not want differentiated pay. Of course, that's why they became teachers. To understand what potential teachers want, you cannot ask actual teachers, but you must ask those who selected other professions.

Then there is the point that if only the more effective teachers were more highly compensated there would be jealousy, lack of cooperation, and nepotism; it would destroy teacher morale. But wouldn't a system that encourages teamwork and prepares teachers for high performance enhance morale? Such negative results are not highly evident or destructive in virtually every other field where effectiveness gets rewarded.

Many people accept additional pay for National Board certification, which may be fine. However, some justify this because it involves extra work and training unrelated to student performance. Why should voters pay for new certifications or extra work if these do not result in significantly enhanced student performance? Why would teachers do these things if not to help students learn? If they get certified and their students don't learn better, is the certification of any use? Recent studies have detected a slight difference in the achievement of students with teachers who are National Board certified. However, "as to whether this observed advantage is of any practical importance (i.e., NBPTS certification could make an important contribution to enhancing student achievement) or whether it is a cost-effective means of improving student achievement, the answer is unequivocally no," J. E. Stone, a researcher on this topic, recently commented. "The NBPTS gains [are] very small and expensive relative to the known achievement gaps" (Stone 2004). Merit pay is criticized as something advanced by people who want to run schools like a business. Businesses are accountable and look to the "bottom line." Shouldn't schools be held accountable for a bottom line of student learning? In virtually every other profession effectiveness gets rewarded.

Finally, there are claims that previous attempts to institute "merit pay" in schools failed. Often that was because it was not implemented properly, that is, it did not gain teacher acceptance, but rather it was imposed from above. Performance standards must be clear, and teachers must be prepared for the assessments they will have to undergo to prove that they are effective. Also, the rewards for all the extra effort must be substantial enough to make all the extra work worthwhile. In most cases, these requirements were not met.

This is surely not an argument for performance pay alone. The opportunity for high pay for high performance would attract more top people into teaching. But if they find themselves in the same old profession with no induction programs, no chance to get better at their craft, no opportunity to advance, little collegiality, little respect from the community, and unpleasant, often dangerous surroundings, they will soon leave. That is what happens now, especially to the best young teachers.

In what other profession does one start with a title and set of responsibilities and retire thirty years later with the same title and same responsibilities? In teaching, you enter your classroom, shut the door, and come out at the end of the day. You don't collaborate with your peers and there is little collegiality. Rarely do your supervisors see how effective you are and there are few opportunities to get better at what you do.

A successful teacher quality initiative must change the school ethos and environment. It must enable capable teachers to progress through a job hierarchy and be rewarded for extra responsibilities without having to move into administration. It must develop an evaluation system with heavy teacher input that educates and then evaluates teachers on the most effective, research-validated teaching techniques. That evaluation should have consequences in that teachers' compensation should be based in part on how well they perform in their classrooms. And a complete TQ model has to provide professional development at the school site to help teachers improve their techniques, prepare for their evaluations, and solve the teaching and learning problems that they face regularly in their classrooms. This would enhance collegiality by enabling teachers to work and learn together.

Most important, the model should base at least part of its performance award on student achievement. It should look not at how smart the students are when they start, but at how much they have learned this year. Such an approach encourages collaboration by rewarding teachers in part based upon learning gains of the whole school. But it also should base part of one's compensation on how much his or her own students learn. It makes teaching more like every other profession where people are compensated for what they produce.

Such programs require fundamental changes in a school, but can provide benefits at least similar to those alleged to come from CSR. In Florida, state economists estimated the cost of CSR, phased in over ten years, to be between $20 billion and $27.5 billion.[3] This is a very expensive way to change schools, especially given the results we have seen so far. The costs of systemic reform to enhance teacher quality are much less. The estimated costs of CSR are too low because they fail to account for the scarcity of quality teachers. They assume, incorrectly, that people who will enter teaching are at the same level of quality we currently see, which is not high to begin with. The *Sarasota Herald Tribune* reported ("Teachers Who Fail: A Survey of Certification-Test Scores Yields Alarming Results," Sunday, December 12, 2004), "More than half a million Florida students sat in classrooms last year in front of teachers who failed the state's basic skills tests for teachers."

The choice is not class size reduction or no reform at all. CSR takes money away from teacher quality initiatives and results in lower-quality teachers being brought into the system. Investing in high-quality teachers costs much less and produces more student learning gains and other benefits, and that makes TQ the preferred policy choice.

EPILOGUE

If class size reduction is not the way to increase student achievement, and teacher quality improvements offer more hope, how do we go about achieving higher teacher quality?

The Teacher Advancement Program (TAP) is a comprehensive school reform developed by the Milken Family Foundation with the goal to attract, retain, motivate, and develop quality teachers, through the implementation of four elements: multiple career paths, ongoing applied professional growth, instructionally focused accountability, and performance-based compensation. TAP schools have changed their structure to better support their most valuable asset: quality teachers.

The most controversial part of TAP is its performance pay component. Quite frankly, performance pay, or merit pay in earlier incarnations, has rarely worked. Everyone knows the reasons offered for those failures: the merit pay system was imposed on teachers without their consent, lack of consensus about who is a good teacher, competition among teachers, nepotism and favoritism by those doling out the awards, and a lot of work for small potential incremental gains (Solmon and Podgursky 2000). In designing TAP, we attempted to deal with all of these issues. TAP involves teachers every step of the way, and requires at least 60 percent of faculty to vote to adopt the program. It is implemented slowly in order to gain and solidify teacher support.

TAP has developed an extensive research-based teacher evaluation system with detailed protocols and rubrics, four to six classroom visits a year, and multiple evaluators. This makes the evaluation system fair and honest. The professional development system—which takes place in the school during the school day on a daily or weekly basis, and deals with problems teachers are facing in their classrooms, prepares teachers to be assessed and then rewarded. The performance pay does not replace the traditional salary schedule, but rather supplements it. Nor is the TAP awards system a zero sum game—the bonuses are criterion referenced rather than relative, so any teacher who meets a standard receives a bonus. And even the least effective teachers earn no less than they would have without the performance pay system. Rather than bonuses in the hundreds of dollars that we see in other plans, we suggest performance pay that averages $2,500–3,000. In general, 50 percent of the bonus is awarded for skills and knowledge as demonstrated in the classroom during the multiple visits by evaluators trained by TAP staff. The other 50 percent is awarded for student achievement (measured by value added or learning gains), 30 percent based on school-wide achievement and given to all teachers, and 20 percent for achievement of the individual teacher's own students. Teachers who score high on the skills and knowledge part can receive bonuses even if their students do not show gains.

TAP is currently operating in ten different states (Arizona, Arkansas, Colorado (Eagle County), Florida, Indiana (Archdiocese of Indianapolis), Louisiana, Minnesota, South Carolina, Ohio, and Texas) and Washington, D.C. By the end of the current academic year, there will be over one hundred schools implementing TAP across the country. TAP is serving more than 45,000 students and more than 3,100 teachers.

We have three years of results from TAP schools in Arizona and two years from TAP schools in South Carolina. We also have analyzed the growth in achievement of students whose schools implemented TAP compared to the growth in achievement of students from similar schools (Schacter et al. 2002). We compared twenty-five year-to-year changes in student achievement in TAP schools to control schools. In seventeen of these cases, or 68 percent of the time, the TAP schools outperformed their controls. The RAND study of Comprehensive School Reform (CSR) schools concluded that 50 percent of the CSR schools outperformed their controls in math and 47 percent outperformed their controls in reading, although the CSR schools had been operating for a substantially longer period of time than TAP. We are still awaiting results of the formal evaluation; however, this year's results appear to be as good as last year's. One important anecdotal explanation for the success of TAP is that teaching in TAP schools is improving significantly.

Some more "intermediate outcomes" that we have observed in TAP schools include that in Arizona, some very talented teachers moving from high–socioeconomic status schools that are not doing TAP to low–socioeconomic status schools that are doing TAP. Over the past three years, sixty-one teachers have started working at the two lowest–socioeconomic status TAP schools in the Madison School District, Camelview and Park. Of these, thirteen (21 percent) have come from high–socioeconomic status schools in Madison or nearby districts, and are among the very best teachers from the area. Teachers in TAP schools are generally more content and feel more professional than is usually the case.

In addition, we have analyzed the effects that TAP had on teacher attitudes and satisfaction. Providing teachers with a career path and opportunity to advance, compensating expert teachers for their skills, knowledge, and responsibilities, restructuring school schedules to ensure time during the school day for teacher lead professional development and coaching, and paying teachers based on how well they instruct and how much their students learn led to increased student achievement. Moreover, the results persisted in Title I and non–Title I schools, in initially high-achieving and initially low-achieving schools, and in schools in large and small urban communities.

We also surveyed teacher attitudes toward various components of TAP. In particular, we were interested in how teachers felt about TAP's accountability and performance pay after these became a reality in their schools. In fact, after implementation, teachers felt less positively about these two innovations than they had indicated feeling prior to implementation, although they still were more positive than the "typical teacher" is presumed to be. However, despite lower levels of support for performance pay and accountability, teachers are reporting high levels of collegiality. This finding is contrary to many who argue that performance pay leads to increased competition and divisiveness. TAP teachers' attitudes confirm that the implementation of TAP requires a commitment to change what has traditionally been taking place in classrooms; however, the payoff in terms of collegiality and professional support is clear. This is the type of climate that we believe will motivate high quality teachers to stay in teaching and will attract new teachers to the profession. For a reform that cost on average $400 per pupil,[4] approximately 5 percent of the average cost to educate a child, TAP appears to be paying large dividends.

REFERENCES

American Federation of Teachers. 2004. "2003 Survey & Analysis of Teacher Salary Trends." http://www.aft.org/salary/index.htm.

Glass, G. V., and M. L. Smith 1979. "Meta-analysis of Research on Class Size and Achievement." Educational Evaluation and Policy Analysis.

Bohrnstedt, G. W. and B. M. Stecher 2002. *What Have We Learned About Class Size Reduction in California.* CSR Research Consortium.

Lazear, Edward. 1999. "Education Production." Working Paper number 7349. Cambridge, MA: National Bureau of Economic Research.

Milken, L. 2002. *Growth of the Teacher Advancement Program: Teaching as the Opportunity.* Santa Monica, CA: Milken Family Foundation.

Mishel, Lawrence, and Richard Rothstein, eds. 2002. *The Class Size Debate.* Washington, DC: Economic Policy Institute.

Nelson, F. H., R. Drown, and J. C. Gould. 2001. *Survey and Analysis of Teacher Salary Trends 2001.* Washington, DC: American Federation of Teachers.

Florida Department of Education. 2002. "Proposed Constitutional Amendments."

Schacter, J., et al. 2002. *The Impact of the Teacher Advancement Program on Student Achievement, Teacher Attitudes, and Job Satisfaction.* Santa Monica, CA: Milken Family Foundation.

Solmon, L., and M. Podgursky. 2000. *The Pros and Cons of Performance-Based Compensation.* Santa Monica, CA: Milken Family Foundation.

Stone, J. E. 2004. E-mail to Lew Solmon, December 13.

The Teaching Commission. 2004. Teaching at Risk: A Call to Action.

Word, E., et al. 1990. "Project STAR Final Report, 1985–1990" Tennessee State Department of Education.

NOTES

1. For example, Krueger argues that Hanushek gives a disproportionate amount of weight to a single study that contains a large number of estimates. Krueger claims that with an appropriate weighting it would show that class size is a determinant of student achievement.

2. Although it is not clear that a credential assures a quality teacher, the necessity to hire teachers quickly will likely result in the need to bring in people with characteristics less conducive to being a good teacher. It seems certain that increasing the numbers of teachers will force school systems to hire those they previously would have rejected.

3. Note that the voters in Florida passed the class size proposition in the November 2002 election. As state officials start planning for the implementation of class sizes they have been able to reduce costs from the original estimate; however, they are still substantial. For example, original estimates of the costs in year one were $3 billion and revised estimates are closer to $628 million.

4. We have found that TAP in Florida costs roughly $300 per student. The approximate total cost over ten years, if TAP were implemented in all Florida schools and phased in during the first four years (25 percent of schools in year 1, 50 percent in year 2, 75 percent in year 3, and 100 percent in year 4) is approximately $5.9 billion. This is less expensive than the estimated class-size reduction costs in Florida. Even if the two reforms produced the same results, although we argue TAP has a larger effect on student achievement, TAP is a much more cost-effective reform.

7

Why So Many Arizona Certified Teachers Aren't in the Classroom

Rebecca Gau and Louann Bierlein Palmer

As part of a larger project examining Arizona's potential teacher shortage, a statewide survey of Arizona inactive certified teachers provides some insight into the question of why teachers leave the profession or never enter the classroom (O'Neil and Associates, Inc. 2002; Morrison Institute 2003). While many teachers leave the profession for personal reasons such as raising a family or retirement, others leave because of unsatisfactory aspects of the classroom environment or school system. Even so, as much as one-third of this pool may "seriously consider" teaching again, especially if pay were increased or class size reduced.

Until this study, inactive certified teachers had not been carefully tracked or surveyed in Arizona. In the spring of 2002, O'Neil Associates, Inc., under the direction of the Morrison Institute, conducted a random sample survey of Arizona inactive certified teachers to determine why they left the profession or never entered it, and also to test the efficacy of proposals to recruit these teachers back into the classroom. Responses by the 804 interviewees are within ±3.5 percent of figures likely obtained (with a 95 percent level of confidence) had every inactive certified teacher in Arizona been interviewed. (The survey methodology and full results are detailed in the report *Is There a Teacher Shortage? Demand and Supply in Arizona*, available at www .morrisoninstitute.org.)

POTENTIAL LABOR POOL

By field-testing an Arizona Department of Education's Teacher Certification Division database, this study estimates that Arizona has 11,000 inactive certified teachers. Of 804 respondents from this universe, 35 percent indicated they would "seriously" consider becoming employed or reemployed as a public school teacher. Thus, as many as 3,850 certified teachers currently not teaching could be seriously interested in returning to the teaching profession if the right conditions existed. But let's first examine why they left in the first place.

Survey respondents were asked to supply their main reason for leaving or not entering the profession. Close to half said they left the profession either for personal reasons, such as raising a family (24 percent), or for retirement (21 percent). These individuals may not be strongly influenced by changes in school district or charter school policies. Nevertheless, a portion of these teachers are likely to return when their children start school or if retirement "doesn't work out." A significant number of other respondents, however, left for reasons that may be preventable—reasons such as disillusionment and stress (16 percent), low salary (10 percent), frustration with administration and bureaucracy (6 percent), and lack of respect or support (3 percent). Stress, administrative burden, and lack of respect and support are considered components of overall "classroom environment." Thus, about one quarter of Arizona's inactive certified teachers might not have left the profession had their work environment been more acceptable.

A closer look at these data show:

- Of the 24 percent of teachers who said they left the profession for personal reasons, most were pregnant or taking care of their children.
- Of the 21 percent who retired, almost half were under the age of sixty.
- Only 10 percent of teachers said that low pay was the main reason they left teaching or never started.
- Almost 20 percent of respondents are not lost to the profession. They either took a different job such as administration or they wanted to stay in the profession (e.g., applying for teaching positions or taking classes to further their education career).

INACTIVE CERTIFIED TEACHERS WHO MIGHT TEACH (AGAIN)

Two survey questions provided data on what policies or factors might motivate inactive certified teachers to either start or return to teaching. Survey respondents were given a list of potential policies and other ideas and asked to indicate how likely each proposal would be to motivate them to teach. In a follow-up open-ended question, respondents were also asked to name one key factor that would most likely lead them to return to the profession.

Over 70 percent of respondents said increased pay would "very likely" make them reconsider teaching. This appears contradictory to the previously mentioned finding that only a small percentage of these inactive teachers said low pay was their main reason for leaving the profession, which indicates that compensation is a complicated issue.

The next most favored proposals concerned classroom environment—reducing class size (66 percent), reducing paperwork (56 percent), and making schools safer (54 percent). The most recent national Schools and Staffing Survey corroborates the paperwork issue. Arizona ranked second highest for the percentage of teachers who said that routine duties and paperwork interfere with their teaching—78 percent in Arizona compared to 71 percent nationally (U.S. Department of Education, 2002).

Finally, inactive certified teachers noted that providing tuition reimbursement (53 percent) would be an important incentive for them to return. Teachers make more money as they gain formal education, yet such courses can be costly.

RESPONDENTS' ONE KEY FACTOR

In response to the open-ended question regarding the one key factor that would motivate inactive certified teachers to return to the profession, the most frequent answer was increased pay (29 percent), followed by personal/ life choices (15 percent), and factors related to public support and respect (12 percent). Other open-ended responses included reduced class size (8 percent), improved classroom environment (8 percent), and increased administrative support (6 percent). On the other hand, 10 percent said that nothing would bring them back.

Importantly, a substantial number of teachers said they might be interested in teaching where they are most needed—in challenging situations. When respondents were asked if they would consider working in a difficult school with hard-to-educate students if they were paid more for this duty, almost 40 percent said "yes," while about 45 percent said "no."

HISPANIC INACTIVE CERTIFIED TEACHERS

Due to rapid growth in the percentage of Hispanic students in coming years, districts and charters will be looking for additional Limited English Proficient (LEP) trained and Hispanic teachers. Analysis of inactive certified teachers surveyed who identified themselves as Hispanic gives an indication of what led to their departure and what might help retain more in the future. Disillusionment and stress (23 percent) was the leading reason for leaving, followed by taking a different job or wanting to stay in the profession (21 percent), and personal or life choices (17 percent).

The leading incentives that Hispanic inactive certified teachers said would attract them back were salary (75 percent), reduced class size (72 percent), better resources (72 percent), and decreased paperwork (69 percent). These response rates were higher than for non-Hispanic respondents. In addition, 68 percent of Hispanic respondents said they would be interested in returning to tougher schools for higher pay, compared to only 39 percent of non-Hispanic respondents. The number of Hispanic respondents to this survey was low because Hispanics are underrepresented in the teaching pool. However, since the actual number of inactive certified teachers who are Hispanic is unknown, these responses may be reliable.

RELATIVELY INEXPERIENCED INACTIVE CERTIFIED TEACHERS

One-third of new teachers leave the profession within their first three years of teaching (Ingersoll 2001). These teachers give different reasons for leaving the teaching profession than teachers with a little more experience. Inactive teachers with fewer than three years of experience most often cited salary (28 percent), personal or life choices (24 percent), and taking a different job or wanting to stay in the profession (21 percent) as their top reasons for leaving, while teachers with three to five years of experience cited personal or life choices most often (35 percent), with fewer citing salary (17 percent) or a different job or wanting to stay in the profession (15 percent). The two groups generally agreed on the top three proposals most likely to bring them back: increased salary, smaller class size, and tuition reimbursement.

INACTIVE CERTIFIED TEACHERS IN RURAL LOCATIONS

Rural school districts face special challenges in attracting teachers. Among these are generally lower salaries and fewer amenities in many locations. To take a closer look at responses of inactive rural teachers, survey respondents were categorized by the county they lived in as either urban or rural. Data from this analysis show that inactive teachers who currently live in rural areas left teaching primarily to retire (24 percent). (This does not necessarily mean that they taught in rural areas, but simply that they live there now.) Other top reasons for leaving include taking a different job or wanting to stay in the profession (21 percent), personal or life choices (18 percent), and disillusionment and stress (17 percent). The top incentives that could entice them back into the teaching workforce include increased pay (73 percent), reduced class size (70 percent), decreased paperwork (59 percent), and improved discipline and safety (59 percent).

INACTIVE CERTIFIED SUBJECT-MATTER AREA TEACHERS

A number of subject-matter areas, particularly special education and LEP programs were of particular interest to researchers. Analysis of survey responses from inactive certified teachers with certifications and endorsements in these fields reveals that they generally left teaching for the same reasons as other teachers—personal or life choices (23 percent), taking a different job or wanting to stay in the profession (21 percent), disillusionment and stress (20 percent), or retirement (18 percent).

The recruitment incentives of most interest to them also mirrored those for the whole sample—increased salaries (76 percent) and reduced class size (66 percent). However, decreased paperwork (64 percent) was somewhat higher for specialty teachers than for all respondents (56 percent)—not surprising, since these teaching specialties typically require extra paperwork.

SUMMARY: PAY IS A COMPLICATED ISSUE

Survey research conducted in Arizona shows that teachers don't stay away from the classroom because of low pay, but increasing pay would bring them back. One explanation could be that pay is not enough to compensate for negative factors related to classroom environment, or the condition of education. Increasing pay without changing these factors could retain and attract more teachers. But increasing pay is a "big ticket" item. Improving the classroom and professional environment in order to attract and keep teachers costs less, and has the added effect of improving the environment in which children learn.

REFERENCES

Ingersoll, R. M. 2001. *A Different Approach to Solving the Teacher Shortage Problem. Teaching Quality Policy Briefs* 3. Seattle, WA: Center for the Study of Teaching and Policy, University of Washington.
Morrison Institute for Public Policy. 2003. *Is There a Teacher Shortage? Demand and Supply in Arizona.* Tempe, AZ: Arizona State University.

O'Neil and Associates, Inc. 2002. *Arizona Teacher Retention Survey: Report of Survey Research Conducted for the Morrison Institute for Public Policy, Arizona State University.* Tempe, AZ: O'Neil Associates, Inc.

U.S. Department of Education, National Center for Education Statistics. 2002. *Schools and Staffing Survey 1999–2000: Overview of the Data for Public, Private, Public Charter, and Bureau of Indian Affairs Elementary and Secondary Schools.* Washington, DC: U.S. Department of Education.

8

Where's the Alternative?
Identifying, Training, and Certifying

Amy Ashley and Mike Kayes

To say that measuring teacher quality is a vital element in strengthening our national education policy and assuring the success of "No Child Left Behind" is something of an understatement. NCLB requires the hiring of "highly qualified" personnel, yet there is no consensus on what specific characteristics, education, and experience define the teachers everyone seeks. The only major point of agreement is the need to find alternate methods for identifying, recruiting, and training these individuals.

Alternative programs to certification have drawn dedicated individuals, willing to commit to teaching in schools that have struggled to attract and retain good teachers due to poor location, below-average pay, and underprivileged students. There is little doubt that many public schools in economically and geographically substandard areas of the country would find staffing extremely challenging without alternative certification programs.

But what is different about alternative certification? Have these programs really done as well as they should in providing quality skills to nontraditionally trained educators? Or are we merely looking for the same standards we have come to expect from graduates of traditional college of education programs without attempting to find and assess other special qualities that may better predict effective teaching? Alternative certification, in most states, does not draw on anything other than the same expectations of beginning teacher aptitude and skill that has been used for years. It allows credit for degrees and work experience in fields outside of education, but then attempts to standardize pedagogy and classroom management to meet the teaching methods of teaching colleges. It is time to evaluate and learn from programs redefining the term "highly qualified," and seek new ways of granting certification based on these analyses.

BACKGROUND

The 1996 report by the National Commission on Teaching and America's Future found that knowledge and skill with regard to the profession of teaching was important, but not so important as having highly educated individuals teaching in their major area of study. Most education experts seem to agree. NCLB's goal is to have measurably qualified teachers in all schools, thereby ensuring that any child in any socioeconomic or geographic situation is properly educated. The NCLB cornerstones for certification are a bachelor's degree and passage of a rigorous test in either core curriculum or the subject to be taught. These are the basics.

Other qualities, however, are just as or perhaps more important, but harder to discern from surveys and multiple-choice questions. There needs to be a way to define specific traits, such as love of imparting knowledge and the desire to see all students succeed, and make evaluations on teachers' mastery of these skills in the same way states now test for classroom management and knowledge of subject.

The problem is not just about the description and demonstration of "highly qualified." How can potential be recognized, nurtured, and encouraged so it culminates in a teaching career? If alternative certification is to be a magnet for those who would otherwise not consider teaching, it needs to truly offer alternatives. Proponents of strict, one-directional paths to teacher certification argue that there are no alternatively certified doctors. If licenses or certificates are going to be issued for professional skills, why "cheapen" them by allowing entry of some based on half the education and experience another receives? Their opponents say that if individuals with engineering or scientific backgrounds decide to make a career change to high school physics teacher (an increasingly common event), why should they have to start all over again? Would a skilled professional, willing to take a large pay cut in order to teach young people, also be willing to go back to school for another four-year degree with emphasis on general studies and pedagogy? If not, is our faith in the state certification system so strong that we will not notice or care when these individuals instead opt to teach in a community college or private school?

The arguments over certification are fueled by the lack of an ideal that aspiring public school teachers can emulate. When asked to recall favorite teachers, most people remember personal traits or unique assignments that made learning seem fun and valuable. The student never saw the time spent by the teacher in ensuring that what appeared fun and quirky was actually based on known methods of effective teaching. Favorite teachers are remembered for their unique presentation of subject and the enthusiasm and creativity expended in delivery. In *What Makes a Good Teacher?*, Marie F. Hassett describes an "inherent sameness of good teachers, regardless of the substantial differences between them in terms of style, personality, goals, and pattern of interaction with students." A semitangible attribute apparently exists, but it is increasingly evident the current form of state certification is not capturing that elusive quality.

For decades few vocalized doubts about the way teachers were trained. State certification and colleges of education date back to the nineteenth century. The baby boom years of the mid–twentieth century produced a huge demand for elementary school teachers, and the overwhelming majority of applicants followed the traditional path to the classroom. Enrollment in education degree programs grew steadily until the early 1970s, when the end of the military draft and new options for women in the workforce made teaching a less attractive career choice. Bright students who excelled in math and science were increasingly drawn to technology careers rather than teaching. Recruiting New Teachers Inc. (RNT), has found persistent perceptions about teaching as a profession of low pay, poor working conditions, discipline problems, school violence, and lack of support from colleagues. Admission to a teaching program is not considered competitive, as evidenced by the minimal academic requirements needed to enter most university teaching programs. Even at the graduate level, in academic year 2000 only 20 percent of applicants to UCLA's law school and 4 percent of applicants to medical school were accepted, compared to a 58 percent acceptance rate for the masters of education program (Hess 2001). Certification is often viewed as a way to keep "just anyone" from gaining access to the great responsibility of educating our young people, yet there is almost no attempt by teachers' colleges to enforce selectivity. The Education Trust (1999) concluded that with over 90 percent of those who graduate from teaching colleges going on to receive licenses, only the most egregious of misfits are excluded from classrooms. Those same baby boomers, who clogged elementary schools in the fifties and sixties, are in some cases reevaluating their careers and see teaching as a rewarding and altruistic alternative to the corporate treadmill. Many have become monetarily successful, and even more are now losing jobs in the technological downsizing of the past several years. Concurrently, there is a great demand for teachers at the secondary level in the fields of math and science. The teacher demographic has been sharply altered as a result of this convergence. Recent statistics from the National Center for Education Information (NCEI) show that 28 percent of new teachers already had a four-year degree upon embarking on their teacher training, and more than half were previously employed in fields other than education.

The experience and maturity of many applicants to alternative certification programs improves the overall quality of the teaching profession and in states such as Texas and California, where these programs have been in operation for a number of years, more minorities, males, and older individuals are entering the workforce. Alternative programs require refinement, but they at least do not reject out of hand the possibility that the second-careerists have something valuable to offer. Traditional certification eschews these individuals' talents as irrelevant, instead requiring courses and texts of questionable value as the only way to gauge teacher preparedness. Most alternative programs are centered in geographic areas of greatest need, poor rural and urban neighborhoods. Attracting and retaining new teachers to small towns and the inner city has been very hard, but the NCEI found more teachers from alternative programs willing to teach in rural and urban schools. In the Troops to Teachers program, 39 percent were willing to teach in an inner city school and 68 percent would teach in a rural school if asked to do so. Of the traditionally certified new teachers, only 16 and 23 percent respectively replied positively to potential inner city and rural teaching assignments (NCEI 2003).

ALTERNATIVE QUALIFICATIONS

If charter schools are to live up to their promise, they must be innovative and results oriented. If they offer better education than at district schools, then clear standards must be set, results measured, and changes implemented if goals are not achieved. Certification of highly qualified teachers is definitely a part of this process, but as applied today, it rarely touches upon those personal traits that in part define good teachers. The current state-regulated set of standards, used all by themselves without regard to an individual's motives, maturity, strength of personality, or degree of commitment, is not capable of identifying the gifted and talented teachers.

While all states now require a certification exam in addition to an education degree, the alternative certification procedures in the thirty-seven states that have routes to teaching through alternative means, are quite varied and administered by different entities. California alone has fifty-three different projects. Some candidates are recruited and trained at the local district level, some through state colleges, some in private programs. These variations are problematic when trying to evaluate program effectiveness on a national scale to compare the success or failure of traditionalist and nontraditionalist schools of teacher training. The traditionalists champion coursework based on pedagogy and strictly defined, stringent state regulations. The nontraditionalists argue that formal education without real world experience does not guarantee teacher quality, and that the school or district should be ultimately responsible for the success or failure of its teachers, not the state (Lockwood 2002).

The Education Excellence Network (EEN), sponsored by the Thomas B. Fordham Foundation, proposes allowing school administrators the freedom to select their teaching staff in whatever way delivers the best results. According to EEN (1999), if success is measured in student assessment scores, why should there be regulatory barriers of dubious validity blocking potentially good teachers committed to improving public education? If regulations were minimized to allow greater diversity in hiring, programs that have succeeded at teacher training, whether traditional or alternatively based, would be recognized and could be duplicated nationwide. In searching for a national standard from which to predict who has the potential to become a highly qualified teacher, a diversified teaching pool on a national level would provide far more data than that which is currently in place.

Educator and philosopher Parker Palmer observes that teachers are "people who have some sort of connective capacity, who connect themselves to their students, their students to each other, and everyone to the subject being studied." He is talking about a person who displays a long list of healthy personality traits that culminate in good teaching. In other words, good teaching comes from an emotionally stable, logical thinker gifted in interpersonal communications, who has a diverse enough background to connect random facts and ideas into information that anybody can understand.

Language facility is key to this skill, and is certainly measurable. The Abell Report, conducted a few years ago, found teachers who scored the highest in vocabulary tests were also considered the most effective. But vocabulary by itself is just a small portion of the entire package called communication. The breathing of life into words, the desire to convey information and be understood goes far beyond just making the right sounds. Everyone has had the experience of hearing a new idea explained in such a clear way that it awakens the brain like an alarm clock: one is immediately able to connect it with other ideas and experiences and make sense of it on many different levels. Teachers and public speakers can see sudden comprehension light up the faces of their listeners, and can analyze what they did or said to make that happen. Undoubtedly, a good portion of this ability is grounded in an advanced understanding of the subject being taught. But something else has to happen. There has to be a passion with a purpose in the presentation that ensnares the student and makes them rapt, because without listener engagement, there can be little meaningful delivery of information.

Public speakers are tested on their ability to communicate based on demand for their time and financial success. They are educators of a sort, but in a much more specific way. Elementary and secondary teachers are not just giving a seminar, they are teaching life skills over the course of a year that hopefully will stay with a child forever. Their ability to communicate is vitally important and there should be better ways to gauge how good they are at it.

Tests of critical thinking skills are built into some state certifications, but creative thinking seems to be overlooked. Creative thinkers go beyond the obvious patterns of problem solving used by critical thinkers. Instead of being objective, impartial, and reasoned, they use humor, fiction, and other "outside the box" stimuli in the quest of new solutions to common problems. They are not afraid of information that may be considered prejudiced, irrelevant, inconsistent, or distorted. Robert Harris (2002), an educator for twenty-five years and author of *Creative Problem Solving: A Step-by-Step Approach*, says that people who think creatively are curious and enjoy challenges. They embrace change, suspend judgment and criticism when evaluating new ideas, are comfortable with imagination and fantasy, and are optimistic. Engineering and technology schools know that creative thinking is the main initiator of technological innovation and scientific research, and have progressed faster than others at the university level to offer "creativity classes" as part of their degree. If a concept as abstract as creativity can be taught in engineering school, then there is clearly a way to evaluate who is succeeding in applying creativity in real or simulated situations. Dr. E. Paul Torrance at the University of Georgia College of Education is the author of the Torrance Test of Creative Thinking. He developed his first creativity test in 1943 and has since revised it hundreds of times to be relevant for people of all ages and education levels. Those who have been trained to administer and score the tests have noted instances where students in the lowest percentiles on standardized tests score in the top 20 percent in creativity testing. It would be interesting to apply the same methods in an effort to understand the creative process, not only among learners, but also and specifically in teachers.

CURRENT PROGRAMS

There are dozens of tests for personality types, nonverbal communication, adaptation and coping, listening, writing, and various other aptitudes, yet few attempts are made to incorporate them into the definition of highly qualified teachers. Much has been written, but little innovation has been implemented in the two decades following the publication of *A Nation at Risk*, a document challenging the quality of public education.

The National Board for Professional Teaching Standards (NBPTS) was founded as a direct response to *A Nation at Risk*. It offers certification to all interested teachers who embrace the five core propositions NBPTS sees as fundamental to proficient teaching: a commitment to students and learning; knowledge of subject and how to teach it; responsibility for managing and monitoring learning; the ability to learn from the experience of teaching; and the desire to remain an active lifelong learner. NBPTS acknowledges, however, that these are not the sum total of that which is required to teach: "Teaching ultimately requires judgment, improvisation, and conversation about means and ends. Human qualities, expert knowledge and skill, and professional commitment together compose excellence in this craft."

Certification by NBPTS is only available to veteran teachers who already hold a state license. The goal is to create "highly qualified" teachers out of the core group already committed to teaching. It does nothing, however, to attract new blood to the profession or address the issue of reforming initial certification standards that are no longer relevant to a diverse and eclectic teaching workforce.

The American Board for Certification of Teacher Excellence (ABCTE) is focused on both new teachers and veterans, and hopes to develop both an initial nationally recognized certification that can be adopted at the state level, and an advanced certificate for experienced teachers. Their requirements are being honed, but for new teachers seeking the Passport Certification, passing a Content Area Knowledge exam and a video-based Professional Teaching Knowledge exam are the key elements. The idea is to create a library of new teachers exhibiting different levels of teaching skill and subject knowledge from which schools can match their needs. By stressing the importance of individuals teaching in their degree major, yet requiring that they also receive knowledge and practical experience on how to teach, ABCTE hopes to significantly decrease the barriers now standing between teacherless classrooms and educated career changers lacking formal classes in pedagogy. An additional benefit is the creation of an alternate teaching credential that isn't "easier" than state certification, but provides uniformity and mobility in the state licensing process.

CONCLUSION

Alternative certification is not about allowing anyone who applies for a job to become a teacher, but neither should it seek ways of reeducating nonconformists so they will fit into the traditional certified teacher mold. Alternative means offering a choice, and if the choice isn't better why change? Conversely, if the choice isn't different why is it better?

The traditionalists, such as Linda Darling-Hammond, argue that alternative certification turns the profession into the equivalent of the Peace Corps, a place to work until a "real job" comes along (National Commission on Teaching and America's Future 2002). But nobody on the other side of the debate is saying it should be easy to become certified. In fact, if rigor is the issue, make alternative certification harder with the caveat that essential skills and knowledge, not just more paper and transcripts, be clearly defined. Talented and committed professionals will embrace assessments used to measure good training and natural aptitude.

According to the Abell Report, the most consistent finding among effective teachers is that they score highest on standardized tests of verbal ability. Verbal ability, as measured on intelligence tests, is a strong measure of cognitive ability, and cognitive ability is a use it or lose it proposition. It increases when individuals are active learners and declines during times of mental inertia. Verbal ability may accurately show temperamental predilection for teaching, but having no connection to college coursework or pedagogy, is overlooked by the great majority of states during teacher certification. Studies have identified specific methods and skills that can dramatically increase student achievement, such as the Educational Testing Service's study that points to hands-on learning exercises, laboratory experimentation, and examples of high-order thinking processes demonstrated on frequent tests, as the foundation used by exceptional math and science teachers (Wenglinsky 2000). For someone already holding a science or math degree, it will not require another four years of classroom training to understand and become proficient in these methods.

The ideal alternative situation would be for a school administrator, recognizing the potential for an already well-educated individual (who also displays the usual qualities of intelligence, commitment, and energy found in any viable prospective employee) to be trained based on the needs of that particular school. Training would be done in the environment according to the standards maintained by veteran teachers who also serve as mentors and provide a support system that will be in place as long as the fledgling teacher remains at that school.

In other fields this is called professional development, and good companies spend large amounts of money perfecting their programs. They do not expect their employees to come to them complete with an understanding of the company culture, the cutting-edge trends shaping their industry, or even a complete picture of how to do their day-to-day job. Employees are hired because they exhibit personal traits that are found in people who succeed in a particular occupation and have the requisite skills.

Teacher certification makes the mistake of trying to remove this professional development stage of training from new teachers. It seeks to send individuals trained to a one-size-fits-all model out into the real world of teaching, "certified" to already be expert at what they do. Even the licensing of doctors and lawyers does not make this claim. A licensed doctor is certified to not be a criminal and to have received a good education on how to make sick people well. There is no implied guarantee of being an accomplished healer, nor is there any guarantee that the certification encompasses proficiency at heart surgery or knowledge of the latest techniques in eradicating communicable diseases. The doctor needs to have further training, hands-on experience, and work closely with others in the specialized area in order to become highly qualified.

The exclusionary nature of state certification is one of its main weaknesses. Despite the fact that candidates have attributes proven indicative of a high quality teacher, without certification they cannot gain access into the profession. Why exclude out of hand those who may have the most promise? As the very pro-educational establishment American Association of School Administrators (2002) says, "What's the harm of exploring the alternative certification route to teaching, as long as quality-control measures are in place?"

It is possible to meet the goal of having highly qualified teachers in every classroom, if the option is open to all who are interested and can pass initial screening. Some will decide not to measure up. Some will decide not to complete the program. However, the pool from which to draw and train these important professionals will have been greatly expanded and enriched by removing the artificial and irrelevant barriers that stood in the way, thus making alternative certification a viable and respected choice for schools and teachers alike.

EPILOGUE

As we conceived and assembled preliminary ideas for this article, we expected to delve into the literature to search out and describe those specific qualities and strengths that define a well-qualified teacher. Like Parker Palmer, we believe that teaching is the function of a healthy personality. We thought (hoped?) to reveal those essential personality traits in an effort to further understanding about whom to recruit, train, and mentor in whatever ultimate certification schema may be employed.

Instead, we are left knowing that an ability to master verbal language and communicate well makes quite a difference. Other than this single specific set of characteristics, the literature appears devoid of guidance. Thus it is perhaps our single most important finding that much remains to be learned and tested when it comes to defining a "highly qualified teacher." We doubt "I'll know one when I see one" will find much acceptance, but neither will the simplistic "this person is state certified and therefore highly qualified." So we offer this article to help promote and further a national conversation that, utilizing NCLB language itself, needs to be research based and data driven.

REFERENCES

Abell Foundation. 2001. "Teacher Certification Reconsidered: Stumbling for Quality." Baltimore, MD. www.abell.org/pubsitems/ed_cert_1101.pdf.

American Board for Certification of Teacher Excellence. 2002. "Passport to Teaching Certification." Washington, DC. www.abcte.org/passport.html.

Feistritzer, C. Emily. 2001. "Alternative Routes to Teaching." Washington DC: National Center for Education Information. www.ncei.com/Testimony010521.htm.

———. 1999. "Teacher Quality and Alternative Certification Programs." Washington DC: National Center for Education Information. www.ncei.com/Testimony051399 .htm.

Harris, Robert A. 2002. *Creative Problem Solving: A Step-by-Step Approach.* Los Angeles, CA: Pyrczak Publishing.

Hess, Frederick M. 2001. "Tear Down This Wall: The Case for Radical Overhaul of Teacher Certification." Progressive Policy Institute, 21st Century Schools Project. www.educationnext.org/unabridged/20021/hess.pdf.

Lockwood, Anne Turnbaugh. 2002. "Who Prepares Your Teachers? The Debate Over Alternative Certification." Arlington, VA: American Association of School Administrators. www.aasa.org/issues_and_insights/issues_dept/alternative_certification .pdf.

Mitchell, Ruth, and Patte Barth. 1999. "How Teacher Licensing Tests Fall Short." Washington DC: The Education Trust. www.edtrust.org/main/documents/k16_spring99 .pdf.

National Board for Professional Teaching Standards. www.nbpts.org/about/coreprops .cfm.

National Center for Education Information. 2003. "Alternative Teacher Certification— An Overview." Washington, DC. www.ncei.com/2003/overview.htm.

National Commission on Teaching and America's Future. 2002. "No Dream Denied: A Pledge to America's Children." www.nctaf.org/dream/dream.html.

Thomas B. Fordham Foundation. 1999. "The Teachers We Need and How to Get More of Them." Dayton, OH. www.edexcellence.net/library/teacher.html.

Wenglinsky, Harold. 2000. "How Teaching Matters: Bringing the Classroom Back into Discussions of Teacher Quality." Princeton, NJ: Educational Testing Service www.ets.org/research/pic/teamat.pdf.

9

Revenge of the (Nerdy) Professors: Scholarly Research on Charter Schools and Why It Matters[1]

Robert Maranto

In social science as in life, the answers you find depend on the questions you ask. Some look at "failing" schools and ask how to improve them; others insist that such schools have a hopeless job until we perfect society to make schooling easier. Still others insist that illiterate students have not failed; they are merely "different."

Such it is with research on charter schools. Researchers who like charter schools ask these questions:

- Why do so many parents want education alternatives, and why do most charter schools have waiting lists?
- How do charter parents and teachers rate their schools? How do district school parents and teachers rate theirs?
- Can charter schools terminate incompetent teachers? Can district schools?
- Do students in charters learn more than students in district schools?
- Do charter schools provide curricula that are hard to get in district schools?
- Are charter schools safer than district schools?
- Does competition with charters make district schools better?
- Are charter schools *more* accountable than district schools?
- What presumably nefarious forces oppose charters?

Researchers who dislike charter schools ask a very different set of questions:

- Do charter schools serve the poorest students?
- Do charter schools use progressive teaching methods?
- Do charter teachers have tenure?
- Do charter schools invent new curricula never before seen on earth?
- Do some charter schools fail?
- Do charter school teachers have less experience than district school teachers?
- Do charter school stakeholders often disagree about school missions?
- Do charter schools embarrass or inconvenience district school officials?
- Are charter schools *perfectly* accountable?
- Have charters lived up to the most ambitious promises of their supporters?
- Do charter school teachers and operators think they are better than the rest of us?
- What presumably nefarious forces support charters?

Either set of questions can be justified, but of course, whether charter schools succeed or fail depends almost entirely on which questions one asks. In graduate school, I learned that the only real social science is comparative social science. You cannot evaluate an institution without knowing how it compares to other institutions. For example, as Winston Churchill pointed out, democracy is the worst system of government except for all the others that have been tried by human beings. Similarly, compared to perfect (and nonexistent) traditional public schools, charter schools fail miserably. Compared to actual district schools, however, most charter schools work pretty well.

Why does this matter to charter operators? For two reasons. First, charter school opponents, traditional district school staff, school boards, unions, and most state boards of education want to strangle the charter baby in its crib. They feed stories to the media to assure that each failed charter gets dozens of newspaper articles while a successful charter school gets no copy, hoping to build enough support to regulate charters out of existence. As charter supporters, we need to know enough to counter their claims. Second, charter opponents are not always wrong. They identify ways to make us better. Indeed, the Arizona Charter School Association once gave its chief detractor, State Senator Mary Hartley, the "Wolf at the Door Award" to honor all the wolves who keep us deer in running shape.

First-wave charter school research books came from charter supporters, and naturally found the initial reports promising. The first, and in some respects still best such book is Joe Nathan's *Charter Schools* (San Francisco: Jossey-Bass, 1996). *Charter Schools* is a fun read, the perfect introduction to charterdom. Academics criticize Nathan as more advocate than social scientist, but in fact, nearly all his findings were subsequently confirmed by "objective" researchers. In particular, Nathan lauds charters' success in focusing on students and in involving parents, while warning about start-up difficulties, particularly the need to agree on a common vision *before* rather than *after* school starts. Another fine treatment of charters, *Charter Schools in Action* (Princeton University Press, 2000), by Chester E. "Checker" Finn, Jr., Bruno Manno, and Gregg Vanourek, presents findings from a multiyear study of charters, including extensive surveys showing parents and students far happier in charter schools than in their previous district schools. This too is a highly readable book, arming any charter operator with facts and figures to rebut myths about charters.

A decade into the movement we have a second wave of charter books, these by opponents. Among the better of the charter-skeptic books is Amy Stuart Wells's edited *Where Charter School Policy Fails*. The culmination of UCLA's five year charter school study, this book could be titled *The Ed. Schools Strike Back*. Indeed, Wells edits *Teachers College Record*, probably the best education scholarly journal.

Wells et al. have written a logical, coherent anticharter polemic. *Where Charter School Policy Fails* never fails to accentuate the negative. This is not to say that the book lacks value. *Where Charter School Policy Fails* is an important work since it shows how the traditional education establishment views charters; thus, those who ignore it do so at their peril. These people have clout, and in the long run may quash the whole charter movement. Further, Wells's well-funded team studied seventeen California charter schools and conducted more than five hundred interviews, generating some very sound insights in the process.

Since Wells et al. present a district school view of charter schools, it is not surprising that one of their best chapters details districts' relationships with charter schools. Basically, charter schools inconvenience districts by making enrollments and revenues tough to predict. In California, at least, district schools are also understandably wary that charters may commit wrongs for which districts will be sued. (Most states have different laws.) Further, all public schools have much in common. Neither district nor charter schools understand the thousands of regulations they suffer under, neither are free of ego battles, and neither want to be held accountable. The authors maintain that neither district nor charter schools *are* held accountable, failing to understand that while troubled district schools face "school improvement plans" (paperwork!), poor charter schools face *oblivion*—about 5 percent have closed and many more came close—costing teachers and administrators their jobs! Which accountability method does more to motivate someone—filing school improvement plans, or filing for unemployment?

Wells et al. also detail how charter teachers love their schools' small communities, which foster close relationships with students and staff. They wisely warn, however, that charters may demand too much of their teachers, particularly in a school's first year. As one teacher put it, a new charter teacher should "be in very good physical shape. Inform your family you won't be seeing them as much as you intended until it gets off its legs" (2002, 169). Similarly, charter parents seek and usually find a sense of community and identity in charter schools. Yet Wells et al. fear that such communities bring exclusivity. Of course, though the authors do not seem to see it, traditional, bureaucratic public schools can be highly impersonal, causing students and staff to react by forming their own exclusive communities (gangs!) within schools, a phenomenon noted by a long line of education writers from Arthur Powell to Elinor Burkett.

The authors' central concerns involve equity. They care little about middle-class parents who want Montessori options their districts choose not to provide. Rather, Wells et al. think the only proper mission for charters is helping low-income students. Here Wells's team makes important points. In particular, schools founded by and serving upper-class parents have huge advantages over those serving poorer communities; thus, the authors urge more funding for the latter. Yet the authors fail to recognize that such inequities have even more pernicious consequences in traditional public schools. As University of Washington Professor Paul Hill reports, most school districts allow senior teachers to transfer to "desirable" (meaning upper-class) schools; thus, within the same district some schools spend nearly twice as much as others! These traditional school resource inequities dwarf those in the charter sector. Indeed, charter schools may lessen inequities by allowing low-income parents to choose their schools, choices middle-income parents make through private schools and by deciding where to buy a house.

The authors also make much of limited data suggesting modest segregation within the charter sector, saying almost nothing about segregation in conventional public schools. They fail to note the *within-school* segregation in district schools, a matter chronicled since *The Shopping Mall High School* was published in 1985. (My large public school was 15 percent African American, but my classes were all white.) My fieldwork suggests that in charter schools, unlike in district schools, whites and minorities take the same classes and sit at the same lunch tables.

Most important is what Wells and her collaborators choose *not* to study. They note only in passing that parents choose charters mainly for academics and safety, and never attempt to discover whether California charters succeed on these terms. Instead, they imply that academics and safety are nothing more than code words for racism and snobbery—even when sought by low-income minority parents. Indeed the authors seem to think minorities can't handle academic work; thus academic standards are inherently racist. They also fail to make much use of statistics: these social scientists use not a single statistical table (though they do use some stats in the text).

Despite its own failings, *Where Charter School Policy Fails* does indeed find real problems with charter school policy, at least in California. It has a wealth of great anecdotes, and does a good job presenting how conventional educators view the charter menace. *Where Charter School Policy Fails* is a very worthwhile read, even though as a charter backer you may not enjoy it.

Gary Miron and Christopher Nelson have written a better charter-skeptic book in *What's Public About Charter Schools?*, an extended study of Michigan charters.The authors may not like charters, but as researchers at Western Michigan University they do ground their analyses in data; thus, their work can be described as skeptical but not hostile. Still, at times they seem to selectively interpret findings so as to overstate potential charter failings. Miron and Nelson particularly dislike profit-seeking education management companies (EMOs), hence the book's title.

Michigan is interesting since its charter school law allows a relatively large number of charters. As of 2000–2001, 180-odd charters accounted for about 4 percent of public school enrollment. Also, over 70 percent of Michigan charters are EMOs; thus, the state tests whether business really can do education better. EMO domination distinguishes Michigan charters from those in other states. The median Michigan charter is twice the size of the typical charter, though still 40 percent smaller than public school counterparts. More importantly, Michigan charters often focus on easy-to-educate kids: elementary school students without serious disabilities. Notably, while non-EMO Michigan charters enroll proportionately as many secondary as elementary school students, the business-based charters are overwhelmingly elementary. In the elementary market, a shrewd EMO can both provide a quality service and make money.

Still, Michigan charters are hardly "elitist." Despite mighty efforts by the authors to find segregation, charter schools as a whole enroll percentages of low-income and minority students rather similar to those of their host districts. (The authors underplay this by making much of small differences and focusing on two Detroit exceptions.)

In accord with every other study on the subject, the authors find that charter parents choose their schools for academics and safety. Regarding academics, Miron and Nelson find that charter schools do not outgain district schools on standardized tests; indeed they do slightly worse. This is mainly since new charters have start-up problems. On reading and math, older charters do as well as but no better than district schools. (As they fail to note, charters often serve kids who have failed in district schools, so they have tough customers.) Interestingly, Miron and Nelson find that independent charters do better than EMOs; indeed independents do as well as their host districts. Older independents probably do better than their host districts, though the authors do not run that statistical comparison. (Why not?) I suspect that in the education biz, both profits (in EMOs) and bureaucracy (in traditional schools) come before people.

Wisely, Miron and Nelson also look at the non–test based measures of school effectiveness. Their surveys show that charter school students like their schools more than their previous public schools, and feel they learn more. Parents also like charters.

Miron and Nelson find that most charter teachers chose their schools for their educational philosophy and small class size. Moreover, teachers *like* charter schools. For example, by a 63–18 percent margin teachers were satisfied with their principals; by a 55–17 percent margin they approved of school governance. Having done two large-scale surveys of district school teachers, I can say that these are impressive ratings. Yet Miron and Nelson seem determined to underplay charter success:

> Initially, charter school teachers/staff had high expectations that their school would support innovative practices (78 percent); but after working in the schools for at least a half year, only 65 percent thought that was true. Initially, 81 percent of the teachers/staff expected autonomy and creativity to be evident in their classrooms; but only 71 percent indicated that they found this to be true. (2002, 108–9)

As my students say, *like duh!* Surely the authors know that new teachers enjoy a honeymoon, and so answer more positively. And how many traditional public schools earn 60–70 percent positive ratings from *their* teachers?

Miron and Nelson reluctantly admit that charter schools innovate, at least in the common use of the term. While charters rarely invent new curricula, they do spread practices eschewed by traditional schools, including Montessori curricula, team teaching, block scheduling, and multigrade classrooms (2002, 127).

Miron and Nelson end with reasonable warnings about EMOs. Michigan public schools are fairly well-funded, but charters get little start-up money; thus the state has high barriers to entry keeping out parent/teacher operators, while offering potential profits for those with money up front, usually businesses. Michigan charter authorizers actually encourage EMOs, raising concerns about tight relationships between chartering bodies and state regulators. Miron and Nelson worry that EMO domination commingles public and private funds, gives businesses power over small operators, and weakens the communitarian nature of charter schools. This gets to the heart of the question of the *publicness* of charter schools, at least in Michigan. The authors fear that "extensive EMO ownership of school facilities, equipment, curricula, and brand names may place significant limits on charter school autonomy and flexibility, thus violating notions of site-based management in the charter school concept" (2002, 196). From fieldwork, I know that the authors are onto something. Miron and Nelson offer useful recommendations to rein in the EMOs, including pegging state charter funding to variations in the cost of educating different groups of students, providing additional start-up funding to lessen dependence on EMOs, and making oversight more transparent, the latter good advice for all schools.

In short, despite undue skepticism, *What's Public About Charter Schools* offers an interesting and comprehensive study of a significant charter sector. Policy makers looking for ideas about what to do and not do would be wise to read *What's Public About Charter Schools*.

Amazingly, some social scientists transcend bias. Ohio State University Education Professor Joseph Murphy and Vanderbilt University graduate student Catherine Dunn Shiffman have produced a comprehensive and fair-minded overview in *Understanding and Assessing the Charter School Movement*. This book is a wonderful survey of the research on charter schools in understandable language, without the usual ideological baggage. It makes a great reference on all things charter.

Murphy and Shiffman start by summarizing pre-charter education reform, noting that charters are politically attractive as "a single policy construct that can be used to attack a host of problems" (2002, 13) by allowing different kinds of education—different strokes for different folks. Of course, the very newness of charters makes them difficult to study, rendering all pronouncements tentative (2002, 19). They go on to outline the 1980s writings of Ray Budde, Ted Kolderie, AFT president Al Shanker, and other developers of the charter idea, the passage of the first state law in Minnesota, and the charters' spread to other states. They explain how Shanker and other union leaders shifted from guarded support to opposition to charters because "the current environment in which multiple charter school models coexist is quite different from the single prototype envisioned by Shanker, who saw a system of charter schools overseen by school district-union panels" (2002, 37). Apparently unions see power as zero-sum: more for parents means less for unions. Indeed, the Michigan Education Association allegedly spent $2 million trying to defeat charters—something not noted by Miron and Nelson. School boards and administrators are even more hostile. Charter supporters seem most able to overcome the opposition in states with lower NAEP scores: desperation promotes innovation.

Chapter 3, the most useful section for a charter novice, offers a succinct but comprehensive outline of what makes charter schools different. Murphy and Shiffman summarize studies of who attends charters (and why), how charter teachers differ, who starts charters, charter curricula, and of course, financing. As noted above, charter founders and parents usually seek services not provided by their district schools: specialized curricula, safety, and small classes. Teachers are most attracted by school missions. Notably, charters pay about as well as traditional schools (at least for new teachers) and tend to hire certified teachers, though this varies by state.

Chapters 4 and 5 outline the public policy theories behind charter schools. While these discussions are outstanding, they might have fit better earlier in the book. Charter schooling in part reflects decreased trust in government bureaucracies, but also new conceptions of democratic governance favoring parents rather than elected representatives and lay expertise rather than education professionals. Charters also import postbureaucratic and postindustrial organization forms into education (2002, 106–11), and focus on outcomes rather than inputs (115–19). In effect, charters "reweave" traditional democratic institutions, in part by using market methods and recasting accountability. Charter supporters also hope to increase the *supply* of good schools. With their autonomy and mission focus, charters offer small communities contrasting traditional public bureaucracies.

Finally, chapters 6 and 7 describe the likely costs and benefits of charters. Chapter 6 offers a good overview of the as yet unresolved debate over whether charter schools enhance efficiency and equity. Murphy and Shiffman give a less informed discussion, however, of whether charters are likely to enhance the income and status of teachers. They seem partial to arguments that as market-based schools, charters threaten teachers. In fact, as Edward Dirkswager's *Teachers as Owners* makes clear, charters may give teachers control over schools. (See chapter 5 in this book.) Indeed, many of the best charter schools are started by teachers who felt frustrated by traditional education bureaucracies.

Chapter 7 offers a sensible rubric by which to evaluate charter schools (2002, 171–72), and summarizes charter research. As noted above, charter schools are more nimble than district schools, with relatively empowered (and happy) teachers and customers. Yet it is not clear that charters produce greater academic gains. Murphy and Shiffman offer a somewhat limited discussion of accountability, as when they write that "other than the reward of not being put out of business, there is almost no evidence of positive consequences . . . incentives and rewards are conspicuous by their absence" (2002, 194). Presumably awards, praise, bragging rights, a long waiting list, and the simple satisfaction of a job well-done count for little! More sensibly, the authors warn that charters lack the resources for high-cost special education services, though so far they enroll percentages of special learners comparable to district schools. Most studies show charter schools no more segregated than district schools, though findings depend on the analytic methods employed. Finally, charters have had some limited impacts pushing traditional schools to improve. Murphy and Shiffman sensibly conclude that "charters at this point in time are probably working a good deal better than might be expected given the barren landscape of school reform in the United States and the constraints laid upon charters through the political actions of their opponents and the zealous pronouncements of their advocates" (2002, 217).

Though clearly written, its emphasis on theories of policy change makes this book more suited to the college classroom than the general reader. Still, in its accuracy, intelligence, and scope, *Understanding and Assessing the Charter School Movement* is a great work of reference on charter schools. Keep it on your bookshelf for whenever you have a question about the state of charterdom.

I've saved the best for last. As good as *Understanding and Assessing the Charter School Movement* is, Rand Education's *Rhetoric Versus Reality: What We Know and What We Need to Know about Vouchers and Charter Schools* is even better. (It's also cheaper, just $15!) Written by Brian Gill and a collection of Rand colleagues, *Rhetoric Versus Reality* summarizes the state of the research on charters and vouchers with sense and simplicity. If you read only one book on school choice, Gill et al.'s *Rhetoric Versus Reality* should be it. This slim volume is a must for both educators and policy makers.

The Rand team excels since it explicitly compares charters and vouchers to existing public schools, certainly the most sensible way to proceed. It also outlines, critiques, and synthesizes existing studies by both choice opponents and detractors in a manner simultaneously sophisticated and understandable—no easy feat! The authors zero in on the most important questions:

- Do schools of choice teach better?
- Do they improve district schools?
- Is there a demand for and supply of education options?
- Will school choice help the neediest?
- Will school choice promote ethnic and income integration?
- Will school choice promote tolerance and common citizenship, or intolerance and Balkanization?

As one would expect, the findings are more positive than negative, though hardly so positive as choice supporters promised. Indeed as the authors note, controversies may continue for years to come. Still, taken as a whole, research finds that school choice brings improvements; thus, choice programs should be gradually expanded in scope.

The authors start with a well done and historically grounded contrast of traditional public schools and market education. As they note, "whether the common school model in fact serves its avowed purpose is an empirical question" (2001, 19); possibly school choice will in fact better serve all students. In chapter 2, Gill et al. compare charters and vouchers and strong and weak charter laws.

Chapter 3 gets to the heart of the book's empirical issues: do students in schools of choice learn more? Here, the authors present a wonderful explanation of the complexities of program evaluation. In particular, they discuss the difficulties of comparing annual academic gains for students who won lotteries for vouchers to private schools with those who lost the lotteries and so (usually) remained in public schools. For sound experimentation, one must assume that the two groups are equivalent, something difficult to do given the high mortality of the treatment group (many drop or flunk out of the program) and control group (many do not show up for later testing). Still, studies from six cities suggest that African American students learn more with vouchers, while other students do about the same. The authors speculate about why (2001, 86–91).

Gill et al. also discuss academic gains in charter schools. Summarizing studies from Michigan (including Miron and Nelson), Texas, and Arizona, the authors report that charters seem to do slightly worse than district schools in Michigan, slightly better than district schools in Arizona, and about the same in Texas (though better for at-risk children). As noted above, findings suggest that first-year charters have serious start-up problems while older charters do better academically; thus, "judging the long-term effectiveness of the charter school movement based on outcomes of infant schools in their first two years of operation may be unfair, or at least premature" (93). The authors also note evidence that school choice pushes traditional district schools to improve, though not nearly so much as proponents claim.

Chapter 4 explores the demand for school choice. Unlike most analysts, the Rand team understands that school choice cannot be viewed in a vacuum. Already, over a third of parents exercise school choice by deciding to live in certain school districts, while another 10 percent use private schools; thus, the question is not whether new school choice policies are more "elitist" than some theoretical common school, but rather whether they are more elitist than existing school choice based on family income (2001, 118). The Rand authors report that most charter schools and all voucher programs have long waiting lists, suggesting a demand for education options. Parents also rate their schools of choice highly. But can the number of schools of choice expand to meet demands? The Milwaukee experience suggests that voucher programs can expand the supply of private education. In most states, the number of charter schools is limited by caps, low capital funding, and substantial regulatory burdens. With reform, charter laws too might increase the supply of good schools.

Chapters 5 and 6 discuss access. Not surprisingly, whether charters and vouchers help the poor depends on how laws structure the programs. Existing voucher programs target low-income students. Both charters and vouchers attract mainly low-achieving students, suggesting that they serve the underserved rather than "elites." In the best discussion of the issue extant, the authors find that voucher programs seem to slightly promote integration, while charter schools do not. The authors also note, however, that traditional public schools probably have more internal segregation than charters. Further, charters might promote integration in areas with high levels of residential segregation.

As chapter 7 details, public schools are expected to teach American values. Could school choice undermine this? Of course, as the authors note, the common school model often repressed Catholics and other minorities. Still, on balance it is probably more a positive than negative legacy. Since the mid-1800s:

> the schools were assigned a variety of social and democratic missions: to contribute to economic progress through agricultural and manual trades programs, to spearhead the Americanization of immigrants, and to help counteract the effects of industrialization on children and communities. More recently, the schools were given particular responsibility for overcoming the educational ill effects of poverty and discrimination—providing equal educational opportunity and targeted assistance but also preparing all students more effectively in terms of social development and exercise of citizenship. (2001, 186–87)

Do schools of choice threaten to balkanize America by undermining this legacy? Or do they strengthen it? So far we have insufficient data about whether charter schools produce better citizens. Catholic schools, however, outperform public schools in producing citizens who vote and do community service; they do no worse than public schools in producing tolerant citizens.

Gill et al. conclude with sensible recommendations about future research and future school choice policy. In particular, voucher and charter programs need more resources to assure a range of choices, participating schools must practice open admissions, and hard to educate students should receive higher levels of funding. Like all education programs, school choice schemes must better track student achievement, so that we can divine and reward what works.

A SLOW NEW WORLD

When political scientists debated school choice after the publication of John Chubb and Terry Moe's *Politics, Markets, and America's Schools* back in 1990, the two sides initially polarized. Proponents (like me) insisted that school choice would rapidly transform public education, making schools safe, academically successful, integrated, and innovative. In contrast, school choice opponents insisted that expanding education markets would bring segregation, academic failure, and widespread corruption. A decade later, both sides have been mugged by reality.

Increasingly school choice supporters, at least the more honest and insightful ones, grudgingly admit that markets bring evolutionary rather than revolutionary gains. Increasingly school choice opponents, at least the more honest and insightful ones, grudgingly admit that school choice does more good than harm, the only fair test of any reform. Political scientists now spend less time debating school choice, and more time debating what choice schemes work best, how much good they do, and whether other reforms can better help students. (Education professors, who have strong ties with traditional public schools, are a few years behind political scientists on this.)

While research is slow, our decentralized political system is slower still. From ending the spoils system, to the civil rights revolution, to welfare reform, big policy changes always take decades. It may take a few decades more to embed charter schools (and perhaps vouchers) into American public education. That will be too late for my young children, but as more research comes in and as more policy makers listen to that research, for my unborn grandchildren I have hope. One always has hope.

NOTES

1. Published July 2003 in *NCSC Review* 3: 22–28 at www.nationalcharterschool-clearinghouse.net

REFERENCES

Burkett, Elinor. 2001. *Another Planet*. New York: HarperCollins.
Chubb, John E., and Terry M. Moe. 1990. *Politics, Markets, and America's Schools*. Washington: Brookings Institution.
Gill, Brian P., P. Michael Timpane, Karen E. Ross, and Dominic J. Brewer. 2001. *Rhetoric Versus Reality: What We Know and What We Need to Know About Vouchers and Charter Schools*. Santa Monica: Rand Education.
Miron, Gary, and Christopher Nelson. 2002. *What's Public About Charter Schools?* Thousand Oaks: Corwin Press.
Murphy, Joseph, and Catherine Dunn Shiffman. 2002. *Understanding and Assessing the Charter School Movement*. New York: Teachers College Press.
Powell, A.G., E. Farrar, and D. K. Cohen. 1985. *The Shopping Mall High School: Winners and Losers in the Educational Marketplace*. Boston: Houghton Mifflin.
Wells, Amy Stuart, ed. 2002. *Where Charter School Policy Fails*. New York: Teachers College Press.

10

Personnel Policy in Traditional Public, Charter, and Private Schools

Michael Podgursky[1]

INTRODUCTION

A major policy discussion in K–12 education today concerns the issue of teacher quality. Research suggests that one of the most important contributions of schools to student achievement gains is the quality of classroom teachers. The No Child Left Behind Act reflects this concern in its requirement that schools employ only fully qualified teachers to be eligible for Title I compensatory education. Much of the policy debate focuses on the issue of teacher licensing. However, recruiting, retaining, and motivating a high-quality teaching workforce depends fundamentally on the personnel policies of public schools and not on teacher licensing. One area of innovation for charter schools is in the area of personnel policy. This paper reports results comparing personnel policies in traditional public, private, and charter schools from a major national survey conducted by the U.S. Department of Education.

DATA

The Schools and Staffing Survey (SASS) is a representative national survey of schools, districts, principals, and teachers conducted regularly by the National Center for Education Statistics of the U.S. Department of Education. The 1999–2000 survey is a major source of information on public and private K–12 teachers and schools in the United States. Earlier waves of the survey were conducted in 1987–1988, 1999–1991, and 1993–1994. However, the 1999–2000 school year was the first time that SASS included a separate charter school survey. The following are descriptive statistics on the 1999–2000 SASS.

- *Traditional Public Schools*
  - Districts (4,690), schools (8,432), principals (8,524), teachers (42,086)
- *Public Charter Schools*
  - Schools (870), principals (891), teachers (2,847)
- *Private Schools*
  - Schools (2,611), principals (2,734), teachers (7,098)

BACKGROUND: SIZE OF WAGE-SETTING UNITS: TEAMS VERSUS BUREAUCRACIES

Before comparing personnel policies across traditional public, charter, and private schools, it is important to note one important difference in these systems. The wage-setting unit in private and charter schools is typically the school, whereas in traditional public schools wage-setting is at the district level. Indeed, most personnel policy concerning teachers—the level and structure of teacher pay, benefits, hiring decisions—is centralized at the district level in traditional public schools. Researchers who study personnel policy in business find that the size of an establishment plays an important role in the type of personnel policies firms use (Brown 1990).

Figure 10.1 illustrates the major differences in the size of the wage and personnel units in traditional public and private schools. One quarter of teachers in traditional public schools are employed in districts with at least 2,100 FTE teachers, and half of traditional public school teachers are in districts with at least 561 FTE teachers.[2] Yet, the typical charter school teacher finds 16 FTE teachers, barely larger than the average private school (15 FTEs)—teams versus bureaucracies.

This difference in the size of the employing unit goes a long way in explaining the differences in personnel policies. In small teams, it is much easier for supervisors or fellow workers to monitor job performance. This makes merit or performance-based pay less controversial. On the other hand, large school districts have a great deal of trouble implementing merit pay systems. In part, this is because they must come up with evaluation systems that guarantee horizontal "equity" across the many schools in the bargaining unit—essentially a hopeless endeavor. Private and charter schools are under no requirement that their performance assessments be identical to those of other schools. They need only assure their teachers that they are treated fairly within the school. Teachers unhappy with the pay system at the

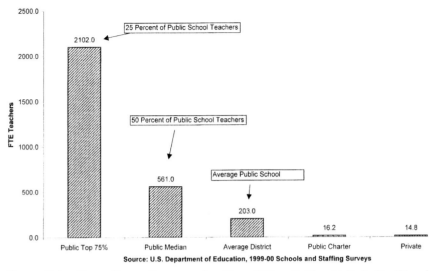

Figure 10.1.   Teams Versus Bureaucracies: Size of Wage-Setting Units in Traditional Public, Charter, and Private Schools.

school can always "vote with their feet" and go to another school with a more compatible pay regime.

A second important difference between traditional public and charter schools is teacher collective bargaining. The percent of teachers covered by collective bargaining agreements in charter schools is far lower than in traditional public schools. (SASS does not bother to ask this question of private schools since very few private schools bargain collectively with their teachers.) As seen in figure 10.2, 69 percent of public school districts, employing 73 percent of teachers, have collective bargaining agreements covering their teachers. This contrasts with just 14 percent of charter schools (employing 18 percent of charter school teachers). The absence of a binding collective bargaining agreement is an important source of personnel flexibility in charter schools. Teacher unions in general have been strongly opposed to more flexible market or performance-based pay systems. Grievance procedures in collective bargaining agreements also make it more difficult to dismiss poorly performing teachers.

RECRUITMENT

Private schools, particularly at the secondary level, routinely hire uncertified teachers (Ballou and Podgursky 1997, chapter 6). Many states permit charter schools to hire uncertified teachers. Administrators in the charter school

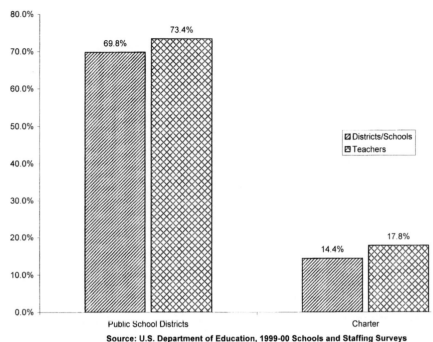

Source: U.S. Department of Education, 1999-00 Schools and Staffing Surveys

Figure 10.2.   Percent of Schools and Teachers Covered by Collective Bargaining Agreements.

survey were asked a series of questions about state regulations from which they were waived ("Does your school's charter include waivers or exemptions from the following state or district policies?"). They were also asked about various hiring criteria used by the school (e.g., full standard state certification, graduation from a state-approved teacher education program). Figure 10.3 reports results from a cross-tabulation of these two questions.

We split our sample of charter schools into two groups—schools that had the flexibility to hire noncertified teachers and schools for whom this requirement was not waived. Schools for which the requirement was waived were much less likely to use certification as a necessary condition for hiring. For schools with a waiver, 65 percent used certification as a criteria to consider for hiring, but only 23 percent actually required it.

LEVEL AND STRUCTURE OF COMPENSATION

Once source of concern to reformers has been the rigid and inefficient pay structure for public school teachers. Pay for nearly all teachers in traditional

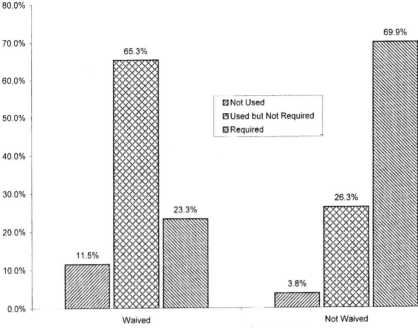

Source: U.S. Department of Education, 1999-00 Schools and Staffing Surveys

Figure 10.3. Charter School Recruitment with Certification Requirement Waived and Not Waived.

public schools is set according to a district-wide schedule that bases salary virtually entirely on years of experience and graduate credits and/or degrees. These rigid schedules have several costs. First, they exacerbate teacher shortages by field, since they do not permit differential pay in shortage fields like math, science, or special education. They also act to lower teacher quality and increase shortages in less desirable schools in a school district. Since high-poverty schools are typically less attractive places to work and all teachers in a district are paid according to the same schedule, teachers will often use their seniority to transfer out of high-poverty schools, or simply quit the district altogether. In either event, the poorest students tend to get the least experienced teachers. Finally, the single salary schedule suppresses differentials by effort or teaching quality. Some teachers, whether due to innate talent or greater effort, are better teachers than others. The single salary schedule rewards all teachers the same regardless of the quality of their teaching performance hence provides no incentive for the best teachers to stay in the profession.

Figures 10.4 and 10.5 present data on methods of teacher pay in the three sectors. In figure 10.4 we see that 96 percent of public school districts

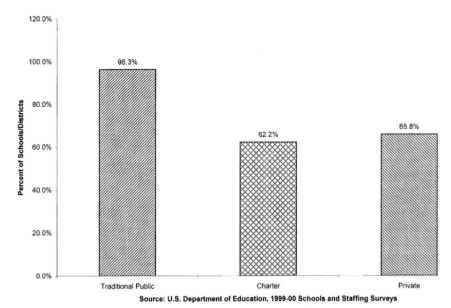

Figure 10.4.   Is There a Salary Schedule for Teachers in this School/District?

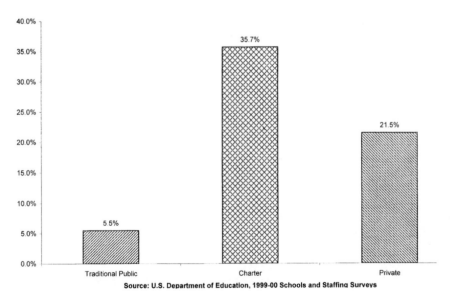

Figure 10.5.   Does this District (School) Currently Use any Pay Incentives such as Cash Bonuses, Salary Increases, or Different Steps on the Salary Schedule to Reward Excellence in Teaching?

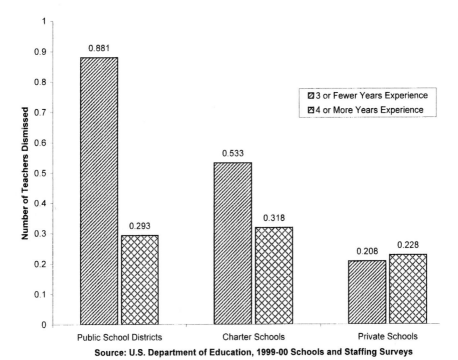

Figure 10.6.   Number of Teachers Dismissed Annually for Poor Performance in Public School Districts, Private Schools, and Charter Schools by Years of Teacher Experience.

(accounting for virtually 100 percent of teachers) report that the district has a salary schedule for teachers. In contrast, only 62 percent of charter and 66 percent of private schools report using a salary schedule to set teacher pay.

School administrators were asked a series of questions about incentive pay. In figure 10.6 we focus on one of these: "Does the district (school) use any pay incentives such as cash bonuses, salary increases, or different steps on the salary schedule to . . . reward excellence in teaching?" Only six percent of district administrators responded in the affirmative. The rates for charter (37 percent) and private schools (22 percent) were much higher.

DISMISSALS FOR PERFORMANCE

Another contentious issue in teacher personnel policy is tenure. Teachers in traditional public school districts receive automatic contract renewal or tenure after three to five years on the job. After receiving tenure it can be very difficult to dismiss a teacher for poor job performance. Moreover it is not at all clear that public school districts take full advantage of the opportunity to weed out poorly performing probationary teachers. Interestingly, although there has been much discussion of this problem, I am aware of no systematic data collection. The most extensive survey I have found on this is Bridges (1992) who surveyed 141 mid-size school districts in California. He found annual dismissal rates for probationary teachers of roughly one percent.

For the first time, the 1999–2000 SASS included items on teacher dismissals. School or district administrators were asked the number of teachers dismissed for poor performance over the previous year. Respondents were asked about total dismissals of teachers with three or fewer years experience (typically untenured) and more than three years (usually tenured). These totals are reported in figure 10.7. The typical public school district dismissed just .9 low-experience teachers and only .3 high-experience teachers. The average charter school dismissed .5 low-experience and .3 high-experience teachers. The total dismissals for private schools were lower for both groups (.2).

As we saw in figure 10.1, the teaching workforce in public school districts is far larger than for charter or private schools. Thus the dismissal rate for traditional public school districts (i.e., dismissals as a percent of the teaching workforce) is far lower than for charter or private schools. The annual dis-

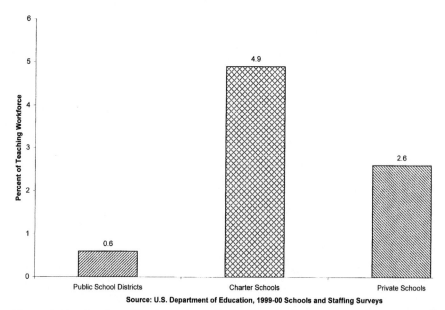

Source: U.S. Department of Education, 1999-00 Schools and Staffing Surveys

Figure 10.7.   Teachers Dismissed Annually for Poor Performance as a Percentage of the Teaching Workforce.

missal rate for all teachers in traditional public schools is just .6 percent of the teaching workforce.[3] For charter schools, the dismissal rate is 4.9 percent and for private schools the dismissal rate is 2.6 percent. Of course, at the time of this survey, the vast majority of charter schools had been in existence just one or two years. One might expect higher dismissal rates as part of the "shakeout" of staff involved in opening a new school. After all, in such schools, virtually all the teachers are probationary. Multivariate analysis of the charter school dismissal rate finds that it tends to decline sharply with the age of the charter school and approach the rates of private schools after several years of operation.

CONCLUSION

One criticism of charter schools has been that they are not particularly innovative and, in terms of classroom practice, tend to resemble traditional public schools (e.g., Wells 1998).

Whether this is a correct assessment awaits further data collection. However, in the area of teacher personnel policy, analysis of the 1999–2000 Schools and Staffing Surveys suggests that there are major differences between traditional public schools and charter schools. These findings reinforce those found in our earlier survey research (Podgursky and Ballou 2001). Charter schools seem to be using the regulatory flexibility they have been granted in this area to forge very different policies. Our analysis finds that in many respects, personnel policy in charter schools more closely resembles that in private schools than traditional public schools.

NOTES

1. The following material was originally prepared for the U.S. National Charter School Conference in Milwaukee, Wisconsin.

2. There are approximately 15,000 public school districts in the United States; however, the size distribution of these districts is very highly skewed. In 1999–2000, 658 districts (5.5 percent of all districts) enrolled 10,000 or more students. However, these large districts accounted for just over half of student enrollments (50.5 percent). On the other hand 3,910 districts (22 percent of all districts) enrolled under 300 students. These tiny districts accounted for just 1 percent of student enrollments (U.S. Department of Education 2002, table 90). This skewness is also seen in figure 10.1. The average public school district employs 203 teachers, whereas 50 percent of teachers are in districts with at least 561 teachers.

3. Unfortunately, the SASS school survey did not ask school administrators the number of teachers with three or fewer or more than three years of seniority. Thus, we cannot compute dismissal rates for the two groups separately.

REFERENCES

Ballou, Dale, and Michael Podgursky. 1997. *Teacher Pay and Teacher Quality.* Kalamazoo, MI: W. E. Upjohn Institute for Employment Research.

Bridges, Edwin. 1992. *The Incompetent Teacher: The Challenge and the Response.* Philadelphia, PA: Falmer Press.

Brown, Charles. 1990. "Firm's Choice of Methods of Pay." *Industrial and Labor Relations Review* 43 (Special Issue): 165S–182S.

Podgursky, Michael, and Dale Ballou. 2001. *Personnel Policy in Charter Schools.* Washington, DC: Fordham Foundation. www.edexcellence.net.

U.S. Department of Education. National Center for Education Statistics. 2002. *Digest of Education Statistics 2001.* Washington, DC: U.S. Department of Education. www.nces.ed.gov/pubs2002/digest2001/.

Wells, Amy Stuart. 1998. *Beyond the Rhetoric of Charter School Reform: A Study of Ten California School Districts.* Los Angeles, CA: University of California at Los Angeles.

11

Future of Chartered Schools— The Supply Side[1]

Bryan C. Hassel[2]

Consider this: most of the dramatic success stories from the charter world come from schools founded by teachers or community members. For example:

- *KIPP Academy, Houston.* At KIPP, a middle school founded by two former Teach for America members, one recent class entered with passing rates of 35 and 33 percent on state math and reading tests. The following year, the class's rates rose to 93 and 92 percent.
- *The Accelerated School, Los Angeles.* Opened by two teachers in 1994 and named *Time* magazine's "Elementary School of the Year" in 2001, the school reported that its scores on the Stanford Achievement test had jumped 97 percent since 1997.
- *North Star Academy, Newark, New Jersey.* Based on results from the spring 2000 state test, 88 percent of the school's first eighth grade class scored proficient or above in language arts (compared with 47 percent citywide) and 66 percent scored proficient or above in math (versus 21 percent citywide).

Numbers like these are eye-catching. But can these stand-alone, typically small chartered schools serve as the basis for a sustainable, large-scale movement for educational change? Or are they likely to remain the exception rather than the rule? After all, starting an innovative, successful chartered school is extraordinarily difficult, and few entrepreneurs seem cut out for the job.

There are certainly reasons to think of successful stand-alone chartered schools as an interesting but ultimately marginal phenomenon. Starting a public school from scratch is, in a word, difficult. It has become a cliché that chartered schools, in addition to being educational institutions, have to succeed as small businesses—balancing their budgets, negotiating leases, financing packages, and contracts, and making payroll. In states where chartered schools are independent, they have to function as mini–school districts as well, with all of the attendant reporting and regulatory burdens. Individuals and small teams—often teachers, parents, or community activists who have never run schools—are apt to possess some but not all of these skills and backgrounds.

Opening a new school also requires capital. Most chartered schools receive federally funded start-up grants of $10,000 to $150,000 for one to three years. Beyond that, they cannot expect any public funds to flow until, if they're lucky, the July before they open. However, expenses can't wait. Principals need to be hired a few months before school starts. Ideally, teachers start at least a few weeks before students arrive. Then there are books and bookshelves, desks and desktop computers, and all the other supplies that need to be purchased. And all of that doesn't include the big kahuna of start-up costs: the chartered school facility.

The first decade of charter school policies has unearthed entrepreneurs who are willing and, in some cases, able to take on these Herculean tasks. They've proven themselves able to secure the requisite start-up capital—by becoming enterprising fundraisers, by "partnering" with others who have deeper pockets, by finding creative ways to keep start-up costs down, or by going without amenities that are standard issue in the typical district school. Even with all these changes, there are now about 3,000 open charter schools, educating about 750,000 students.

Nonetheless, this supply of entrepreneurs can work only if we're talking about a reform that captures just 1 percent of the nation's public school market share. But what if we're interested in creating a set of schools that educate 10 percent, 20 percent, or an even greater share of American students? Are there enough social entrepreneurs out there to do *that?*

Nationally, the growth of chartered schools was dramatic in the years following the passage of the initial charter laws. In 2001 and 2002, however, the number of new chartered schools opening in the fall actually declined compared with the previous year.

Statutory caps on chartered schools have caused some of this leveling, but not all of it. Even in jurisdictions with few restrictions on new starts, the numbers tend to decline over time. It appears that within a given geographical area lives a limited supply of entrepreneurs willing to undertake starting a chartered school, a supply that peters out over time. Not to zero, but to what amounts to a drop in the bucket of public schooling in a city or state.

ARE EMOs THE ANSWER?

Education management organizations, or EMOs, are sometimes touted as the solution to these challenges. According to the Center for Education Reform, 19 of these companies ran 350 chartered schools in 2001–2002, about 15 percent of the nation's chartered schools. Since EMO-run schools are typically larger than the average chartered school, EMOs actually educate an even higher percentage of *students* in these schools—perhaps 25 to 30 percent.

Most EMOs today are for-profit companies, such as Edison Schools and Nobel Learning Communities, but not all. Aspire Public Schools, for example, is a nonprofit seeking to operate a large chain of public schools, at least initially in California. The nonprofit New Schools Venture Fund has established a "Charter Accelerator" initiative to invest in more nonprofit EMOs.

EMOs offer many answers to the leadership supply question:

Expertise and systems. Starting and operating a school requires expertise across a range of fields—from curriculum and instructional design to facilities management to community relations. EMOs can hire experts in these areas or develop expertise over time, and then share knowledge and capacity with their constituent schools. They can turn expertise into systems so that every school doesn't have to reinvent the wheel.

Economies of scale. As they operate more and more schools, EMOs can use their growing buying power to obtain favorable terms for goods and services. By negotiating bulk purchase contracts with suppliers, they can reduce the per-student cost of equipment, furniture, transportation, food service, accounting, human resources functions, and the like.

Capital (for research and development and possibly facilities). At least for for-profit EMOs, the prospects of long-term profitability make it possible to raise capital from venture investors or, in a smaller number of cases like Edison Schools, the public markets. For nonprofits, philanthropic funds serve a similar purpose. This capital allows the companies to make substantial investments in R & D—such as Edison's multiyear curriculum design project, which took place largely before the company operated a single school. Some EMOs have also deployed capital to help meet the challenge of financing facilities.

Incentive and capacity to cultivate leaders. As important as a company's expertise and systems are to its schools, the quality of the school-level leadership is still critical for the success of EMO-run schools. EMOs have strong incentives to seek out high-potential leaders and develop their capabilities over time. And because they operate multiple schools, they are in a position to develop a "farm system" and create opportunities for career advancement that would not be possible in grassroots charters.

Incentive and capacity to sustain schools over time. If a stand-alone chartered school experiences troubles, the founders or current leaders may try strenuously to get the school back on course. But if they fail, no institution is likely to do the hard work of saving the school. The school district may be glad to see the school go; the charter authorizer may not have the capacity or the philosophical inclination to intervene. But if an EMO school begins to sink, the EMO has strong incentives to rescue it. And they may have the resources to do so, by sending in new leadership or expertise.

THE DILEMMA OF SCALE

Still, it would be a mistake to rely on EMOs alone to sustain the charter sector over time, for three reasons.

First, though EMOs bring substantial monetary and human resources to the table, they are not immune from financial and management challenges of their own. One of the major national EMOs, National Heritage Academies, recently reported an annual profit. But most of the scale players in the market have been nonprofits without the tax advantages. Investments in capacity and marketing have swamped revenues for the typical EMO.

Second, for-profit EMOs exacerbate the built-in political challenges of creating chartered schools. Under any circumstances, chartering ignites political controversy. But when schools are operated by for-profit entities, they become even more of a lightning rod. Grassroots organizations like ACORN, which have supported charter schools—even started their own—have led vigorous campaigns against Edison Schools' involvement in troubled public systems like Philadelphia, New York, and San Francisco.

These experiences raise questions about the political viability of a charter school movement that becomes largely composed of schools run by for-profit EMOs. Chartering has attracted unlikely coalitions that include free marketeers and business leaders, but also community-based organizations, civil rights groups, and other nontraditional allies. It seems that the support of nonconservative charter advocates depends, in part, on the fact that up to now the movement is mostly composed of grassroots, community-based schools—not franchises of profit-seeking companies.

Finally, and perhaps most importantly, EMOs may not be the most likely source of innovation—and thus of the kind of dramatic gains in performance that we need to see in schools. For several reasons, the drive for scale mitigates against out-of-the-box approaches. To begin with, attracting sufficient enrollment is vital for EMOs; the need to fill seats is bound to drive companies to appeal to the "median" consumer, who might balk at strange new grade configurations or pedagogical approaches.

The companies' internal dynamics also push toward the conventional. EMOs face the substantial challenge of scaling up an educational and organizational model across multiple sites, perhaps across a wide geography. It makes sense in that context to select the familiar, the easily conveyed. The same goes for personnel. If a company needs thirty principals, the average hire is more apt to resemble the typical principal than the renegade that a stand-alone chartered school might seek.

Herein lies a great dilemma facing the charter movement. To become a serious force for educational change, chartered schools as a group need to achieve greater scale. The most obvious path to scale is the proliferation of chains of schools run by education management organizations. For financial and political reasons, though, looking exclusively to EMOs for scale is a poor strategy. In addition, the kind of breakthrough innovations that are part of the great promise of chartering may be more likely to emerge from schools that are, at least initially, single-site start-ups. But such schools are limited in number and small in size—hardly the basis for a large-scale movement.

Resolving this dilemma requires thinking about "scale" in two new ways. First, what would it take to enable more successful, stand-alone schools to "scale up"—by replicating themselves or through other means? Second, what would it take to create an environment in which much larger numbers of successful, stand-alone chartered schools can form and thrive?

ENABLING PROVEN MODELS TO SPREAD

Education is notorious for single-school success stories that serve as fodder for *60 Minutes* and feature films, but are never "replicated" elsewhere. Within traditional school systems, it's not hard to see why. The incentives to adopt good ideas from other schools are weak, and the constraints on change—from policy and culture—are strong.

Chartering has the potential to overcome this conventional failure, by providing a space within which it's easier to scale up what works via the creation of *new* schools. But most effective chartered schools remain single-site successes. Charter leaders have their hands full even several years into start-up. Their "model" may actually be heavily reliant on the personal leadership of one or more founders and/or local ties and circumstances, which are difficult or impossible to "bottle."

Still, a small number of successful chartered schools are beginning to explore scaling in one way or another:

KIPP Academies. Based on the success of the two initial KIPP Academies in Houston and the Bronx, KIPP decided to scale up with support from the Pisces Foundation and other philanthropists. KIPP's approach to scale relies on developing *leaders* to open and operate new public schools—both charter and district-based. The highly selective Fisher Fellows program inducts twenty to twenty-five aspiring school founders per year and provides them with a summer training program that includes classroom instruction at Berkeley's Haas School of Business—half focused on business matters, and half on academic and school issues. Fellows then do a four-month residency in an existing KIPP network school. By spring, fellows go to work founding a school—with intensive assistance from KIPP national. Support continues over three years, ending with an "inspection" to assess how well the school lives up to KIPP's "five pillars"—the general principles that define a KIPP school.

By 2010, KIPP aims to have started a total of two hundred schools nationally. If successful, the resulting network will be an interesting model. It won't be an EMO—each school will be an independent entity, subscribing to the five pillars but very unique. But it will capture some of the advantages of scale, primarily in the start-up phase. At this point, KIPP does not seem focused on reaping other potential values of scale, such as the power of joint purchasing or the centralization of certain routine functions.

Minnesota New Country School/EdVisions. Minnesota New Country School in Henderson, Minnesota, is quite unique in two respects. First, its learning program is very unusual. Almost all of its high school instruction takes place through personalized project-based inquiry, facilitated by teachers and relying heavily on the computers sitting on nearly every child's desk. More traditional forms of instruction are used as well, but only as needed to ensure the mastery of basic skills. Second, the school is run by a cooperative of teachers, who make all the key decisions about the school—from the learning program to the budget to hiring and firing. With funding from the Bill and Melinda Gates Foundation, the EdVisions cooperative is now seeking to spread this dual model to fifteen new secondary schools over five years. Gates funding will go both to the new sites and to EdVisions central, which will provide intensive start-up assistance. Six sites are currently involved at different stages.

High-Tech High. Founded by tech industry leaders and educators in San Diego, High-Tech High is undertaking various efforts to scale up its design, which offers a rigorous, personalized program focusing on math, science, and technology, and providing extensive connections to the "adult" world through internships and other means. Like KIPP and EdVisions, part of High-Tech High's scale-up work involves helping others found similar schools in nine sites around the country, another initiative funded by the Gates Foundation. But High-Tech's approach includes other elements as well. It has developed a Learning Resource Center, a detailed online source of information about the school's approach that allows anyone in the world to access and use the school's resources. It is engaged in various initiatives to prepare teachers to use its approaches in their own schools. And it is participating in a local effort to design fourteen new high schools to be built in San Diego over the next decade.

Nevertheless, expanding beyond a single campus or city presents added challenges—challenges that so far have prevented most successful chartered schools from seriously pursuing scale. What's needed is a new infrastructure that makes scale-up more feasible—a diverse range of service providers capable of helping schools with the whole array of service needs. If such a system existed, it would be easier for successful schools to scale up, just as it would be easier for brand-new stand-alone schools to start.

CREATING AN INFRASTRUCTURE THAT SUPPORTS STAND-ALONE SCHOOLS

Presently, starting a new school from scratch is just too difficult and painful to do, even for people who are capable of pulling it off. Much of the work goes into activities that are *not* where education needs innovative, fresh thinking, like transportation, food service, accounting, regulatory compliance, zoning battles, mortgages, and the like. It seems likely that there is a large reservoir of entrepreneurial educators and noneducators who would be willing to engage in school start-up—*if* it were not such a nightmare.

Part of the answer certainly lies in the policy arena—giving chartered schools equitable access to funding (including capital funds), cutting unnecessary regulations, ensuring that institutions other than local school boards can issue charters in every jurisdiction.

But just as important are internal or "supply side" solutions. Stand-alone chartered schools need access to the same high-quality, pooled expertise that the best school systems and EMOs provide to their schools. They need a set of institutions that can shoulder the burdens of school start-up and management, allowing entrepreneurs to focus on building an excellent educational program. However, to retain their independence, stand-alone schools need to come to these service providers as voluntary, paying customers—not as units controlled by a larger system.

The creative challenge, then, is to imagine a "system" of providers that can deliver this kind of service. Within such a system, three attributes, besides quality, seem most important: scope, intensity, and diversity.

Scope. Since operating a school is a complex undertaking, the service infrastructure needs to cover a wide range of issues on which chartered school operators may need help. In many service areas, an industry of providers already exists—because school districts and private schools already demand the service. Prime examples include textbook and software publishers, information management systems, developers of curricula and "comprehensive school reform models," and transportation providers. In other areas, like accounting, payroll, legal services, and facilities development and financing, a host of general-purpose providers already serve nonprofits and small businesses. Many of these companies see great potential in the chartered school market and have already begun offering their products and services to charter customers.

However, even where a sector of service providers already exists, its offerings may not be well tailored to the charter context. Chartered schools tend to be small, have limited budgets, and face uncertain futures due to the vicissitudes of the market and the threat of nonrenewal or revocation of their charters. As a result, conventional providers may find chartered schools unattractive in the end. Facilities financing stands out as one illustration, but the same holds true for many curriculum and "whole school reform" providers. While learning programs like Core Knowledge and Expeditionary Learning/ Outward Bound have seen real opportunities in the charter sector, others have shied away.

So new institutions will need to arise—both to meet needs that are unique to chartered schools and to design service packages in older service areas that make sense for chartered schools.

Intensity. Every state with chartered schools has at least one "technical assistance center" for the schools, and many have more. These organizations tend to provide assistance to schools on all the issues they may face. Chartered schools call them with every question imaginable. They publish handbooks, newsletters, and websites that seek to address chartered schools' concerns soup to nuts. One, the California Charter School Development Center, runs "boot camps" for new school leaders, running them through a litany of topics.

However, helpful as they are, technical assistance organizations often are not able to provide *intensive* services to many schools. With their limited resources and broad mandate to serve all schools, it's not possible for most of them to roll up their sleeves day in and day out or to provide full services, like accounting or special education, to chartered schools.

Several answers to the need for intense start-up help are emerging in the marketplace. One is the school "incubator," exemplified by the Education Resource Center in Dayton, Ohio. The ERC gets more involved in particular schools' start-up efforts than most TA providers, serving as temporary adjunct staff. It's also more selective. Like a venture capital firm, it sizes up a client's prospects diligently before providing help. Incubators have succeeded in the small business world, but charter incubators are too new to show results. Another avenue is a growing number of fee-for-service start-up providers, such as the Minnesota-based nonprofit School Start. Charter entrepreneurs contract with these organizations to provide all-purpose help in the start-up phase— help in preparing the charter application, writing the budget, finding a facility, selecting an appropriate learning program, and hiring teachers. The Education Performance Network (EPN), the professional services affiliate of New American Schools, is taking a different tack by creating an "education management support organization." EPN offers clients a menu of services including data management, accountability and evaluation, education program design, and charter start-up and implementation. A key aim of EPN is to help build schools' capacity to manage themselves over time.

A third development is the emergence of leadership development programs for would-be charter entrepreneurs. Examples include the Fisher Fellowship program, New Leaders for New Schools, and the Massachusetts Charter School Resource Center's Leadership Institute. These organizations seek to provide in-depth training to potential school leaders, including both classroom and on-the-job components. Some follow up the learning with hands-on start-up assistance for graduates.

Finally, several national organizations have begun to help their local affiliates start chartered schools. The YMCA is one. Another is the National Council of La Raza, a leading Hispanic advocacy and development organization. La Raza has put together the most intensive package of services—including hands-on consulting for community-based groups starting chartered schools, joint professional development opportunities, and the creation of national partnerships that can be useful to all of the network's schools.

Diversity. Third, schools need access to a variety of providers so they can shop around for the best quality, fit, and prices. In contrast to district-based service systems, in which the central office or its chosen contractors provide all services to schools, the essence of the charter service system must be diversity and choice.

On this front, early trends are promising. Across the different domains of service, many different types of providers are emerging. Besides the for-profit and nonprofit providers already mentioned, chartered schools in some places have formed cooperatives and associations to take advantage of economies of scale. Special education has been an especially fertile area for charter cooperatives, with models emerging in the District of Columbia, Texas, Minnesota, and Indianapolis. For example, the D.C. Public Charter School Cooperative, with twenty-one members, aims to provide information to members about the complexities of special education, employ specialized staff that no school would want to employ alone, and develop a Medicaid billing system to increase reimbursements for special education services.

Developing the range of service providers necessary to expand the charter movement will require investment on the part of firms, philanthropists, and governments at the local, state, and national level. And, it's important to note that investments in scale will have little impact if the policies and institutional environment that make chartered schools possible are not strong. Without multiple authorizers who are willing and capable, full funding for chartered schools, and broad autonomy, no amount of investment in scaling capacity will pay off.

With the right policy supports and investments, though, we can imagine a charter sector characterized by both scale *and* a diversity of entrepreneurial schools, a future in which grassroots chartered schools remain the heart of the movement, but in a sustainable fashion.

NOTES

1. An earlier version of this piece appeared in *Education Next*'s Winter 2003 issue (3: 1, 8–15) under the title "Friendly Competition."

2. Lucy Steiner provided valuable research assistance for this article.

12

Charter School Accountability Issues—Pragmatic or Political?

Heather Zavadsky

PURPOSE

Accountability has become the single most important focus in education reform. Increased attention on student performance has sparked the opinion that traditional public schools are failing our nation's children. As a response, charter schools have become one of the most rapidly growing solutions for providing innovative public school systems of choice. Now operating for almost a decade, debates have shifted to how charters can demonstrate their effectiveness and accountability.

The importance placed on testing by the No Child Left Behind Act of 2002 has led legislators and policy makers to support holding charters to the same accountability systems as traditional public schools. Concern rises that charters are being compared and equated to the same system they were designed to improve upon, creating tension between the purpose of charters—providing innovative flexible programs—and the political challenges of public choice and charter regulation. This results in a one-size-fits-all evaluation system, limited by standardized test scores, that penalizes educational programs that vary from the norm.

This paper informs policy makers and practitioners about accountability challenges of charter schools and illustrates how politics and policy can affect the evaluation of charter schools. This case study of one charter campus—the Texas Campus—demonstrates the dangers of comparing charter programs to traditional public schools, and contributes to the knowledge on charter school accountability from inside an actual charter school district.

111

Although this paper presents one case, there are numerous cases of charter schools struggling with similar accountability issues.

PERSPECTIVE

The charter school movement utilizes the premise of "building innovative programs for specific types of students with minimal adherence to the rules and regulations of traditional schools" (*Education Week*, 3/21/02). Charter school accountability for most states is built upon three rationales: a) bureaucratic oversight and efficiency, b) performance accountability, and c) market efficiency (Garn and Cobb 2001; Manno, Finn, and Vanourek 2000). Fusarelli (2001) and Hess (2001) assert a fourth rationale, political responsiveness, which drives charter accountability systems.

Bureaucratic accountability is a system driven by compliance to a standard set of rules or practices that can be easily linked to behavioral rules, which in turn produce desired outcomes (Garn and Cobb, 2001). This focus, driven by easily defined bureaucratic inputs, produces little public agreement on desired outcomes. Outputs drive performance accountability by applying standardized tests to "reliably and validly measure student achievement" (Garn and Cobb 2001, 118). Some researchers criticize the judgment of performance by standardized tests as leading to unfair comparison between schools, thus potentially leading to a narrowing of the curriculum.

The third accountability framework, market efficiency, relies on consumer control, the assumption being that if parents or children do not like a school, they can leave that school the next day. A more veiled form of accountability, political accountability, describes an accountability system driven more strongly by political rather than technical issues (Fusarelli 2001).

On the surface level, charter schools in Texas adhere to the same state accountability standards and policies as public schools, which are largely driven by performance indicators. However, politics have played a strong role in the charter school movement for the past few years, primarily in terms of limiting expansion. Representatives of the Texas House Education Committee on Charters assert that Texas charters with campuses rated as Low-Performing should not be allowed to add additional campuses, or, in some cases, be granted renewal. Although everyone agrees that the charter system needs a measure of quality control, these high-stakes policies hinging upon one performance output alone ignore the differences in inputs between charter and traditional programs. Representing fewer than 1 percent of the public school enrollment statewide, charter schools have markedly less students taking state accountability tests, and almost two-thirds more at-risk students (Fusarelli 2001). For a charter school district serving primarily at-risk students, this system can, at best, judge campuses using questionable statistics, and at worst cause irreparable damage not only to campuses and districts, but to students as well. Based almost solely on the issue of performance and comparison to traditional schools, performance accountability ignores the differences between the two systems.

METHODS

This study differs from other research on charter schools and charter school accountability since the perspective comes from a practitioner in an actual charter school district, rather than an outside researcher who might be either influenced by special interests or biased against change in public education. Developed as insider research, the researcher is a "full participant," a functioning member of the community undergoing investigation (Glesne 1999). The researcher's role in this context is as an administrator who completed the comprehensive charter renewal application, frequently consulted the state agency with accountability concerns, attended legislative sessions to analyze political motivations surrounding accountability issues, and worked closely with the director of the case study school.

Built as a descriptive case study of a charter district, there are no prescribed methods for data collection or data analysis (Merriam 1988). The analysis of current charter school and accountability policies in Texas is used as the background for outlining how politics and policy affected this charter district. Data includes interviews from administrative personnel within the charter district, interviews with the director of the facility that houses the case study school, observations of legislative sessions, and communications from state agency personnel, as well as a document review.

CASE STUDY: TEXAS ACCOUNTABILITY SYSTEM

The Texas public school accountability system grew out of a 1993 mandate by the Texas Legislature to create a system to rate school districts and evaluate schools. The system was built upon a preexisting student-level data system (PEIMS) and an assessment system, the Texas Assessment of Academic Skills (TAAS), that tested knowledge of the state curriculum defined by the State Board of Education (TEA 2001a). The statewide curriculum, the Texas Essential Knowledge and Skills (TEKS), was implemented in 1998. Components of the accountability system include integration of the statewide curriculum and the state criterion-referenced assessment system; district and campus accountability; district and campus recognition for high performance and significant increases in performance; sanctions for poor performance; and school-, district-, and state-level reports. The 2003 accountability system will transition from the TAAS test to the newly developed Texas Assessment of Knowledge and Skills (TAKS).

Accountability information is compiled into the Academic Excellence Indicator System (AEIS). The base indicators in the AEIS include TAAS rating standards for reading, writing, mathematics, and, added in 2002, eighth grade social studies. For all subject areas except social studies, district and campus ratings fall under four basic categories:

- *Exemplary*: at least 90 percent of "all students" and students in each group meeting minimum size requirements must pass each section of the TAAS.
- *Recognized*: at least 80 percent of "all students" and students in each group meeting minimum size requirements must pass each section of the TAAS.
- *Academically Acceptable* (district) or *Acceptable* (campus): at least 55 percent of "all students" and students in each group meeting minimum size requirements must pass each section of the TAAS.
- *Academically Unacceptable or Low-Performing*: Those districts or campuses not meeting the standard for Academically Acceptable.

Social studies standards are similar except that Academically Acceptable or Acceptable was lowered to 50 percent. In Texas, charter schools are rated by the accountability system after two years of operation. They must meet the same standards as traditional public schools on the statewide test, the TAAS/TAKS, including the requirement that they pass the test to graduate (Fusarelli 2001).

BACKGROUND ON "TEXAS CHARTER DISTRICT"

The Texas Charter District (TCD) represents a successful charter system that suffers from the consequences of a performance accountability rating system. Beginning its fifth year serving students with unique needs, the majority of TCD campuses serve students in residential treatment facilities. Included in the student population at TCD are: teenage mothers and their babies living in residential facilities, adjudicated teenagers in residential centers, abused and neglected children residing in facilities at the request of the Department of Protective and Regulatory Services, and children with medical disorders living in private hospitals.

TCD's profile includes over 94 percent at-risk, 60 percent special education, and 55 percent mobile students. This challenging student body is served by certified administrators with many years of service in public schools, and nearly 100 percent certified teachers, with most certified in special education. Despite TCD's successes in raising overall achievement, moving students to less restrictive environments, and stabilizing challenging behaviors, their evaluation hinges upon standardized test scores. Texas does have an Alternative Education Accountability system designed primarily for programs serving at-risk students; however, TCD does not qualify, as their campuses cannot meet the attendance requirement of eighty-five consecutive days due to students moving in and out of residential care. Additionally, the state agency has indicated that the Alternative Accountability system may be abolished under new regulations coming out of the No Child Left Behind Act.

TCD constantly runs the risk of having campuses labeled Low-Performing due to the few numbers of students who fall within the accountability capture date. As of 2003, two campuses have received Low-Performing ratings because one or two residential treatment center students on a given campus score below seventy on the state achievement test. Relative to the total student population of that campus, in spring 2002, a single student not passing one exam represents a 20 percent campus failure rate. Although the state agency asserts that our rating presents no problem, and they understand our dilemma, the fact remains that we are still being punished by the accountability system. We are not eligible to apply for certain grants, we lose instructional time preparing for monitoring visits, and could potentially lose the capability of adding campuses. Individual campuses suffer the greater risk of losing their financial supporters, forcing them to leave our system of experts for a less regulated and possibly unaccredited private system. And finally, students feel they are failing their schools and ultimately, themselves.

BACKGROUND ON "TEXAS CAMPUS"

Housed within the Texas Residential Treatment Center, Texas Campus (TC) serves boys with moderate to severe behavioral issues. The treatment center program can accommodate up to twenty-two boys in three campus residences, with an average stay of two years. Parents or legal guardians voluntarily place their children in the program and are required to participate in program activities on selected weekends. In addition to the director and treatment personnel, house-parent couples reside with the boys and guide them in their daily family-style routines at the facility. Lessons at Texas Residential Treatment Center—cooperation, trust, and family values—often begin with their day-to-day routines. In addition, core subjects for middle school and high school students are offered, as well as a full range of courses in agronomy, raising livestock, and horticulture. Finally, students are required to participate in a daily routine of horsemanship skills and activities that require self-discipline, patience, and practice.

According to the TC director, who has over twenty years of experience in child care and over twenty-six years using therapeutic animal programs, horses have the ultimate ability, more than other animals, to bring about positive changes in children and youth. He asserts that horses can

> bring smiles to their faces and happier hearts during periods of the day. The boys become more confident in relationships and bonding issues and they relate it to Education. Socialization and communication skills and bonding starts with the horses and allows them to relate that to their families, which has been very exciting to us. They learn how to catch a horse and not get stepped on, they do competitions and team roping, and we see them grinning from ear to ear.

In addition to many challenging activities and academics, family involvement and counseling provide an important component of the program. Counselors work individually with the boys and their families on an ongoing basis. Four-day interactive workshops are scheduled with parents and boys on a quarterly basis to prepare the boys for their return home.

Many TC boys have learning disabilities or challenges such as attention deficit disorder or hyperactivity disorder. Frustration with these challenges has often led to extreme behavioral problems in the classroom. Many are behind their peers in at least one subject, and have fallen below their appropriate grade level in their overall achievements. With this in mind, the Texas Residential Treatment Center provides a unique, on-campus school program to help the boys to progress academically and move up to grade level. The boys attend classes year-round, each weekday morning directed by certified teachers. They complete self-paced learning materials to earn Texas public school credits. As they discover that they can perform academically, the boys become more motivated to succeed. The boys can receive transferable public school credits, and can test for a GED or receive a high school diploma if they finish their curriculum while in residence.

The TC director affirms that his program has been developed from years of experience in working with troubled youth, and describes many successes his students have achieved as they graduate from the program. The data he has gathered over the past five years shows that an average of 80 percent to 90 percent of the students completing his program graduate from high school or complete their GED. One graduate from TC became a talented horseman, joined the military, and was the single selection out of five hundred candidates to join the Washington Honor Guard Program. The director attributes this student's successes to his "ability to control his emotions and apply himself." Clearly this and other students exemplify the successes of this program.

ACCOUNTABILITY CHALLENGES

The TC program at Texas Residential Treatment Center illustrates an example of a highly successful educational program for at-risk students that has fallen victim to a one-size-fits-all accountability system. By serving so many "nontraditional" students, TCD continually falls between the cracks of Texas accountability policies. Limited numbers of test-takers per campus allows the state agency to use a "Special Analysis" of our test scores, which analyzes trends and makes rulings based on professional judgment. For charter schools with less than or equal to three students in each TAAS subject and fewer than ten dropouts reported, the charter school is assigned a "Not Rated" due to insufficient data (personal communication, TEA Accountability, May 2002). TC had six students take the TAAS exam in spring 2001. The students did well on all the exams except the composition section of the writing exam, where two of the six failed, earning that campus a rating of Low-Performing. This year TC had one student out of five fail the social studies TAAS exam, again earning an accountability rating of Low-Performing. According to the state agency, TC was allowed a Special Analysis; however, a trend could not be established because the campus has only been rated for two years and a trend cannot be established on one student. If that campus had been registered as "Alternative Instruction," TC would have received a "Not Rated" because the allowable minimum limit of three students would be raised to ten or fewer students. We have applied for that status for spring 2003.

The unique needs of our students and the environment of a residential treatment facility warrant, in our opinion, the need for a different type of assessment system. However, TC does not qualify for the Alternative Accountability system (which would allow us to select an additional indicator for assessment), because our students do not all attend for eighty-five consecutive days, due to their high movement rate to other treatment programs and back to the mainstream. Thus the policies written to accommodate small numbers and unique student populations do not seem to help our district.

REALITY CHECK

When asked about the impact of being rated Low-Performing, the director of TC responded that he had to explain to parents, who have seen exemplary academic performance from their children prior to the spring TAAS, why their campus is rated Low-Performing. Although the parents seem to understand the issues with small numbers, the programs' financial supporters still show concern. However, the loss of funding pales in comparison to the director's concern about the students themselves. As stated by TC's director:

> The worst outcome of all of this last year was with the two boys that failed the composition portion of the writing exam. Everyone knew who failed, and it set those boys back at least three to six months. They have since graduated, but I really believe it lowered their self-esteem. That's the worst part of all this, is how it affects the kids.

When we explain our dilemma to the state agency, they claim that they understand our unique situation. The monitoring team sent to evaluate TC in 2003 showed no concern with their findings and verbalized their understanding, and in fact admiration, for the program. However, their comments to us remain unpublished and do not offset the effects of press publications labeling the campus Low-Performing.

As of 2004, TC received two years of Low-Performance ratings, based on the performance of two or fewer children each on one test subject. In addition to the potential loss of financial support and confidentiality due to public notice, TCD and TC also wasted valuable time gathering documents in preparation for monitoring visits that occurred long after the students in question had left the program. Fortunately, TC won an appeal to the 2004 Low-Performance rating, and avoided being put on a "Student Improvement Program" by the state agency. Had the appeal been lost, TC would have been required to work with a team of outside consultants on their educational program, a practice that is not feasible within a specific treatment program based on individual student needs.

We must also consider what this case means to the many statistics put forth in publications and touted by legislators about charter performance. Literature counting the number of Low-Performing charter schools compared to Low-Performing traditional campuses claim their evidence points to the failure of the charter school movement. In the Texas Subcommittee meeting on Charter Schools (June 27, 2002), a senator continually quoted statistics on the number of Low-Performing charters compared to Low-Performing traditional schools when discussing charter school performance. Stating that a moratorium should be placed on charter schools until "the state tightens its grip on them" the same senator suggested that public schools are "dumping" at-risk students into these programs (Embry 2002). However, this case study shows that such statistics include cases similar to TC's—a Low-Performance rating based on the performance of one test and one unique student. As for being "dumped" into the program, the director will attest that parents place their children in this program voluntarily.

Fortunately not everyone believes the comparison of charters to traditional schools represents a fair or reasonable comparison. In the same session,

State Representative Harold Dutton retorted that we should not compare charters to the "system that previously failed these students" (June 27, 2002), as many students seek out charters for a different type of program to help them gain back ground lost in public schools.

As stated by one TCD administrator, "It's not that we don't want to be held accountable and provide the best education possible. It's just that the traditional system doesn't work when you are talking about highly mobile special needs students."

CONCLUSIONS

TCD has suffered from the current state accountability system. Although the state system has policies to address specific issues such as low numbers of test-takers, or alternative assessment for high percentages of "at-risk" students, TCD does not qualify for these exceptions due to other stipulations associated with these policies. Future plans by the state agency to reform these exceptions may be hampered by political pressures to limit charters or go completely ignored, as energies are focused on implementing new regulations from the new No Child Left Behind education policy.

This study illustrates the need for a charter accountability system that evaluates programs by more comprehensive methods than state assessment scores alone. One suggestion would be to use an abbreviated form resembling the state's multifaceted charter renewal application, which reviews fiscal practices, governing practices, instructional methods, test scores, and alternate measurements defined by the charter. Rather than the current method of limiting the performance rating to state achievement test scores, absences, and dropout rates, charters could align their evaluation system to their overall purpose and focus. The possibility of developing such a system would require politicians and policy makers to become more familiar with the operations and programs of different charter schools beyond statistics on paper. Such a system would also need to acknowledge that charters, developed as a different method of educating students, cannot be effectively compared to the traditional public school system using state accountability exams as the only measuring method. Charters should be held accountable, and even compared to traditional schools, with comprehensive, valid measures.

REFERENCES

Education Week On the Web. 2002, March 21. "Charter Schools." Retrieved March 22, 2002. www.edweek.org.

Embry, J. 2002, June 27. "Dunnam Says He'll Call for a Moratorium on Texas Charter Schools." Waco access.com.

Fusarelli, L. D. 2001. "The Political Construction of Accountability: When Rhetoric Meets Reality." *Education and Urban Society* 33, no. 2, 157–69.

Garn, G., and C. D. Cobb. 2001. "A Framework for Understanding Charter School Accountability." *Education and Urban Society* 33, no. 2, 113–28.

Glesne, C. 1999. *Becoming Qualitative Researchers* (2nd ed.). New York: Longman.

Hess, F. M. 2001. "Whaddya Mean You Want To Close My School? The Politics of Regulatory Accountability in Charter Schooling." *Education and Urban Society* 33, no. 2, 141–56.

Manno, B. V., C. E. Finn, and G. Vanourek. 2000. "Charter School Accountability: Problems and Prospects." *Education Policy* 14, no. 4, 473–93.

Merriam, S. B. 1988. *Case Study Research in Education—A Qualitative Approach.* San Francisco: Jossey-Bass.

Texas Education Agency. 2001a. *2002 Accountability Manual.* Department of Quality, Compliance, and Accountability Reviews.

Texas Education Agency. 2001b. *2002 Alternative Education Accountability Manual.* Department of Quality, Compliance, and Accountability Reviews.

13

Teacher Quality Leadership from Public Charter Schools

Michael B. Poliakoff

At the conclusion of his first annual report to Congress on teacher quality, U.S. Secretary of Education Rod Paige called for "radically streamlining the system." He observed that traditional (education school) certification requirements "impose significant costs on talented individuals interested in teaching." "The tragedy," he noted, "is that none of these hurdles leads to improved quality."[1] Public charter schools, however, generally have more flexible hiring policies, and provide an important laboratory for the "radical streamlining" that Secretary Paige envisioned. We will see that there is every reason to believe that charter school personnel policies will demonstrate their effectiveness.

A teacher's success is ultimately proved by his or her ability to increase student achievement, and the institution that hires a teacher needs to base its decision on attributes that predict effective teaching. *Teacher certification* is by itself a poor predictor of successful teaching. Although reliable educational research is notoriously sparse,[2] certain types of *teacher preparation* do have a high correlation with student learning gains. Teachers' strong subject area preparation positively correlates with student achievement. (Here research data supports common sense: as Will Rogers observed, you can't teach what you don't know.[3]) Some state-approved certification programs appropriately include a rich, uncompromised preparation in the subject area to be taught; others do not.[4] Second, teachers who receive their degrees from demanding, selective colleges and universities tend to be more effective in the classroom.[5] It is not, of course, the elite status of the college that matters here, but the admissions process that gives preference to students with higher admissions test scores and higher verbal ability. Consistent with other evidence that a teacher's intellectual strength is highly correlated with student learning gains, we find that college entrance examination scores are strong predictors of teacher effectiveness.

In one large study based on over 29,000 students in 690 Alabama schools, teacher ACT scores accounted for 15 percent of the variance in student achievement, double the effect of class size, two and a half times the effect of having teachers with master's degrees, and over five times the effect of years of experience.[6] Yet education schools—the engine of teacher certification—routinely attract and graduate students drawn from the lowest achievers on these examinations: the National Center for Education Statistics discovered that 28 percent of education majors had SAT or ACT scores in the bottom quartile—the highest share of low achievers among college majors.[7] Education majors accounted for only 14 percent of the graduates who scored in the top quartile on SAT or ACT exams, compared with 31 percent for humanities majors and 37 percent for mathematics and science majors. The National Council on the Accreditation of Teacher Education (NCATE), touted as the "gold standard" for teacher preparation programs among proponents of education schools, merely prescribes in its standards that teacher candidates should be assessed with "multiple indicators" (www.ncate.org/2000/2000stds.pdf). NCATE's failure to articulate real quality measures makes relying on education school–based teacher certification an exercise in leaning on a broken reed.

To the extent that subject area examinations can indicate a teacher's proficiency at a given subject, the results should make us very suspicious of traditional teacher preparation. Although a number of states massage the results of their teacher licensure exams to conceal failures, a visit to the websites (www.title2.org) that report the results makes it abundantly clear that a shocking number of aspiring teachers go through quite a lot of schooling and are still unable to pass, at least on their first attempt, relatively basic tests in the subjects they intend to teach.[8] What does this mean for the abilities of those certified and employed as teachers? Former governor Tom Ridge led Pennsylvania to become the first state in the nation to test in-service teachers for their subject area proficiency. Vehemently opposed by the teachers' unions and colleges of education, these very basic tests, designed to screen for competence, not high-level skills, provided data at the district and school building level and a blueprint for where professional development was most urgently needed. The results also showed which education schools produced graduates falling below state norms. The two weakest average performances in the state came from education schools accredited by NCATE.[9]

The charter school world is in many quarters taking a different path. Of the forty states (plus the District of Columbia) that have passed legislation enabling charter schools, half permit some percentage of charter school teachers to be uncertified. In other words, their teacher quality measures cannot be based simply on what their state licensure system prescribes. Arizona, the District of Columbia, Florida, and Texas place no requirement on charter schools to hire certified teachers. Unfortunately, this freedom to hire outside the established system is sometimes held up as a deficiency of charter schools, and some agencies pressure charters to conform to district school practices. Charter schools that seek accreditation from regional bodies often face demands to hire certified teachers as a condition of accreditation. (The American Academy for Liberal Education's new charter school accreditation is unique in defining and requiring teacher quality measures independent of any state certification system.)[10]

In reality, personnel and compensation policies in charter schools make it much more feasible to recruit and retain teachers whose quality is demonstrated by qualifications rather than credentials. When economists Michael Podgursky and Dale Ballou surveyed two hundred randomly selected charter schools (getting a 66 percent response rate), they found that 31 percent provided bonuses for teachers in hard-to-staff subjects and 46 percent used merit or performance-based compensation for 5–10 percent of teacher base pay. Charter teachers also tend to work longer hours over a longer school year. Critics will note that charter teachers have higher turnover than their counterparts in district public schools,[11] but is this necessarily undesirable? Teachers who are not intellectually or emotionally suited to the profession should find other pursuits. Although teacher experience has a positive impact on student achievement, it does not outweigh factors such as subject-area preparation, verbal ability, and general academic achievement as a predictor of successful teaching. Charter schools, which are much more likely to terminate an unsuccessful teacher,[12] are clearly more able to trade experience for academic promise in their teaching force. And they are less bound by collective bargaining restrictions to retain the unsuccessful.

What has this higher level of freedom in staffing meant for the charter school teaching force and, more importantly, for charter school teacher quality? More research is needed, but initial small-scale studies suggest that charter schools use their prerogatives to choose teachers they deem qualified whether or not they hold state certification. Compared to district schools, a greater percentage of the charter teachers show more of the predictors of effectiveness. Caroline Hoxby has compared the selectivity of the colleges attended by charter and district school teachers.[13] Approximately 20.3 percent of the teachers in public schools graduated from a college ranked by the Barron's Profiles of American Colleges as "competitive plus." For charter schools, that figure is 36.1 percent, nearly the same as that for private schools (36.4 percent). Another remarkable finding is that 36.7 percent of the public school teachers majored in a subject area, while 56.1 percent of the charter school teachers completed a subject-area major—a figure higher even than that for private schools (41.9 percent).

It is in this light that education policy makers should review recent criticism of charter schools. The American Federation of Teachers report, *Do Charter Schools Measure Up? The Charter School Experiment After 10 Years*, concludes that "Charter school teachers are inexperienced and have less formal education compared to their colleagues in other public schools."[14] The recent PACE Working Paper, "Charter Schools and Inequality," considers two "gaps" between charter and district public schools: teacher certification and years of experience.[15] Again, it is necessary to ask, to what extent do these factors matter, relative to other indicators or predictors of teacher effectiveness? As noted above, a teacher's demonstration of strong academic skills outweighs both experience and master's degrees (especially master's degrees in education)[16] as a predictor of success. The recent NAEP report, *America's Charter Schools*, also noted that more charter school students have uncertified teachers but found that whether or not a teacher was certified showed no statistically meaningful relationship to student performance. More research on charter school teacher attributes and student learning gains will be very useful for charter school policy decisions: the NAEP report may be particularly helpful in pointing out the unusually high importance of experience for charter school teachers and the consequent importance of mentoring for new teachers.[17]

When the *American School Board Journal* asked "What do you think of teacher certification?" 24 percent of those who responded favored scrapping their state's system and 59 percent wanted to open it up to "nontraditional" candidates. Some respondents noted the need for site-based decisions. One superintendent, for example, wrote, "If we all really believe in local control, let us decide who can be in our classrooms and judge us on our results. Process is good, but it can be repetitive and get in the way of learning by wearing out teachers and administrators."[18]

Charter school principals often articulate these sentiments, and indeed they can go beyond merely wishing for wider hiring authority. Two Massachusetts principals recently interviewed by former Boston public school teacher William Triant clearly felt that the absence of certification requirements was the most important feature of the state charter law. Triant quoted one, a former district school principal, who explained, "Certification is a guarantee of nothing to me. It doesn't mean that they can teach. It just means that they have taken and passed—possibly with D's—certain courses, and been through some student teaching, but I have no idea of the quality of the mentor teacher. What I need to see is people who are highly intelligent, prestigious college background, articulate, they like kids. They know what it means to work on a team. They are visionaries of a sort that they understand the movement and the potential that it holds and that they want to be part of creating a school. People ask and I tell them 'I don't care if you are certified.'"[19]

There are some notable examples of highly successful staff development at charter schools, where rigorous demands for academic excellence and demonstrated potential for teaching replace reliance on certification. Two will have to suffice for this article, but there are many more stories in the charter school world of similar success.

At Tucson's BASIS School, where all middle school students must take and pass comprehensive exams to be promoted and all high school students must take AP exams in core academic subjects, principal Olga Block seeks teachers with an academic profile that predicts their ability to help students meet these remarkably high standards. Less than a quarter of BASIS's faculty of fifteen teachers hold Arizona state certification (none of the science or mathematics teachers do), but two BASIS teachers have PhDs, and most have subject-area master's degrees. To judge by the average Stanford-9 math scores at BASIS, which at present hover well above the ninetieth percentile, math instruction is rather effective at the school.

At Tempe Preparatory Academy, headmaster Daniel Scoggin has a very straightforward vision for teacher recruitment: he seeks those who are academically proficient, committed to scholastic rigor and excellence, and have a "heart of charity" to serve teenagers. Candidates teach a sample class and must demonstrate high intelligence along with care, humor, and a desire to teach at Tempe PREP. Rather than rely on certification as an indicator of pedagogical preparation, Tempe PREP has developed a master teacher program, providing close mentoring and supervision for new teachers. The high demands have not limited the applicant pool: approximately ten candidates apply for each position, and of the twenty-five full-time and three part-time faculty, four hold subject area (not EdD) doctorates, and fourteen hold subject-area master's degrees.

Charter schools are forging a remarkable and promising model for public schools, one in which teacher qualification and performance are the basis for hiring, retention, and promotion. At the same time that Teach for America is proving through student learning gains that highly motivated, bright college graduates are at least as effective as their certified peers—and often more effective—charter schools provide yet wider demonstration that qualification is not coterminous with certification.[20] The academic "ripple effect" of charter schools has long been noted: when a public charter school's academic performance is better than that of the district schools around it, it often serves as the catalyst for improvements that go far beyond its own walls. There is every possibility that another one of the benefits of charter schools will be their "ripple effect" on teacher quality and the way we prepare, re-cruit, and reward this nation's teachers.

NOTES

I would like to thank Dr. Sarah Cunningham, director of charter school accreditation at the American Academy for Liberal Education for her thoughtful help with this arti-cle. Mistakes remain my own, of course.

    1. U.S. Department of Education, Office of Postsecondary Education, Office of Pol-icy Planning and Innovation. 2002. *Meeting the Highly Qualified Teachers Challenge: The Secretary's Annual Report on Teacher Quality.* Washington, DC: U.S. Depart-ment of Education, 40.

    2. Suzanne Wilson, Robert Floyd and Joan Ferrini-Munday. 2001. *Teacher Prepa-ration Research: Current Knowledge, Gaps and Recommendations.* Seattle, WA: Uni-versity of Washington Center for the Study of Teaching and Policy. See also Michael B. Allen. 2003. *Eight Questions on Teacher Preparation: What Does the Research Say?* Denver, CO: Education Commission of the States.

    3. See especially Dan D. Goldhaber and Dominic J. Brewer. 1999. "Teacher Li-censing and Student Achievement," in *Better Teachers, Better Schools,* ed. Marci Kanstoroom and Chester E. Finn. Washington, DC: The Thomas B. Fordham Foun-dation, 83–102.

    4. See especially Kate Walsh. 2001. *Teacher Certification Reconsidered: Stumbling for Quality.* Baltimore, MD: The Abell Foundation. David M. Steiner and Susan D. Rozen. 2004. "Preparing Tomorrow's Teachers. An Analysis of Syllabi from a Sample of America's Schools of Education," in *A Qualified Teacher in Every Classroom?* ed. Frederick M. Hess, Andrew J. Rotherham, and Kate Walsh. Cambridge, MA: Harvard Education Press, 142 suggests on the basis of a thorough syllabus analysis that there is a deeply engrained anti-intellectualism in many teacher preparation programs: "Based on our sampling of the coursework requirements of some of the country's most highly regarded schools of education, we are not convinced that elite education schools are doing an adequate job of conveying fundamental, broad-based knowl-edge and skills to prospective teachers. The foundations and methods courses we re-viewed suggest that faculty at most of these schools are often trying to teach a par-ticular ideology—that traditional knowledge is repressive by its very nature—without directing their students to any substantial readings that question the educational im-plications of this view." For a description of exemplary programs in teacher prepara-tion, see Michael Poliakoff et al. 2003. *Teachers Who Can: How Informed Trustees Can Ensure Teacher Quality.* Washington, DC: American Council of Trustees and Alumni.

    5. Ronald G. Ehrenberg and Dominic J. Brewer. 1994. "Do School and Teacher Characteristics Matter? Evidence from High School and Beyond." *Economics of Edu-cation Review* 13, no. 1: 1–17.

6. Ronald F. Ferguson and Helen F. Ladd. 1996. "How and Why Money Matters: An Analysis of Alabama Schools," in *Holding Schools Accountable: Performance-Based Reform in Education*, ed. Helen F. Ladd. Washington, DC: The Brookings Institute, 284. Cf. also Ronald F. Ferguson. 1991. "Paying for Public Education: New Evidence on How and Why Money Matters." *Harvard Journal of Legislation* 28, no. 1: 475.

7. U.S. Department of Education, NCES. 1993/1997. "Baccalaureate and Beyond Longitudinal Study, Second Follow-up" (Baccalaureate and Beyond: 1993/1997) discussed in U.S. Department of Education, Office of Postsecondary Education, Office of Policy Planning and Innovation. 2002. *Meeting the Highly Qualified Teachers Challenge: The Secretary's Annual Report on Teacher Quality.* Washington, DC: U.S. Department of Education, 13–15.

8. See Ruth Mitchell and Patte Barth. 1999. *Not Good Enough: How Teacher Licensing Tests Fall Short.* Washington, DC: The Education Trust, and Sandra Huang, Yun Yi, and Kati Haycock. 2002. *Interpret with Caution: The First State Title II Reports on the Quality of Teacher Preparation.* Washington, DC: The Education Trust.

9. Bill Schackner and Carmen J. Lee. 2002. "Teacher Test Results Pressure Universities." *Pittsburgh Post Gazette*, May 25.

10. "AALE standards do not require traditional teacher certification. Instead they establish high qualifications, based on evidence of excellence in preparation and performance: academic distinction in general/liberal education; high verbal quality; advanced knowledge in academic subject areas; classroom effectiveness; and most importantly, superior record of achievement of students. AALE standards accommodate the new corps of highly able individuals who are drawn to teaching in charter schools from various professions and backgrounds." "AALE Charter School Accreditation" at www.aale.org/charters/index.htm.

11. Michael Podgursky and Dale Ballou. 2001. *Personnel Policy in Charter Schools.* Washington, DC: Thomas B. Fordham Foundation.

12. Michael Podgursky. 2003. "Personnel Policy in Traditional Public, Charter, and Private Schools." *NCSC Review* 1, no. 1 (January): 10–13.

13. Caroline Hoxby. 2000. "Would School Choice Change the Teaching Profession." NBER Working paper 7866 (August): 27ff. Dr. Hoxby reported a response rate of approximately 70 percent to this survey of all charter schools in operation in October 1998.

14. The American Federation of Teachers. 2002. *Do Charter Schools Measure Up? The Charter School Experiment After 10 Years.* Washington, DC: American Federation of Teachers, AFL-CIO, 76.

15. Bruce Fuller et al. 2003. "Charter Schools and Inequality: National Disparities in Funding, Teacher Quality, and Student Support." Policy Analysis for California Education Working Paper Series 03-2 (April).

16. Goldhaber and Brewer.

17. National Center for Education Statistics, U.S. Department of Education. 2004. *America's Charter Schools: Results from the NAEP 2003 Pilot Study.* Washington, DC: National Center for Education Information, 6, 9.

18. "You Say: Teacher Certification Needs Help." 2002. *American School Board Journal* vol. 189, no. 6 (June).

19. William Triant. 2002. *Autonomy and Innovation: How Do Massachusetts Charter School Principals Use Their Freedom.* Washington, DC: The Thomas B. Fordham Foundation.

20. Debra Viadero. 2004. "Study Finds Benefits in Teach for America." *Education Week* vol. 23, no. 40 (June 16). See also Margaret Raymond, Stephen Fletcher, and Javier Luque. 2001. *An Evaluation of Teacher Differences and Student Outcomes in Houston, Texas.* Stanford, CA: Hoover Institution.

14

Does Mission Matter?: Exploring a Typology of Charter School Orientation

Jeffrey R. Henig, Natalie Lacireno-Paquet,
Thomas T. Holyoke, and Heath Brown

ACKNOWLEDGMENTS

The authors would like to thank the Spencer Foundation for their generous support of this project and the schools in Arizona, the District of Columbia, Michigan, and Pennsylvania that responded to our survey. Elisabeth Clemens, Brayden King, and Melissa Fry (Arizona); Richard Hula and Chelsea Haring (Michigan); and Rebecca Maynard and Connie Keefe (Pennsylvania) provided assistance with the surveys. Katrina Bulkley, Bruce Fuller, Michael Mintrom, David Plank, and Kevin Smith provided valuable feedback on earlier drafts.

Like the proverbial blind men encountering an elephant, those writing about charter schools provide a curious and contradictory set of accounts. Social scientists using similar data and similar research designs issue sharply different reports, with some declaring confidently that charter schools are performing poorly compared to comparable public schools (e.g., Nelson et al. 2004) and others declaring just the opposite (e.g., Hoxby 2004). Numerous anecdotal and heartwarming accounts circulate about charter schools turning around the lives of students, while others tell horror stories about amateurish and short-lived efforts, fiscal shenanigans, inflated promises, and dismal test results.

One explanation for these inconsistent findings is that "charter school" is an umbrella term that can apply to a wide range of organizational missions, backgrounds, and behavioral tendencies. With this in mind, a few recent studies have begun to unearth systematic differences across types of charter schools. Some find differences, for example, based on whether or not charter schools are associated with for-profit educational management organizations (EMOs) (e.g., Bulkley 2001; 2002; Lacireno-Paquet et al. 2002; Miron and Nelson 2002; Brown et al. 2004; Lacireno-Paquet 2004). Others have found differences between charter schools started de novo and long-standing public schools that converted to charter schools (Fuller et al. 2003; Zimmer et al. 2003). Others suggest that there may be systematic differences between charter schools authorized by local districts and those authorized by states or other bodies (U.S. Department of Education 2004). But almost no effort has been made to probe for finer distinctions within these categories and there have been only limited efforts to link these typologies to broader theoretical foundations about organizational differentiation, behavior, and change.

In this chapter we seek to probe deeper and explore this variation with charter schools by offering a typology that distinguishes broadly between those that by virtue of their experience, norms, and organizational structures are more oriented toward markets and those that pursue more purposive and philanthropic missions as seen in the nonprofit sector. Because types of philanthropic missions may also vary significantly, we draw further distinctions among those following missions of educational professionalism, social services, and grassroots community or economic development. We then test the hypothesis that these organizational types make a difference in how charter schools define, pursue, and respond to their intended consumers with data drawn from a survey of charter schools operating in Arizona, Michigan, Pennsylvania, and the District of Columbia.

A TYPOLOGY OF CHARTER SCHOOLS
BASED ON ORGANIZATIONAL ORIGIN

Charter schooling is just one example of a growing tendency of government to experiment with variations in public-private delivery mechanisms for providing public services (Salamon 1987, 1995; Kettl 1993). The most authoritative proponents of privatization (e.g., Friedman 1962; Savas 2000) have relied on the language of economics to account and argue for this shift in policy direction, suggesting that competitive markets ensure that service providers will be more innovative, responsive, and efficient than government "monopolies." But some favor privatization with a different vision in mind. When they think about private sector alternatives to government, their favored vehicles are not for-profit corporations but community-based organizations and social service agencies. Rather than responsiveness to external signals of supply and demand, this form of privatization is premised on the belief that the social good could be best achieved by tapping into the intense internal commitment found among leaders and supporters of nonprofit organizations motivated by mission, not markets (Henig et al. 2003).

Rooted, as they are, more in civil society than competitive markets, we expect that charter schools founded by mission-oriented organizations may behave differently from those spawned by for-profit corporations. Empirical comparisons of nonprofit and for-profit behaviors in noneducation arenas like health care, nursing homes, and childcare have found evidence that nonprofits often appear to make systematically different choices than for-profits in staffing, pricing, screening of customers, and selection among alternative delivery mechanisms (see Weisbrod 1998; Mark 1995, 1998; Bushouse 1999). The entrance of large for-profit educational management organizations (EMOs) into the charter school area is relatively recent and still not well researched, but some early studies suggest that the market vs. mission distinction may help to explain what are otherwise bewildering inconsistencies in charter school reports. Lacireno-Paquet et al. (2002) found that market-oriented charters serve somewhat less disadvantaged students than do other charter schools. Henig and MacDonald (2002) found that in the District of Columbia market-oriented charter schools were more likely to locate in neighborhoods with high home ownership rates than in areas where there were high concentrations of Hispanic residents. Finally, Brown et al. (2004) found evidence that charter schools initially launched by EMOs are larger and less likely to delegate to the individual schools decisions regarding curriculum, testing, discipline, and facilities.

Nor is it the case that all nonprofits are cut from the same cloth. Some charter schools have been launched by teachers animated by particular pedagogical visions; some by social service organizations that see an opportunity to expand the help they already provide to high-need populations; some by parents unhappy with homogenizing and bureaucratic rules and regulations; some by local businesses that see school reform as a key to stronger economic development. Because such organizations tend to draw their ideologies and staff from distinctly different cultures, the result can be a variety of beliefs, norms, and missions that may translate into different kinds of organizational choices and strategies.

Social service, or "helping," organizations are oriented around missions of providing help to needy populations. This category, which includes organizations that run food pantries, provide job training, work with delinquent youth, etc., is perhaps what most people have in mind when they think of the nonprofit sector. Some long-standing social service agencies were quick to realize that charter school legislation provided opportunities for them to expand the range of services they could offer and simultaneously open up a major new source of funding. For example, the Next Step charter school in Washington, D.C., was established by a nonprofit with a larger mission of providing counseling, training, and support services to primarily Latino single mothers and young adults who have dropped out of public education.

Because social service organizations have clearly defined, highly needy clients, we expect the charter schools they launch to focus on populations defined by particular categories of need and to put more emphasis on effective provision of services than on growth and expansion. Because they and their members are accustomed to relying on philanthropy and government contracts as revenue sources, we might also expect them to be less attuned to conventional marketing strategies, to be more likely to partner with various foundations, and to invest more resources in monitoring developments within the public sector than surveying potential new clients or the activities of competitor schools.

By design *professionally defined organizations* seek to embody the values, body of knowledge, and preferred practices of a profession in the services they produce. Educators' claim to professional status has been more contested than many "higher status" occupations so perhaps for this reason their formal collective organizations—such as the National Education Association and the American Federation of Teachers—have straddled the boundary between professional association and labor union and have invested considerable political capital in traditional systems of public education. As a result, though teachers unions have occasionally launched charter schools, educators who have done so are more likely to have acted individually, or as a small collection of individuals, animated by a shared vision of what good schooling entails. Examples of these schools would be those launched by teachers who are tired of fighting school district bureaucracy and wish to implement new programs aimed at particular types of students.

Because they are invested in the notion that they possess a special expertise that legitimates particular ways of doing things (a "one right way") we might expect charter schools launched by education professionals to be less likely to adapt and change in response to market signals. But unlike charter schools affiliated with social service nonprofits, because they typically claim that key decisions require the exercise of "professional judgment," of which they are the sole or primary arbiters, we might expect such organizations to be less likely to engage in partnerships that entail a sacrifice in their autonomy.

Grassroots community-based organizations are formed to pursue the interests of geographically defined groups of citizens sharing common interests and values relating to ethnicity, race, housing tenure, and socioeconomic class. Typically these are less formally structured than social service or professional organizations, and may even be ad hoc single-issue (e.g., "stop the highway") groups that dissipate once their goals are achieved. In fact, these types of community-based organizations primarily tend to adopt more formal structures when doing so facilitates a desired ability on their part to pursue grants and contracts or play official or advisory roles in governmental proceedings (Berry 1999).

Grassroots community charter schools started by groups of parents or neighborhood leaders discontented with the traditional school system might be linguistically, culturally, or ethnically oriented schools, perhaps focusing on Armenian culture and language, or Afrocentric schools. Because their mission is linked to small and relatively well-defined groups of individuals, we expect charter schools founded by grassroots, community-oriented organizations to also be relatively small, less likely to advertise widely, and less likely to have plans to expand.

Finally, some nonprofit charter schools are founded by *local business and economic development* organizations, such as chambers of commerce or downtown business associations. Of all the types of charter schools we discuss, this one seems least likely to differ in orientation and behavior from for-profit EMOs and, by extension, differ considerably from other mission-oriented schools. Nonetheless, there are at least two reasons why charter schools launched by such organizations may behave more like mission-oriented than profit-oriented ones. First, what typically motivates local business organizations to sponsor charter schools is not profit—a private and material good—but the long-term economic health of the immediate community, a conventional collective good (Peterson 1981).[1] A second reason that charter schools founded by such organizations may tend to behave more like other mission-oriented, rather than profit-oriented, organizations is that the local business leaders who are the members of the chamber or business association may have only a very arm's-length relationship with the charter school itself. After helping to set broad goals, local business organizations often hire conventional educators or others with nonprofit and social service backgrounds to manage the school on a day-to-day basis.

Yet, compared to other mission-oriented groups we would expect charter schools launched by these nonprofits to be more businesslike and efficiency-oriented in their approach. We expect them to focus more on providing job skills to potential entry-level workers; thus, compared to others, these charter schools might be more likely to operate at the secondary school level and to organize themselves around a career or vocational theme. We expect them to be less likely to target populations whose special needs make them potentially less desirable as employees. For instance, in the District of Columbia, one local hotel firm has helped operate a school oriented toward the hospitality industry.

DATA AND METHODS

In January 2002, we sent a survey to all charter schools in Arizona, Michigan, Pennsylvania, and the District of Columbia. These states were selected because each had charter school policies in place for several years and because each was host to at least some charter schools run by EMOs. We included only schools that were open as of the 1999–2000 school year and verified that schools opened before 1999–2000 were still in operation whenever possible. We received a total of 270 completed surveys for a response rate of 35 percent. Comparison on comparable dimensions to charter schools in the 1999–2000 Schools And Staffing Survey (SASS), conducted by the U.S. Department of Education, provides some reassurance that our sample is representative.[2]

Distribution of Schools by Type of Founder

In the school survey, we asked respondents: "Thinking about the individuals and organizations that played central roles in starting your charter school, please indicate which of the following best apply." The question was followed by a list of possible founder types including EMOs and mission-oriented nonprofits.[3] Based on their responses, we categorized each school into one of the seven organizational types discussed above. Figure 14.1 illustrates the percentage of charter schools in each of the seven categories. Seventeen percent of the responding schools were founded by an EMO, either on their own (10.67 percent) or operating along with other organizations (6.67 percent). The remainder of schools, which we categorize broadly

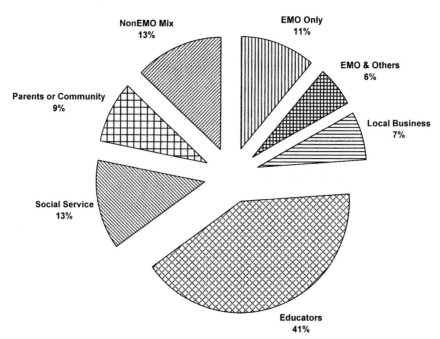

Figure 14.1.   Distribution of Charter Schools by Founder Type

as "mission-oriented," include those formed by educators (40.32 percent),[4] those formed by social service or nonprofit organizations (13.44 percent),[5] community and parent groups (9.09 percent),[6] those founded by local business groups (6.72 percent),[7] and those that checked more than one option but not including an EMO (13.44 percent).

Overall, most charter schools in our sample are found in central cities (61.63 percent), a tendency particularly evident for those founded by local business groups or social service agencies (figure 14.2).[8] Educators and EMOs appear more likely than others to start charter schools in the suburbs. Of the seven types of charter founders, only parent/community-based groups have a significant presence in rural areas.

The seven types of charter schools are not evenly distributed over the four jurisdictions. Michigan by far had the largest concentration of EMO-affiliated schools and two-thirds of all EMO-only founded schools were there as well. On the other hand, only five percent of schools in the District of Columbia reported some type of EMO affiliation.[9] Former educators were important founding groups in all of the jurisdictions, but especially in Arizona, where they constitute almost 55 percent of the responding schools. The District of Columbia had the highest concentration of charter schools founded by social service/nonprofit organizations (30 percent).

Some have suggested that the first types of operators to enter the charter industry would be those with missions of philanthropy or other altruistic goals, followed later by those with profit-oriented ambitions (Solmon et al.

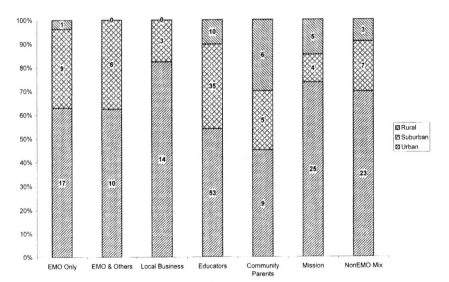

Figure 14.2.   Location of Charter Schools by Founder Type

1999). Essentially, more risk-averse for-profits would be waiting to see how the pioneers did and what models show the best signs of promise. Our findings regarding the age of existing charter schools appears to bear that out. Schools founded by community-based organizations, parents, or social service agencies tended to have been in operation for about four and a half years in January 2002 when we conducted our survey. The newest entrants, those founded solely by EMOs, came onto the scene, on average, more than a year later.

Theme and Target Population

What do these differences in organizational type mean in terms of actual school behavior? Two of the most important questions a charter school founder makes at start-up are whether to feature a special curricular "theme" and whether to target special populations of students such as those at-risk or teen parents. These decisions establish broad parameters that in turn, we suspect, affect the size, location, teacher recruitment and development needs, grade configurations, and even the kind of facility that a school will need.

If founding organizational structures and norms matter, we can expect charter schools founded by educational professionals and parent groups to be the least likely to engage in curricular or student niche approaches: educators because they have training and experience in offering a general education (they would prefer to compete based on quality of service rather than product differentiation) and parent/community groups because their orientation is often around a specific and spatially defined set of families. More market-oriented, EMO-associated schools, because they would be interested in the potential for developing a broad consumer base, would be most likely to aim for the median student; although emphasizing a fairly broad theme that might appeal as a marketing tool, they would be less likely to target a niche population unless it was one that had a particularly favorable revenue-to-cost ratio. Schools with a social service background would define their audience around a high-need population. Local business groups might be most likely to adopt a particular theme, tied to vocational or technical skills. To gauge whether this is true, we asked schools in the survey:

- Does your school target a particular type of student (e.g., at-risk, special needs, gifted, juvenile offenders)?
- Does your school's curriculum focus on a particular theme (e.g., character education, public policy, cultural heritage, technology, vocational, service industry)?

Schools that responded "yes" were asked to specify their target population or theme. As the results in table 14.1 suggest, despite many analysts' concern

Table 14.1.   Target Group and Curricular Themes

	Have Target Group	Target Population: At Risk Number in Each Category (Row %) (Column %) (N=253)	Have Curricular Theme	Three Most Common Themes
Founded by EMO Only	5 (18.52%) (6.02%)	4 (80.00%)	17 (63.96%) (10.18%)	Back-to-basics; character education; technology/computers
Founded by EMO and others	3 (18.75%) (3.61%)	2 (66.67%)	9 (56.25%) (5.39%)	Technology/computers; business; back-to-basics
Founded by Local business	5 (29.41%) (6.02%)	1 (25.00%)	13 (76.47%) (7.78%)	Career path; trade or specific job; liberal arts; technology/computers
Founded by Educators	30 (29.41%) (36.14%)	18 (66.67%)	61 (59.80%) (36.53%)	Back-to-basics; technology/computers; other
Founded by Social Service	18 (52.94%) (21.69%)	15 (88.24%)	16 (47.06%) (9.58%)	Character education; ethnic/identity; technology/computers
Founded by Parents or Community	4 (17.39%) (4.82%)	2 (50.00%)	17 (77.27%) (10.18%)	College prep; character education; other
Founded by Non-EMO Mix	11 (32.25%) (13.25%)	5 (50.00%)	25 (73.53%) (62.08)	Trade or specific job; liberal arts; career path
Totals	83 (30.74%)	53 (68.83%)	167 (62.08%)	

that charter schools might systematically target the most advantaged students (Kahlenberg 2000; Rothstein 1998; Fiske and Ladd 2000), more than half of all the schools that said they *did* target a group indicated that they targeted at-risk students. Overall, social service–initiated charter schools appear much more likely than others to engage in student targeting, with about 53 percent doing so, and their target audience is almost always students with high needs.

Charter schools in our sample were twice as likely to say that they emphasized a curricular theme as they were to identify a target student group (just fewer than two out of three do so overall). Emphasizing a theme was most common among community-based and local business–originated charters and least common among those initiated by social service or nonprofit groups (77.3 percent, 76.5 percent, and 47.1 percent respectively). Community-and local business based–schools differed, though, in the type of theme they emphasized, with business tending to focus on career- or trade-specific themes and community/parent-based schools more likely to emphasize themes that have more to do with symbolically affirming community aspirations (college preparatory; character education) than filtering demand based on particular skill.

Scale of Operation

Early proponents of charter schools envisioned them as intimate communities in which students would get more individualized attention (Kolderie 1990; Nathan 1991), and the evidence to date tends to confirm that charter schools are substantially smaller in scale than the traditional public schools. RPP International (2000), for instance, reported that charter schools had a median enrollment of 137 compared to 475 in traditional public schools. But, because market-oriented schools may be more concerned about achieving economies of scale, we expect that this vision of intimate communities may more accurately describe mission-oriented than EMO-initiated charter schools.

In figure 14.3 we present data on the average size of schools by different types of founders. As the data suggests, schools associated with EMOs are significantly larger on average than are charter schools with other types of founders, with EMOs often exceeding others by well over a hundred students. It is also interesting to see if these differences are expected to continue into the future. To that end, we asked each school to estimate their enrollment three years down the road. While all types of schools plan to grow, those founded by EMO-only or EMO and others anticipate growing the most and plan to remain significantly larger than the other types.

Another aspect of scale is the grade structure offered by schools. There has been some criticism that charter schools predominantly serve lower grades because these students are easier and less expensive to educate. In figure 14.4 we present the percent of schools, by founder type, that do *not* offer high school grades. Over three-quarters of the EMO-only founded schools do not offer the high school grades while schools founded by social service nonprofits were the most likely to offer high school grades. Grades offered by charter schools are not necessarily static; many charter schools hope to expand the number of grades they offer in the future. Thus we asked respondents to project three years into the future and tell us whether they planned on offering other grades. The pattern, however, remained the same, with EMO-only-founded schools remaining the least likely to offer high schools grades and social service–founded ones to be the most likely.

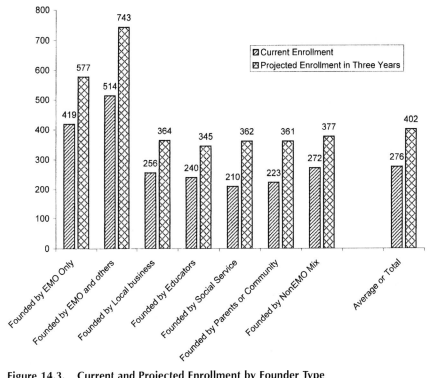

Figure 14.3.   Current and Projected Enrollment by Founder Type

Marketing and Market Research

We have already demonstrated that EMO-originated charter schools in our sample are larger than other types. Seeking to achieve economies of scale it is logical that these schools would market themselves aggressively and widely, using traditional forms of recruitment and advertising. This is not to say that mission-oriented schools may not seek to aggressively recruit; nonetheless, seeking to maintain smaller, more intimate communities, these schools are likely to be more inclined to recruit through informal channels. They are also more likely to lack the management expertise and capital to allow them to grow rapidly, further encouraging a modest and informal recruitment approach. Parent and community-based charters in particular we expect to limit recruitment to more localized and informal arenas.

To test this proposition we asked each school if they regularly, occasionally, or never used any advertising or promotional methods in student recruitment. Somewhat surprisingly, EMO-initiated charter schools were only marginally more likely to use expensive strategies like paid advertisements, websites, and radio (see table 14.2). At the same time, these schools were no

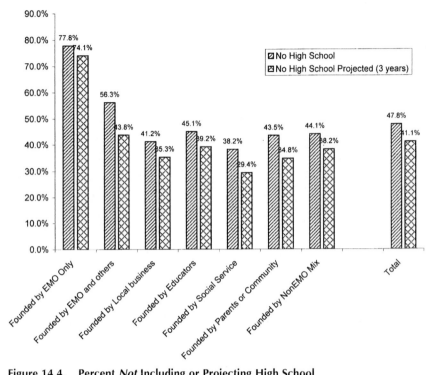

Figure 14.4.   Percent *Not* Including or Projecting High School

less likely than others to rely on informal and cheaper options like word of mouth or flyers. Similarly, though we expected community-based organizations to be the most likely to rely on informal and lower-cost practices such as open houses, EMO and local business–related schools also appear among the most likely to say they use these tools for recruitment as well. Schools initiated by educators tend to use the fewest number of recruitment strategies. There are several possible explanations. Some critics of the professional education community suggest that a history of monopoly status combined with a professional ethos that celebrates their own expertise have led teachers to adopt a "take it or leave attitude" toward consumers; if deeply enough engrained, such an orientation might even be carried by the presumably more entrepreneurial subset that has self-consciously opted to move to the more market-sensitive arena of charter schools. More likely, perhaps, is the possibility that, because they often are headed by principals and teachers already familiar to the local community, educator-initiated schools may feel less of a need to advertise. Schools founded by a mix of partners (whether or not including an EMO) are also significantly less likely than EMO-only-initiated charters to use three or more marketing tools.

Table 14.2. Percent of Schools "Regularly" Using the Following Methods of Advertising/Recruitment

	Paid Ads	Flyers	Web Site	Word of Mouth	Radio	Open House	Average Number of Tools Used Regularly
Founded by EMO-Only	29.6%	44.4%	63.0%	85.2%	14.8%	48.2%	3.04
Founded by EMO-Mix	25.0%	37.5%	62.5%	100.00%	6.3%	43.8%	2.88
Founded by Local business	23.5%	58.8%	41.2%	100.00%	11.8%	70.6%	3.35
Founded by Educators	16.7%	29.4%	43.1%	92.2%	8.8%	28.4%	2.33
Founded by Social Service	26.5%	47.1%	52.9%	100.00%	5.9%	35.3%	2.76
Founded by Parent or Community	21.7%	21.7%	56.5%	95.7%	4.4%	52.2%	2.73
Founded by non-EMO-Mix	17.7%	35.3%	52.9%	91.2%	8.8%	32.4%	2.65

Note: The row percentages do not add to 100 percent because many schools use more than one advertising or recruiting tool.

Finally, if EMO charter schools are interested in continuing to grow and reap greater profits, we would expect them to be more attuned to what parents and students—current and prospective—are looking for. In general, we would expect EMO-originated firms to be the most inclined to engage in such market research, while schools started by educators the least. Indeed, because EMO-originated charter schools might be aiming at more upscale consumer groups, we anticipate that they would be more likely than others to monitor other private and charter schools.

To get at this issue empirically, we asked schools about the frequency with which they conducted surveys of both current and prospective students and their parents. The results are presented in table 14.3. Overall, when it came to actively engaging in market-side research, the only types of charter school that really approached the idealized image of a competition-savvy market actor were those started by local business organizations. As we expected, charter schools founded by educators or community-based organizations were relatively disinterested in carrying out market research on both demand and supply-side issues. Surprisingly, though, EMO-affiliated schools, particularly

Table 14.3.   Percent of Schools Regularly Surveying Parents or Collecting Information about Competitors

	Demand Side				Supply Side Competition		
	Current Students	Current Parents	Prospective Students	Prospective Parents	Traditional Public Schools	Other Charters	Private Schools
Founded by EMO Only	26.9	51.9	11.1	15.5	14.8	29.6	20.0
Founded by EMO-Mix	40.0	62.5	18.8	37.5	50.0	33.3	13.3
Founded by Local Business	70.6	70.6	35.3	35.3	52.9	58.8	25.0
Founded by Educators	36.4	47.5	21.8	25.7	25.7	28.4	10.1
Social Service Founders	56.3	58.8	12.1	11.8	32.4	35.3	11.8
Founded by Parents or Community	39.1	47.8	18.2	17.4	39.1	34.8	13.6
Founded by Non-EMO Mix	45.5	55.9	14.7	23.5	20.6	26.5	15.2

those with an EMO as their sole founder, were also among the least likely to systematically collect supply-side information, though it is possible research being done is carried out at the corporate level. EMO schools also were relatively disinterested in monitoring the competition, but to the extent they did pay attention they were more likely than other types of charter schools to look at private schools and least likely to monitor the conventional public schools. Though charter schools started by social service nonprofits were as disinterested as the EMO charters in surveying prospective students and parents they did closely monitor their current consumer populations.

CONCLUSIONS: ACCOUNTING FOR ORGANIZATIONAL DIFFERENTIATION AND CONVERGENCE

Much of the existing literature on charter schools treats them as an undifferentiated mass. Even those who note that the umbrella term "charter school" encompasses a diverse array of organizations typically have not elaborated typologies to create a more meaningful framework for analyzing the charter phenomenon. We attempt to develop such a typology grounded in the proposition that the norms, traditions, and perspectives of founding organizations may bear upon the kinds of decisions that charter schools make. In several of the decision arenas we examined we found evidence of a sharp distinction between charter schools at least partially founded by EMOs and other types of charter schools. Specifically, there is strong evidence that EMO-initiated charters are much less likely to offer high school grade levels and are often considerably larger than other charter school types. Furthermore, EMO-initiated charter schools appear less likely to target particular subpopulations. At the same time, EMO-initiated schools were not substantially more likely to aim at a median student, aggressively advertise, engage in market research regarding present or potential customers, or monitor competitors.

Expectations based on very simple models of market-oriented vs. mission-oriented behavior are hazardous, but we find enough evidence of patterned differences to retain our belief that making distinctions within the community of charter schools can be elucidating. That for-profit EMOs may behave differently from other charter schools comports with the evidence emerging from other studies (Lacireno-Paquet 2004; Lacireno-Paquet et al. 2002; Miron and Nelson 2002; Brown et al. 2004). The theoretical case for charter schools has too often been based on market-laced notions of efficiency, innovation, and competition. At the same time, much of the political rhetoric designed to reassure critics relies on anecdotal accounts of mission-oriented schools providing nurturing environments designed to lessen social inequities rather than driven solely by profit-making motivations. Both arguments have some merit, but this can only be seen if one looks inside the traditional black box of the charter school community. To the extent that the EMO model for charters is different, legislators, charter authorizers, and charter regulators may need to develop policy instruments designed to acknowledge such distinctions. This is especially the case in light of the apparent trend toward greater involvement by for-profit EMOs, both as founding partners and as new partners for mission-oriented charters that find they need the capital and management expertise EMOs appear to provide. If these schools gradually muscle aside smaller and frailer mission-oriented schools, some attributes evident in the charter school movement as currently constituted may prove short-lived.

We draw our chapter to a close on a new thought. Though significant differences clearly do exist among charter schools, it is possible that a blurring of types may occur in the future, at least partially because external environments matter as much as internal organizational structures and behavioral norms. Regardless of the different reasons founders may choose to charter a school, it may be that the basic task of operation is relatively uniform and competitive pressures so severe that entrepreneurs adopting novel themes and targeting small, unique populations cannot survive for long. DiMaggio and Anheier, for instance, suggest that "differences in the behavior of [non-profit] and other firms in the same industry often flow from industry composition . . . e.g., degree of government involvement in regulation etc." (DiMaggio and Anheier 1990, 150). Also muddying the distinction between for-profit and nonprofit is the fact that some charter schools that were initiated by mission-oriented nonprofits have subsequently contracted with or otherwise allied with EMOs, and while the originators in principle are still setting the goals of the organization, it is an empirical question whether they may lose control of the reins in such relationships.[10] Convergence is also possibly shaped or unwittingly encouraged by the regulatory and policy environment (Witte, Shober et al. 2003; Wohstetter, Malloy et al. 2004). Charter authorizers, for example, play a key role in accepting and rejecting charter school proposals and thus shape what the population of charter schools look like in each state or jurisdiction. Testing requirements, a feature of all charter school legislation, also may lead to convergence in terms of what schools are teaching and how, even if the organizational structure (for-profit or nonprofit) varies. What will matter most are environmental factors such as the intensity of competition, the nature of consumer demand, the preferences of foundations and other sources of philanthropic support, and the funding and regulatory regimes of state and local governments.

NOTES

1. Local business groups often turn to education reform after "cutting their teeth" on more conventional urban revitalization efforts: promoting downtown redevelopment, building convention centers, attracting professional sports teams, and the like (Stone et al. 2001).

2. In our survey the responding schools had a mean enrollment of 276 students, comparable to the mean enrollment of 220 in the SASS data set for the same jurisdictions; 62 percent of the schools responding to our survey reported offering a theme, while 56 percent of the SASS charter schools reported that they offered "programs with special instructional approaches." Although the wording in SASS and our survey is not identical, along several important measures the two groups of charter schools surveyed are broadly similar. Our survey asked two slightly different questions about EMO affiliation. The first asked whether the school was *founded by* an EMO (16.3 percent), and the second asked whether the charter school had *collaborated with or received support from* a for-profit EMO (23.3 percent). The SASS asked whether charter schools were *managed by an organization that manages other schools but was not a school district*, to which 21.6 percent of the schools in the four jurisdictions responded as being managed by for-profit EMOs. Since our "collaboration" question may imply a less formal relationship than the "management" wording used by SASS, and in light of the fact that our later survey might have been expected to find a higher level of EMO involvement, we conclude that our sample may underrepresent the EMO-associated charter schools to a slight degree. We did find possible differences

in grade-level configuration; for example, 26 percent of the schools in our sample are high schools, a lower percentage than in the SASS population (36 percent).

3. They were presented with the following options and told to check all that applied: converted from a traditional public school; converted from former private school; extension of an existing social service organization; founded by former public school teachers; founded by a for-profit education management organization; founded by a group of parents; founded by the local business community; other (please specify). Of the 253 respondents with codable answers, 49, or slightly fewer than 20 percent, checked more than one option. For those that checked only the "other" category," we examined the name or description of the founding group and recodified the organization, where it was possible, into one of seven categories.

4. Including public school conversions, private school conversions, those founded by former public school teachers, and those who checked "other" but indicated they were formed by private school teachers or administrators.

5. Including those formed as an extension of an existing social service organization and those that checked "other" but listed a nonprofit organization, religious institution, or religious leader.

6. Including those founded by a group of parents and those that checked "other" but indicated they were formed by "a community organization" a "community-based organization," or a particular community organization.

7. Including those founded by local business groups and those that checked "other" but listing particular corporations or local business sponsors.

8. We matched schools to their census area using the common core of data (CCD). CCD defines its MSC1 category as comprising districts that primarily serve a central city of an MSA.

9. The 5 percent figure understates EMO penetration in D.C. in at least a couple of ways. None of the Edison Schools in D.C. responded to our survey (Edison Schools did respond elsewhere), and two other schools that have had EMOs as major partners from the beginning nonetheless did not mention them among the founders. We know this because we have been following the D.C. charter school situation carefully, and have conducted interviews at these schools. We chose not to recodify these schools here, since we do not have comparable depth of knowledge about the situations in other states.

10. Rather than look at the nature of the founding organizations, we could have opted to build our typology based on whether the charter schools are currently linked to EMOs. In this analysis, though, we were particularly interested in the question of whether difference in founders' organizational traditions and norms would continue to shape the schools' behavior regardless of whether they later find it more practical to seek EMO services. It is an important question, though, whether mission-oriented charter schools lose their distinctive character when they subsequently ally with EMOs and this is something that we hope to explore further in future analyses.

REFERENCES

Berry, Jeffrey M. 1999. *The New Liberalism.* Washington, DC: Brookings Institution Press.

Brown, Heath, Jeffrey R. Henig, Thomas T. Holyoke, and Natalie Lacireno-Paquet. 2004. "Scale of Operations and Locus of Control in Market- vs. Mission-Oriented Charter Schools." *Social Science Quarterly* 85, 5 (December): 1035–51.

Bulkley, Katrina. 2001. *Balancing Act: Educational Management Organizations and Charter School Autonomy.* CPRE Educational Issues in Charter Schools Conference, Washington, DC.

———. 2002. *Recentralizing Decentralization? Educational Management Organizations and Charter Schools' Educational Programs.* National Center for the Study of Privatization in Education.

Bushouse, Brenda K. 1999. *Motivations of Nonprofit and For-Profit Entrepreneurs in the Child Care Industry: Implications for Mixed Industries.* Annual Conference of the Association for Research on Nonprofit Organizations and Voluntary Action, Arlington, VA.

DiMaggio, Paul J., and Helmut K. Anheier. 1990. "The Sociology of Nonprofit Organizations and Sectors." *Annual Review of Sociology* 16: 137–59.

Fiske, Edward B., and Helen F. Ladd. 2000. *When Schools Compete: A Cautionary Tale.* Washington, DC: Brookings Institution Press.

Friedman, M. 1962. *Capitalism and Freedom.* Chicago: University of Chicago Press.

Fuller, Bruce, Marytza Gawlik, Emliel K.Gonzales, and Sandra Park. 2003. *Charter School and Inequality: National Disparities in Funding, Teacher Quality, and Student Support.* Berkeley, CA: PACE Center, 32.

Henig, Jeffrey R., and Jason MacDonald. 2002. "Locational Decisions of Charter School: Probing the Market Metaphor." *Social Science Quarterly* 83, 4 (December): 962-80.

Henig, Jeffrey R., Thomas T. Holyoke, Natalie Lacireno-Paquet, and Michele Moser. 2003. "Privatization, Politics, and Urban Services: The Political Behavior of Charter Schools." *Journal of Urban Affairs.* 25, 1: 37–54.

Hoxby, C. M. 2004. "Achievement in Charter Schools and Regular Public Schools in the United States: Understanding the Differences." Harvard University Program on Education Policy and Governance working paper, December 2004, at www.ksg.harvard.edu/pepg/pdf/HoxbyCharters_Dec2004.pdf.

Kahlenberg, R. D. 2000. *All Together Now: Creating Middle-class Schools through Public School Choice.* Washington, DC: Brookings Institution.

Kettl, Donald F. 1993. *Sharing Power: Public Governance and Private Markets.* Washington, DC: Brookings Institution.

Kolderie, Ted. 1990. *Beyond Choice to New Public Schools: Withdrawing the Exclusive Franchise in Public Education.* Washington, DC: Progressive Policy Institute.

Lacireno-Paquet, Natalie, Thomas T. Holyoke, Jeffrey Henig, and Michele Moser. 2002. "Creaming versus Cropping: Charter School Enrollment Practices in Response to Market Incentives." *Educational Evaluation and Policy Analysis* 24, 2 (Summer): 145–58.

Lacireno-Paquet, Natalie. 2004. "Do EMO-operated Charter Schools Serve Disadvantaged Students? The Influence of Policy." *Education Policy Analysis Archives,* vol. 12, no. 26 (June 15).

Mark, Tami L. 1995. "Psychiatric Hospital Ownership and Performance: Do Nonprofit Organizations Offer Advantages in Markets Characterized by Asymmetric Information?" *The Journal Of Human Resources* XXXI, 3: 631–49.

Mark, Tami L. 1998. "Analysis of the Rationale for, and Consequences of, Nonprofit and For-Profit Ownership Conversions." *Health Services Research*: 83–101.

Miron, Gary, and Christopher Nelson. 2002. *What's Public About Charter Schools: Lessons Learned About Choice and Accountability*. Thousand Oaks, CA: Corwin Press.

Nathan, Joseph. 1991. *Free to Teach: Achieving Equity and Excellence in Schools*. New York: The Pilgrim Press.

Nelson, F. Howard, Bella Rosenberg, and Nancy Van Meter. 2004. *Charter School Achievement on the 2003 National Assessment of Educational Progress*. Washington, DC: American Federation of Teachers. Available at: www.aft.org/pubs-reports/downloads/teachers/NAEPCharterSchoolReport.pdf.

Peterson, Paul. E. 1981. *City Limits*. Chicago: University of Chicago Press.

RPP International. 2000. *The State of Charter Schools 2000: Fourth Year Report*. Washington, DC: Office of Educational Research and Improvement, U.S. Department of Education.

Rothstein, Richard. 1998. *The Way We Were?* New York: The Century Foundation.

Salamon, Lester. 1987. "Partners in Public Service: The Scope and Theory of Government-Nonprofit Relations." *The Nonprofit Sector*, ed. W. W. Powell. New Haven, CT: Yale University Press, 99–117.

———. 1995. *Partners in Public Service: Government-Nonprofit Relations in the Modern Welfare State*. Baltimore, MD: Johns Hopkins University Press.

Savas, E. S. 2000. *Privatization and Public-Private Partnerships*. New York: Chatham House.

Solmon, Lewis C., Michael K. Block, and Mary Gifford. 1999. "A Market-Based Education System in the Making." Accessed online: www.azschoolchoice.orgs/pubs/06.htm.

Stone, C., J. R. Henig, et al. 2001. *Building Civic Capacity: Toward a New Politics of Urban School Reform*. Lawrence, KS: University Press of Kansas.

U.S. Department of Education. 2004. *Evaluation of the Public Charter Schools Program: Final Report*. Washington, DC. (Prepared by SRI International).

Weisbrod, Burton A. 1998. "Institutional Form and Institutional Behavior." *Private Action and the Public Good*, ed. W. W. Powell and E. S. Clemens. New Haven, CT: Yale University Press, 69–84.

Witte, John F., Arnold F. Shober, and Paul Manna. 2003. "Analyzing State Charter School Laws and Their Influence on the Formation of Charter Schools in the United States." Paper prepared for the American Political Science Association 2003 Annual Meeting, Philadelphia, PA, August 28–31, 2003.

Zimmer, Ron, Richard Buddin, Derrick Chau, Glenn Daley, Brian Gill, Cassandra Guarino, Laura Hamilton, Cathy Krop, Dan McCaffrey, Melinda Sandler, and Dominic Brewer. 2003. *Charter School Operations and Performance: Evidence from California*. Santa Monica, CA: RAND.

15

How the Best Laid Schemes Go Astray: The Agony and (Occasional) Ecstasy of Charter Start-ups

Robert Maranto

An old joke about universities says that it takes two academics to screw in a light bulb, one to screw it in and the other to write the book about it.

So it is with charter schools. Most of the more successful operators I know (and a few of the less successful ones) think their experiences merit a book. More than a few have already written theirs, offering a whole new literature: the charter start-up book. This literature offers us a familiar cycle of woe, from the desperate parents seeking alternatives, to unsupportive school districts and their minions, to hostile zoning boards, to the struggles to build and staff a new school, to battles over mission and how to realize the mission, to (usually) eventual success.

The best, though certainly not the happiest, of the charter starter books is reporter and former inner-city teacher Jonathan Schorr's *Hard Lessons: The Promise of an Inner City Charter School*, a woeful tale of the first year in the life of the two campuses of an Oakland charter school. Schorr offers much to comfort, and as much to discomfort, charterdom.

Even for a big city, the Oakland city schools are awful. Aside from the usual low test scores and violent classrooms, the Oakland public schools were incredibly overcrowded, and featured such oddities as a group of wacky Marxist substitute teachers more interested in class struggle than classroom learning, and of course, the infamous Ebonics controversy. No less a personage than Jesse Jackson declared Oakland schools a "national laughingstock." As one former superintendent bitterly joked, "Why don't we just bend over and say 'we're mooning America?'"

Not only are Oakland schools abysmal, they are also abysmally unequal. While Oakland public schools on the hills overlooking the city capably serve upper-income (and mainly white or Asian) parents, most city schools molder in the "flatlands." As Schorr writes, public school quality depends "on neighborhood, which in turn depends largely on wealth and race": the flatlands schools, by and large, warehouse low-income minority students. Indeed, Mexican American parents complained that the schools in Mexico were far better than those in Oakland, where their children got patronizingly good grades without learning: "The system was telling them everything was fine, but they knew their children couldn't read."

Finally, in 1997 a group of disgruntled flatlands parents, led by the Oakland Community Organization (OCO), pressed for improvements at one of the worst public schools, Jefferson Elementary. Inspired by Deborah Meier, the parents, OCO, and a few teachers spent nine months devising a schools-within-schools plan, with the seeming support of Jefferson's principal. But in a familiar story, the turf-conscious principal undermined the plan at the last minute. The principal instead urged parents to wait for his three-year school improvement plan to show results—of course, he planned to retire in two years! Similarly, on the district level the Oakland teachers' union officially backed site-based management, while in fact sabotaging it behind the scenes.

Failing to work within the system, Jefferson parents and the politically left OCO went outside it to lobby for charter schools, forming an uneasy alliance with School Futures, a Walton-funded nonprofit with a business orientation. OCO, in particular, found it difficult to ally with conservative business against the teachers' union. For its part, the union chief threatened legal action when an OCO organizer talked to teachers about charter schools, leading Schorr to tartly observe that "It was odd that she believed he could get arrested for exercising his free-speech rights, considering that she had taught honors-level civics classes."

With thousands of parent signatures and some help from Oakland Mayor Jerry Brown, who threatened to take over the school district, the reformers beat down opposition from the district administration and teachers' union to gain reluctant school board approval for five charter campuses . . . and then the fun began.

The school board dragged its feet until April, leaving only 150 days for the charter starters to find, rebuild, and furnish a site, negotiate government paperwork, develop school policies, buy supplies, and most important, hire a competent staff. Unfortunately, the Oakland parents and OCO lacked the expertise to open schools, leaving them to the tender mercies of School Futures. Having opened only five schools in its five-year history, School Futures took more than two months to hire principals.

More geared to selling than producing, School Futures staffers were simply not willing to put in the hours to get the job done. Rather than the five campuses promised, School Futures prepared only two buildings and provided those later and smaller than promised, never bothering to inform its partners! Furniture, books, and even paychecks also arrived late, and School Futures's poor communications continued.

Despite School Futures's tardiness, things might have worked out with top-notch principals and teachers. After all, each school had some things going for it. The mainly Hispanic Dolores Huerta Learning Academy gained considerable social capital from the Mexican American community. Similarly, the mainly African American Ernestine C. Reems Academy of Technology and Art gained students and support from Pastor Ernestine C. Reems's church, which owned its building. Indeed, each school started well enough. Despite the failures of their parent organization, heroic efforts by the principals and some of the parents opened the two campuses almost on time, though with teachers "free of whatever baggage came with teaching experience, because most of them had none."

And then, as all too often in school settings, the personalities got ugly. Schorr observes that one of the principals had never before managed others: "As a teacher, independent in her classroom, she had never worked directly under any boss, and certainly not a white one, a situation she viewed with particular annoyance." In contrast, School Futures's top dog, a forceful African American, "had learned his relationship with authority inside giant institutions with clear chains of command: the Marines, IBM, and Xerox," so the sheer "cheekiness of his two Oakland principals—the first women to serve School Futures in that position—bewildered him."

At Dolores Huerta, not only School Futures but also the parents complained about the brusque principal, who had previously served as an administrator in the Oakland public schools. In November School Futures fired her. On the one hand, the whole episode "raised questions about the company's claim of bringing solid business practices to education." On the other hand:

> A November dismissal of a principal was nearly unheard of in the district, and even at the end of the year, a problem principal might well have been reassigned to a small, quiet school where fewer parents would complain. But at the charter school, the managers could remove [Principal] Coates swiftly—a painful but quick surgery that put the needs of children above those of adults.

At E. C. Reems, a more dedicated principal held the school together, but was initially too overwhelmed by other tasks to observe teachers or devise special education programs. By spring, she too was clumsily fired, more because of strained relations with superiors and with Pastor Reems than because of her gradually improving performance. School Futures then placed a single principal over the two sites, choosing Pastor Reems's highly unprofessional brother, a former district school principal who barely lasted out the year. For their part, district bureaucrats tried to close the campuses due to paperwork lateness, largely ignoring academic performance the same or slightly ahead of that in nearby district schools.

Despite this and later adventures, the schools soldiered on as reasonably safe, if academically mediocre outposts in the flatlands. But with capable management, the charters could have been so much more.

Schorr's account is masterful. As a reporter, he can tell a story. Further, as a former inner-city schoolteacher, Schorr *knows* education. He describes the perils of first-year teachers, the attempts of parents to make a difference, and the damage a single troubled child can do to the academic performance of an entire class over the course of a year. He also knows that everything is relative: School Futures charter schools are lousy—except when compared to nearby district schools.

Schorr does best explaining the culture of urban public schools, as when he describes a soon to retire district school principal who, convinced that "the children who attend this school have no background" and thus could not learn, nonetheless "did what he could."

> He wore a tie every day, because a study he read in 1975 said kids perform better at schools where the principal wears a tie. He devised a split shift with his assistant principal so he wouldn't have to come in until about nine. And he made sure that Styrofoam lunch trays weren't mixed in with the rest of the trash, because they took up too much room in the compactor.

Such district school "leaders" make clear the need for charter schools, but charters must do better rather than just as well. A good school needs both an instructional leader and a business leader: School Futures failed at the latter and both principals, to varying degrees, failed at the former.

The sad lessons of *Hard Lessons* seem clear. On the school level, education administrators must practice basic professionalism: do sweat the small stuff, don't promise more than you can deliver, hire carefully, and leave enough time to do the job right. On a policy level, we must not replace duplicitous, insensitive public monopolies with duplicitous, insensitive private ones.

While not quite as memorable, quite a few other charter starter books merit a read. Among the best is Patty Yancey's somewhat incongruously named *Parents Founding Charter Schools: Dilemmas of Empowerment and Decentralization,* which is actually about parents and educators starting charter schools. Yancey, who teaches education at the University of San Francisco, is one of those rare academics whose dissertation is fun to read. She follows two of the first California charters in their first two years, finding, predictably, that parent governance is easier said than done.

While traditional educators give lip service to empowering parents and teachers, they in fact view parents less as partners than as revenue sources and nuisances to be distracted with busywork. Indeed, only 4 percent of teachers' colleges offer a course on how teachers can work with parents! And all too many school administrators treat their teachers no better.

Charters offer the possibility of something more. Yancey purposely studies two charter schools founded by parents and educators. C-Star was founded by a "European American" educator, along with parents from a child care co-op. The educator, "Sara," embraced a whole-child vision of education involving parents and integrating students of all classes and ethnicities. Unfortunately, C-Star's founding parents were "never particularly cohesive, even from the beginning. Parents would come to a flurry of meetings, disappear for a month or so, and then reappear" (2000, 64). Most parents enrolled not for the school's vision, but simply to escape dangerous public schools. Despite the charter's parent-centered model, most parents preferred to leave the work of developing and running the school to the "unfocused" Sara.

Alas, Sara was not up to the task. The school had no written contracts, no official personnel policies, vague curricula, and teachers who viewed teaching as a job, not a calling. Sara's curriculum required teachers to collaborate, but they did not in fact do so, in part because of philosophical differences. The local school district, for its part, did not provide the promised school site, but instead handed over an unprepared building months late. Under pressure, Sara was given to outbursts of temper, leading to parental complaints, a school board investigation, and finally, a leave of absence.

Yancey concludes that for C-Star "the time and energy expended to maintain enrollment, financial solvency, and internal democracy diminished the organization's ability to effectively implement the educational goals of the founding mission and safeguard the objectives of the public at large" (2000, 113). In other words, administration drove out education. Still, the school eventually stabilized by its fourth year.

Yancey's second case, Community Charter, was influenced by C-Star's failures, but in the end fared even worse. Here, a group of overwhelmingly white, middle class, politically correct parents founded a school dedicated more to racial diversity than to any particular educational philosophy. The charter faced the usual political problems, with the local teachers' union president promising to support the charter (once it included collective bargaining), and then promptly reneging. Eventually, after a twenty-month delay, the charter was approved, and the group began battling over site selection.

Once the small school started, a single novice teacher and a lack of parental involvement harmed the first year, as did parental debates over discipline, with African American parents wanting more structure than liberal white parents. Student and staff turnover continued, and eventually, in its third year of operation, the hostile local school district revoked Community Charter's license.

Despite an obsessive focus on racial politics, *Parents Founding Charter Schools* offers dramatic stories with important lessons about how to (and how not to) start a school. Like Schorr's low-income, minority parents, Yancey's more upscale edupreneurs should have planned better, agreed on a vision, and most of all, taken care to hire teachers who supported that vision. Alas, these things are easier said than done, particularly when founders must spend all their limited energy fighting political opposition from outsiders rather than developing internal political consensus.

Luckily, not all the tales of woe are woeful. While Schorr offers a journalistic treatment, and Yancey offers an academic treatise, James Nehring's optimistic *Upstart Startup: Creating and Sustaining a Public Charter School* gives a principal's view. Compared to the other start-up books, *Upstart Startup* has less depth for analysts and policy makers, but is actually more useful for practitioners. Nehring offers an amazing wealth of detail about the inner workings of a progressive school that simultaneously rejects and yet requires administration. If you want to know how to teach in or manage a progressive school, this is the book for you. Indeed, anyone thinking about making the jump from teaching to administration should read *Upstart Startup*.

Inspired by Ted and Nancy Sizer, a group of Massachusetts parents and educators started the Francis W. Parker Essential School, named after a late-nineteenth-century Progressive educator. The Sizers actually served as acting coprincipals the first year. James Nehring, who led an alternative school in Albany, was invited for a visit in Parker's first year and ended up taking the job of part-time principal/part-time teacher, or principal teacher. In *Upstart Startup*, Nehring details his two years as principal and third year as teacher.

Parker, located in a small exurb of Boston, is staffed by Sizer devotees, mainly young teachers just out of Brown or Harvard. Sharing common goals, the teachers usually support each other. Further, there are no regular administrators: Parker "administrators" keep teaching.

Unlike the other schools profiled, Parker is relatively well organized, and conflicts stay manageable. Here, the main story is less about school threatening battles than of the daily grind of continual growth, competing goals, and immense responsibilities wearing down a capable educator, and about growing pains threatening the nonhierarchy. Without regular administrators, duties are inchoate, with the school functioning more out of dedication than order. Parker nearly tripled in size in its first four years, leading Nehring to ponder:

> To what extent might growth necessitate changes in the school's administrative structure? Thus we were left to dwell in the world of ambiguity, partly for lack of adequate time to carefully see the work through and partly of necessity, as we watched the school grow and change before our eyes.

Nehring is another good storyteller, chronicling in great detail the inner workings of school and the typical days for students, teachers, and the principal teacher. He brings to life tales of how his proudly nonhierarchical school struggled to develop a discipline code reconciling democracy and authority, to define curricula, to adjust students to a system with "no grades and no average," and generally to limit administration but still function.

In contrast to the schools described above, Parker mainly succeeds because of its clarity of mission, hiring for mission (and resilience), its supportive network of parents and academics, and because it found an underserved niche market.

Of course, like all the charter schools, Parker must adjust to the demands of the outside world. As Nehring points out, the notion of charters as unregulated schools is "more myth than reality." Aside from mounds of paperwork, Parker suddenly had its budget cut 5 percent because of a change in state busing rules. More important, Parker must adjust a proudly progressive curricula to state demands for more traditional subjects and for those hated standardized tests. As Nehring concludes, traditionally bureaucracy has killed progressive education. Will it this time? Only time will tell, but Nehring makes it clear that the Sizerites will not go down without a fight.

All three authors agree that traditional schools often fail at basic professionalism. Charters usually, but not always, do better. For both charter and district educators, schooling is serious business requiring professionals, planning time, integrity, due diligence, and attention to detail. Unfortunately, especially in low-income districts, people willing and able to do this are in short supply.

BOOKS REVIEWED

Nehring, James. 2002. *Upstart Startup: Creating and Sustaining a Public Charter School.* New York: Teachers College Press.

Schorr, Jonathan. 2002. *Hard Lessons: The Promise of an Inner City Charter School.* New York: Ballantine Books.

Yancey, Patty. 2000. *Parents Founding Charter Schools: Dilemmas of Empowerment and Decentralization.* New York: Peter Lang.

16

Whose Idea Was This Anyway? The Continually Challenging Metamorphosis from Private to Charter

Jim Spencer

In January 1988, we began operating a private Montessori preschool in Flagstaff, Arizona. Before that time, we had intended to do other things in our personal lives and in our careers, but our community's demand for quality child care was so strong that by 1994 we were serving over two hundred children ages two to nine in a three-site elementary program.

Our program was very small, for three related reasons. First, the expense of starting a completely equipped and staffed Montessori elementary program is quite high. Second, Flagstaff lacks the wage base that would allow us to charge the private school tuition necessary to support a new high-caliber Montessori program. Third, being "poor but proud," we couldn't bring ourselves to offer and advertise a second-rate program.[1] Consequently, the elementary students we had were limited to those children who had been with us for several years in our preschool through kindergarten program.

LEXUS: THE RELENTLESS PURSUIT OF PERFECTION

The relentless pursuit of perfection that characterizes the Lexus luxury sedan somewhat imperfectly parallels our own experience. When it first hit the marketplace in 1989, the Lexus was immediately crowned by *Consumer Reports* as the best car on the road. I'd like to say it was the same with us, but it would be more accurate to say that we started out as a rusted Yugo. Even our critics, however, would have to say we have improved every year that we have been in business. I'm blowing my own horn here, but we did grow from an original student population of forty and a staff of five to our present student body of 350 and staff of thirty-five because we've done something right in our own pursuit of excellence.

We opened our school years ago when our community wanted an alternative to traditional child care and elementary education, and since that time we have worked to provide an ever-improving product. I emphasize "ever-improving" because we've worked very hard to upgrade every aspect of our school (and later, our schools) year after year. Each year, our facilities are cleaner and newer, our classrooms are better equipped and furnished, our programs are educationally stronger, and our staff is better trained and more highly motivated. Excellence does not just happen, and we did not "just grow." We *really* knew what we wanted when we started. We've worked extremely hard and sacrificed a great deal—profit, vacations, new "stuff," family time, and sleep, among them—to pursue it. I believe we have attained the degree of excellence we first had in mind, but we continue to strive for an even higher standard, even as I write this.

One might have expected that our plans would have included continued growth into a giant school system with four hundred sites and thousands of students. Nothing could be further from the truth. Our vision was and still is based on the adage that "small is beautiful." This vision has been echoed by the Edison Project's fundamental principles of "schools within schools," but we felt this way long before the Edison Project (1998) developed its approach.

We added a grade a year, limiting growth so that we could concentrate on getting the best possible fit the first time. We expected to grow to a maximum of 450 students at four sites, but again demand changed our minds. We now have two primary schools (preschool through kindergarten), an elementary school (grades 1 through 6), and a middle school (grades 7 and 8). We have no more than thirty children and at least two permanent teachers in every classroom, supplemented by "specialists" in areas such as languages, art, music, chess, computers, and gardening. By establishing relatively small sites, we enable our administrators to operate their educational programs autonomously, with only general guidance. We chose the class size based on the Montessori model which provides for gender balance, age balance, and a sense of community still with a teacher student ratio of 1 to 15.

We still centralize financial operations of the schools and the maintenance of the facilities, however, for two reasons. First, we believe each site should be uniformly operated. Second, our administrators must be free to concentrate on educating children, rather than budgeting, accounting, and "fixing things." Each site is a small community managed by a single person, and no site is so large that it loses its personal approach. Every teacher at every site knows every child and every parent at that site, which really makes a difference. At each site, the teachers and administrators meet frequently to discuss how to achieve our shared goals. In this way, we all know each other and we can work together in our "relentless pursuit of excellence."

After the state legislature passed charter school legislation that was arguably the most progressive of its kind in the country, we applied for a charter by the end of 1994. As private individuals, we could apply to the state for the authority to operate a public school, and we recognized our opportunity to offer Flagstaff a real Montessori elementary program. Shortly thereafter, we became the first applicants approved by the Arizona State Board for Charter Schools and the first charter school in Flagstaff.

Although we were ecstatic about our new status, we had no idea what we had done. What's more, I'm reasonably certain that we weren't alone. Probably most Arizona charter operators with a background in private education have had second thoughts about whatever prompted us to give up the good life. Why we have thought thus is the story that follows.

PRIVATE IS JUST THAT

Imagine yourself the owner of a hardware store. You took out a second mortgage on your home and borrowed money from Aunt Edna to start the store. You ate a lot of beans for a lot of years to get to the point where you were your own boss. You charged what you could to cover the costs of doing business, expensed everything you could to keep your taxes down, and ran the whole thing with a one-write check system and a one-page spreadsheet. No one else but Uncle Sam knew how much you made, and no one else knew how you made it. It was *private.*

Moreover, if you'd done half your job, you had developed a way of doing things that worked for you, given your circumstances and your temperament. Your procedures were tailored to these circumstances and, generally speaking, your policies were "flexible" and had been developed as needed. Then, imagine how you felt the day that the folks from "Ace Home Centers" approached you with a buyout offer. It boiled down to sell or risk losing the business to the "big boys." Actually, it sounded like a pretty good deal: a lot more money coming in, a chance to expand, and they wanted you to stay on as general manager.

All of a sudden you find yourself working for someone else who doesn't understand *your* business, who has his own set of rules that you must now follow, who treats *your* customers like cattle, who now wants *your* business analyzed for him or her six ways from Sunday, and who has eleven different programs from eleven different head office departments that are all designed to implement "company policy."

Your friends ask, "Why did you do it?"

You reply, "It sounded like a good idea at the time."

WE'RE NOT IN KANSAS ANYMORE: DIFFERENCES
BETWEEN PRIVATE AND CHARTER SCHOOLS

Every analogy breaks down eventually, so let's not carry this one too far. Suffice it to say that being a charter school is not like being a private school. In our arena of private Montessori education, the success of our schools largely rested on our ability to create the best class of students from those who applied for admission. It's never been a policy of "take the best, reject the rest" (as suggested by some), but rather an approach that asks in every case who will best benefit from this educational methodology, and who can contribute to the environment shared by the other children.[2]

When it works right, private Montessori education operates a lot like the shop of a craftsman who makes fine violins, one at a time. I believe one key strength of private schools is that most of them have the luxury of addressing students individually rather than like widgets coming off an assembly line. Don't mistake me, I'm not about to harangue and bash traditional public schools. After all, I, too, am a product of conventional public schools and did not even enter my first private school until the graduate level. At the same time, if I thought our traditional public schools had all the answers, I'd be doing something else with my life.

First Big Difference

As a charter/public school we are required to take everyone who comes to us on a first-come-first-served basis regardless of whether we feel they will benefit from the experience or not. We are experienced professionals, yet we cannot tell a parent, "Your child would be better served by the Waldorf Charter School down the street." Nor can we ask, "Given what you have told us about your background and your desires for your child, have you considered Lamb of God Christian School?" Such professional advice is not permitted. It is the parent *alone* who decides where his or her child goes to school.

Consider the impact on a former private school classroom. Presume we are only able to accept twenty-four children. Perhaps three of the first twenty-four to apply can't control themselves in the relatively unstructured openness of the Montessori classroom or are overstimulated by the presence of so many learning aids. These students then disrupt the classroom and the individual work environments of twenty-one other children. The classroom focus shifts to these three; they become discipline problems, are labeled (if only in the minds of the teachers) as problem children, and "fail" in their first experience in school. The teachers are frustrated, at least three children are frustrated, and each of three sets of parents are unhappy with the school, their child, or both. In the end, a very successful private school may have its reputation damaged among both parents and potential teachers.

Second Major Difference: Drowning in Paper

Remember the one-write check system and the one-page budget? They are gone with the wind. It seems like everyone in the Arizona Department of Education wants to know something about what you are doing. Many want to know the same things, but they don't share information between offices very well. Consequently, the time you used to spend at your son's Little League games is now spent filling out reports, creating lists, and completing tables. Yes, you just told somebody that last week, but this time someone else wants to know about it sideways!

It would be wrong, however, to cast all the blame on the "head office." We mustn't forget all the pollsters, professional information crunchers, and doctoral students of education. I swear every doctoral student in education seems to be doing a dissertation on charter schools, the "in" topic in the education field. Each of these students has a survey that will take *only* forty-five minutes to complete. We'd like to help, but the day is only so long.

Third Difference: There Is No Privacy

Public is public. It seems like everyone has access to everything. Unless you can prove that it violates some other law to do so, you are obligated to share every bit of what used to be private information with anyone who asks for it, from the curious to the malicious. For example, when we first started, my wife and I were unaware that we had to notify and invite the media and all outsiders every time we discussed our charter school. Taken literally, we had to invite the world to every one of our family dinners! When we realized this problem, we added three more people to our board, but we still found it hard to adjust to our lack of privacy in discussing matters concerning our school.

Fourth Difference: Some People Hate You

Anytime you get involved in something new that changes or adversely affects any well-established institution, you make enemies. When we were a private school, we were left alone and ignored by those who did not believe in our program. However, when we began "siphoning" off public tax dollars (paid by the parents of the children we educate) and competing with traditional schools, we were called names in the grocery store and personally slandered at public meetings. Sadly, I am not exaggerating.

Then there is the local newspaper reporter who is convinced you got into this "racket" to destroy public education and who sees it as his or her mission to ask you just the right questions in just the right way so that he or she can prove it to one million loyal readers. With hundreds of vendors constantly mailing me for my business, even the *mailman* has expressed his ire at having to stuff about three times as much mail into the larger mailbox I had to buy.

Fifth Difference: Beware False Profits

I wish I had a dollar for every time I heard someone make reference to all the money charter school operators were making. I'd love to have them all talk to my CPA to learn the truth, but I couldn't do that to her. The bottom line is that if you are thinking about becoming a charter school operator to make more money than you do as a private school owner, you would do much better by opening a liquor store.

Sixth Difference: Big Brother is Watching You

This difference is almost self-explanatory. As a private school, the parents of your enrolled children watch you. If they don't like what they see, they stop watching because they have moved their children somewhere else. As a public school, not only does Big Brother watch, but so does big sister, big aunt, big uncle, big second cousin twice removed, and so on. Everybody watches, and everybody has an opinion, a comment, a criticism, and an investigative reporter for a brother-in-law. The Democrats watch because they believe charter schools are getting away with murder and killing the traditional public schools; the Republicans watch to prove that the Democrats are lying. The traditional public schools watch to find weaknesses in charter schools on which they can capitalize in order to reclaim their lost sheep. The Department of Education watches because they have to; it seems like everybody at the Department of Education has to watch. The media watches because that's how they eat, whether what they say is true or not. And the State Board for Charter Schools watches because they sponsored you and don't want you to make them look bad. In fact, you'd be hard pressed to find any identifiable group that doesn't have an interest in watching charter schools. When we were private, it was just the parents of our children who watched (he sighed).

Seventh Difference: The Question of Fit

Private schools with methodologies that are nontraditional must change their approach or add another one. Montessori children, to cite only one example, are individually monitored and evaluated in every subject area every day by their teachers. For this reason, Montessori students rarely take tests. As a result they are *relatively* unfamiliar with test-taking strategies and are at a disadvantage in standardized test-taking contests, such as the Iowa series or the Stanford 9. Because Arizona is seeking to improve its standing on the "Who's Who in Education Among the States" list, a great deal of emphasis has been placed on each school's standardized test scores. Double that for us unproven charter schools. So now, instead of focusing on the traditional Montessori goals of developing character, self-esteem, self-reliance, self-discipline, and on directing independent study at the student's own pace, we find ourselves "teaching to the test" so that we won't look bad when we are compared to the other schools which we have worked so hard to not imitate all these years. Having to fit our octagonally shaped peg into the traditional round hole has cost us some of our shape and, sadly, some of our distinctiveness.

NEW WINE IN OLD WINESKINS

This question of fit brings me to one of my favorite analogies, a biblical parable which explains the inadvisability of putting new wine in old wineskins. A new wineskin is soft and pliable. New (unfermented) wine, when put into a new wineskin, causes the skin to stretch as the wine ferments. By stretching, the new skin contains the juice, helping the wine reach its full potential. An old wineskin, on the other hand, has already been stretched out. If you put juice into an old wineskin, the already stretched skin can't stretch anymore; both the skin and the wine are lost as the liquid ferments and the old skin bursts.

Charter schools are like a new wine. Because Arizona (and every other state, I suspect) lacks a new model to contain and enable these schools, they have been placed into the old wineskin of the traditional public education system. Privately, many of these schools could survive, perhaps even thrive, in the form their founders envisioned. I fear, though, that forcing these schools to operate within the confines of outdated traditional system regulations will cause much of the innovation and freshness of this "new wine" to be lost. If we miss the chance at real *educational* reform, and even of renaissance, that the charter school movement represents, we may irreparably harm the only educational system we have.

To use yet another analogy, remember Michael Jordan's attempt to succeed at baseball? The new skills required eluded him, and he performed poorly under a different set of rules that required different skills. Thank heaven for the strike that year, or he might still be a second-rate baseball player instead of a basketball legend. The same lesson holds for schools: forcing a private school to operate in a public school environment can turn a great school into a mediocre one.

"WHOSE IDEA WAS THIS, ANYWAY?":
PROBLEMS WITH IMPLEMENTING THE NEW LAW

When I get into a particularly whiny state of mind, I sometimes ask, "Whose idea was this, anyway?" Sometimes I ask it of my wife and sometimes she asks it of me. We usually ask it right after we've opened the dreaded brown envelope from the Department of Education, or logged into our e-mail to find all those messages from the Department's employees (most of whom we've never met). Sometimes, though, we intend it as a broader inquiry, and what we're actually asking is, "Did the folks who thought this up really think it through?" I truly don't think so.

Being what it is, the political process prevents issues from being adequately studied before they become laws. The legislative session is only so long, legislators have a number of obligations, and most terms of office in the state are only two or four years in length. When the well-meaning legislators created charter schools in Arizona, I'm convinced they did so without all the data they needed and without all the "what ifs" answered. Forget that they very possibly enacted charter school legislation to avoid dealing with the question of school vouchers. Simply consider whether they really created what they thought they were creating, and, if they did, whether they knew how much turmoil would result.

For example, I wonder if anyone thought about what the term "route mile" meant when charter schools (most of whose students are transported to school not by school buses, but by individual automobiles) applied for transportation support funds.

I wonder how a school district with under a hundred children (read "charter school") pays for a law-abiding special education program.

I wonder how students of a charter school, whose teachers do not have to be state certified, can participate in interscholastic sports when the sports authority requires that the teachers at participating schools be accredited, and the accrediting agency requires that all the school's teachers be state certified.

There are a lot more questions I wonder about. Sometimes I feel like wailing, "When we were private, we didn't have these problems."

THE "ROUTE MILE" WHAMMY

"They" tried to keep it quiet, but some enterprising charter school operator who applied to the "Stimulus Fund" for start-up capital discovered that the law governing transportation funding was a gold mine. Apparently, the law, which was written for school districts with school buses, said that schools would be funded for transportation on the basis of how many "route miles" were traveled getting kids to and from school.

For example, let's say you have a small school with four hundred children attending. If you had ten school buses that each traveled a ten-mile route while picking up and dropping off forty children apiece each day, the district would be paid for the cost of ten buses traveling ten route miles a day, 175 days a year. The state pays $1.50 per route mile. A brief calculation shows that the state's formula suggests that $26,250 is needed to maintain the bus fleet. Enter the charter school. Most charter schools require that parents drop off and pick up their children as part of their "contract" with the school. Each of four hundred children are ferried to and from school by private auto, with each car traveling an average of five miles each way. Instead of ten vehicles each traveling ten miles, you have four hundred vehicles traveling an average of five miles. Calculating these costs with the state's figures shows that four hundred "buses" for five route miles, 175 days a year, at $1.50 per route mile provides the charter school with $525,000 for transportation. Needless to say, this would have blown the state education budget.

The state was saved by a quick law change and by the relatively small number of charter schools who filed for the funds, but only after losing several million dollars in excess transportation costs and providing "stimulus funds" to several schools that otherwise would have done without the money.

SPECIAL EDUCATION OR "THE HIDDEN SIPHON"

Private schools do *not* have to accept everybody, and they try to serve the segment of the market they can best address and whose needs they *can* meet. If the private school simply cannot afford to provide complete care for children with disabilities, the private school operators explain that fact to parents of prospective students and tells them what services can be provided. Some parents still choose to enroll while others choose to go to another school they believe is better suited to meet the needs of their child.

Charter schools have to accept everyone who applies, up to their capacity, and they have to provide whatever that child needs to learn in the school environment. The state fractionally supports special education. The expectation, I presume, is that its provision eventually will cover the cost of building a special education program. The state does not provide nearly enough funding to create a special education program from scratch on opening day. It does, however, legally require that one be in place. Small schools, like charter schools, that have no bonding authority or credit history, can literally be put out of business by a relatively few students with special needs.

So as not to exaggerate the problem by using the example of a child with multiple physical, psychological, and emotional disabilities, simply consider the needs of a young child with Down's syndrome. The child must be evaluated by a specialist ($350). The child will very likely require ongoing speech therapy ($150/month), ongoing physical therapy ($150/month), and ongoing occupational therapy ($150/month). The child will be the subject of several progress evaluation meetings with specialists, school officials, teachers, and parents ($100/month), and will probably require special tutoring ($150/month). The child will require these services monthly, whether the school is in session or not. This child's needs will cost the school $8,750 per year over and above what it costs to educate the child. The school probably receives a total of $5,000 to educate this child and meet his special needs ($2,500 if the child is a kindergartner). If the school does a good job with this child and attracts several others with more severe problems, given the current funding mechanism, the school will not survive long enough to do any lasting good.

How does our school pay for special education, you ask? We cut the budget in other places. We reduce the salaries of teachers, administrators, and the business manager, and we sell chocolate. And frankly, if this section lacks the playfulness of the other parts of this chapter, it's because it's very difficult to find any humor here.

HEY MOM, WHERE'S THE TEAM?

"Hey Mom, why doesn't my school have a soccer/track/volleyball/etc. team?" Good question; a lot of charter high school students probably ask it. This is not a big issue with the elementary schools because younger children are just as happy to rely on local community programs. With high school students, though, athletic competition is more complicated. It's not just a game; it's a social imperative. Many charter high schools are not accredited, however, because all of their teachers are not certified. And unaccredited schools are not allowed to participate in authorized competitions with other schools.

Currently, the accrediting agency is addressing this issue. If a change in policy is made, the problem of competing with district schools may simply become one of size and funding. These issues are not easy ones, but they are more understandable. After all, why should a teacher who is fluent in five languages have to be state certified to teach Spanish? And why should an experienced biochemist have to be "state certified" in education to teach high school biology and chemistry? If the accreditation problem remains, charter schools may soon be numerous enough to form their own interscholastic athletic association. Alternatively, charter schools may simply continue to compete with other charter schools and the private schools in their surrounding area, schools that tend to be unaccredited but excellent.

THE BENEFITS OF "GOING PUBLIC"

So, apart from "it sounded like a good idea at the time," why did we become a charter school?

First, as a private school in Flagstaff, we could count on receiving about $3,200 a year per child to meet all the school's expenses and put food on my family's table. As a charter school, we receive what every other public school receives from the state: last year that was about $5,000 per student. This additional funding enabled us to pay our teachers a good bit more and to outfit our classrooms more completely with new Montessori equipment. Given these additional outlays, the special education requirements, and the start-up expenses associated with adding new grades and new equipment every year, we are making only a very little bit more than we did as a private school. As operators of the school, we hope and expect to reap a better return eventually, but only after we are certain we are providing what is expected of us.

Second, it's rewarding to be able to offer people something that they never had before, and even more rewarding when it's better than what they were getting elsewhere. I do believe that our charter school is a better choice for most children than the traditional public school. If I didn't believe that, I'd be running the liquor store. We take pride in what we are doing and experience a level of satisfaction that we did not experience when we relied entirely on equipment we would purchase at garage sales.

Third, it's exciting to be a pioneer. Yes, the pioneers tend to get hit by all the arrows, but they also get to be the first to cross the Rockies, see the Pacific, and raise their children in a new world. There is something to be said for dreaming, but so much more for using the dream as your blueprint and building something tangible. My spouse and I believe we have a truly excellent school. One of our students even created a "field trip sticker" that says "Visit my school; You won't believe what goes on in this place!" Others agree with us.

IN CONCLUSION: WOULD I DO IT AGAIN?

There are days when I could go either way, but, on balance, I'd do it all again. I say this because the new facility is finished and the battles with the city are over. I say this because the annual financial report has been submitted and the upload problems I had were on THEIR end. And I say this knowing, even expecting, that even though the next arrow won't hurt any less than the last 178, they are coming less frequently! Being a private school definitely had its advantages, but now that we are a charter school, I wouldn't go back.

At least, not today.

NOTES

1. Author's note: I've been told that my writing tends toward the outrageous, makes copious use of hyperbole, and is generally tongue-in-cheek. For this reason, proceed at your own risk!

2. For more information on Montessori methods, see the American Montessori Society website atwww.seattleu.edu/~jcm/montessori/menu_link.html. Or, for those more comfortable with the printed page, there is Maria Montessori's [1978 (1941)] *Dr. Montessori's Own Handbook.*

REFERENCES

Montessori, Maria. 1978 (1941). *Dr. Montessori's Own Handbook.* New York: Shocken Books.

The Edison Project. 1998. www.edisonproject.com/menuframe.html.

The website of the American Montessori Society:www.seattleu.edu/~jcm/montessori/ano_bib.html.

17

If You Build It, They Will Come

John Buck

Here's everything you need to know about facilities management: how to get that big loan, whether to buy, build, or lease, where to go for money, and, most importantly, what you need to have figured out for yourself before you get there.

I once heard at a charter school conference that the top three issues in the charter school world were "Facilities, facilities, and then facilities." As one who specializes in helping charter schools finance their projects, I must admit that even I was taken aback by that idea. (Note: you'll see several examples of shameless self-promotion [SSP] throughout this article. Please pay close attention to them.) No doubt facilities are important, particularly when trying to attract students and their attendant revenues. But surely there are equally important issues for charter schools! After all, Abe Lincoln was educated in a one-room school, and he turned out pretty well.

There are other issues affecting charter schools, many of which are completely over my head. For example, I couldn't devise a curriculum any more than I could walk on water. (And besides, that's been done.) What I do know is the core issue ensuring a charter school's success, including success in obtaining facility financing.

IT'S A BUSINESS!

One must give James Carville credit for focusing on the thing that, more than any other except perhaps Ross Perot, helped propel Bill Clinton to the presidency. "It's the economy, stupid!" allowed Clinton to come from nowhere (politically speaking) to unseat a reasonably popular incumbent president. This analogy from the 1992 election is relevant to your charter school. The most important slogan for your charter school is "It's a business, stupid!"

Now, I know some of you reading this think of yourselves as educational do-gooders, frustrated with the traditional public schools, and out to save the educational world. If you had wanted to run a business, you would have opened a Subway franchise. But when you chose to open a charter school, you accepted stricter accountability in return for several freedoms. This accountability includes proving yourself to prospective facility lenders, as opposed to voters, if you want your own facility. The fact is, unless you are the long-lost relative of Bill Gates or Malcolm Forbes (or Ross Perot), you will likely need other people's money to do so. Obtaining other people's money usually means they expect you to actually pay them back, and to demonstrate your ability to do that means you have to run your school as a business.

Another fact is that charter schools that don't make it bail because they couldn't manage the business, not because there weren't students willing to enroll. Many parents want another choice in education. But, despite this, charter schools have failed. In most cases, it was classic self-destruction, which means if you can get a handle on the business, your odds of success are pretty good.

Did Perot go out and leverage future revenues to build facilities before making EDS into a going concern? No! He built his business first, by developing a product customers wanted, by putting in the correct business infrastructure to run the business, and then by marketing the heck out of it. Then he built his facilities. And that is what you need to do with your charter school: build your school before you build its facility.

BUT I HAVE AN ACCOUNTANT!

That's a start, whether you are large enough to have one on staff, or you must contract out those services. But that's just a basic prerequisite, necessary even for the most mundane state reporting requirements. It doesn't mean you actually understand the numbers, or your school. Establishing your school as a going concern to satisfy a potential lender in your facility involves much more. Charter schools have been around for only about ten years, and most of your schools are much younger than that. Most permanent facility financings will have a term between twenty and thirty years, and the real estate collateral is often suspect for use as other than as a school, unlike many other businesses. Your charter can also be revoked, which means a charter school must be established as a going concern.

CAN YOU HEAR ME NOW?

I recently saw a poster showing President Bush and Saddam Hussein on the phone, with the president asking the former dictator that very question. Not only did I laugh out loud, but I also thought it demonstrated what can happen when one misjudges a situation. So don't misjudge yours.

How can you get a handle on your charter school business and lay the groundwork for successfully obtaining facility financing in the process? I'll try to outline a few pointers. If you pay close enough attention, you might not even need the services of someone like me to obtain your facility financing. Not!

Realistically, you will probably not be able to do it all yourself. And it's in my self-interest to truthfully show you how to run a business. First, I typically earn the majority of my compensation when a transaction closes, and if you don't know how to run your business, there will be no transaction to close, forcing me to go out and get a real job. And we can't have that!

Secondly, because I am an independent financial adviser (SSP alert), I can work with you over a period of years, if necessary, to help get you ready for a financing to obtain the facility of your dreams. But if you don't install the proper business infrastructure, it's unlikely either of us will succeed. Last, to some extent some of you have already received financing, particularly from the public bond markets. If you then fail, you would make it harder to finance other schools as a result of the pullback on the part of lenders. Again, these pesky lenders actually want their money back (with interest, no less).

So, since we are in this together, perhaps we should review some of the basics with respect to your charter school business. I'll discuss some of the considerations in leasing facilities. After that, we'll get into the general steps it takes to own your own facility, no matter how it was financed, paying close attention to managing construction risk. Then, the really fun stuff: the nuts and bolts of financing your facility and the potential sources of funds. Many of these issues are excruciating to read (and write) about. But, hey, that's why I love what I do: few, very few, want to deal with these issues.

BUILDING YOUR SCHOOL

Who are you?

In addition to being a great song by one of my favorite groups, it is the central question to your charter school. Sometimes this runs counter to what a lender is looking for. For example, many analysts prefer bigger schools because it gives them a sense of comfort regarding the demand for the school as well as your ability to withstand a shock in enrollment. But, ensuring that your school is a going concern may require a smaller focus. It's more

important for the school to be what it should be rather than what some financial analysts would prefer.

You have to know your market. Fortunately, you should be good at doing
your homework, or you wouldn't have gone into the education business.
What are you trying to accomplish? Whom are you trying to serve? (Hopefully, the answer to that is not yourself!) What is your niche? What are the service area demographics for that market? How many kids within a reasonable
distance of your school need the type of educational product you offer?
These are questions a reasonable charter operator would want answered
prior to expending the effort to open a school, and questions your lender
will want you to answer to their satisfaction prior to turning over their money
to you for your facility. While charter authorizers often ask many of these
same questions, they don't have quite the stake in your success a lender
does, and may in fact decide your charter authorization based on their own
self-interest rather than yours.

Part of this also means knowing your competition. What is the condition
of the local school district, in terms of educational quality and overcrowding?
How many other educational alternatives lie within your service area? Are
you complementary to other charter schools in the area, or in direct competition? Why would a parent choose your school over other alternatives?

After considering the above questions, you may be ready to define your
school's mission. I was always suspicious when they talked about defining
missions in grad school, but I can now say I understand its importance to a
charter school. Chalk up my grad school experience to poor learning.

Defining who you are as a school also means describing to anal-retentive
financial types the educational model you employ. Most of us are clueless
about such things, or we would not have had to become financiers. You may
think you understand it, but make sure you can distinguish it from the competition.

Finally, knowing "who you are" means clearly understanding the implica-
tion for which grades you serve and the class size you desire. If you are K–6,
why do you choose not to include 7–8? If you serve K–12, how does that fit
with your mission? Do you need a class size of fifteen to serve the niche, or
of thirty to make the numbers work? If thirty, what does that do to the educational quality and desirability of the school? All these are interrelated and
need to be clearly understood so you can explain them to potential lenders.

TO BE, OR NOT TO BE!

Once you have become self-actualized, a first consideration is to decide
what kind of entity to utilize. The majority of schools are either nonprofits
themselves, or have an established nonprofit shell corporation that is instru-

mental to the school. These shells own the facility on behalf of the school and lease the facility to the school. State law typically determines whether your school is nonprofit or you need a shell corporation. Whatever the case, it's usually easier to decide this in advance of a financing, particularly since most of you will want to obtain the financing yesterday. Nonprofit versus for-profit affects what type of financing you can consider. For-profit entities cannot borrow on a tax-exempt basis. Tax-exempt financing has a lower interest rate than a comparable taxable financing.

You also received, or will receive, a charter from an authorizer. Authorizers take various forms throughout the country. School districts, universities, and state agencies are the most prevalent. It's in your interest to foster a good relationship with yours. They can make your life easier or harder, and control whether you get to continue or not. In the case of school districts, who can think of your charter as unwanted competition for state dollars, this becomes particularly important. In the case of some other types of authorizers, be aware of "empire builders." The better you run your school, the less likely they will impose on your operation.

If you can, try to negotiate an "evergreen" charter. This approach involves tradeoffs, but provides more certainty in the renewal process. It seeks to set out certain benchmarks, or accountability items, for your school at various points in your life cycle, and calls for the authorizer to extend your charter *prior to the year in which your charter expires* if you meet these benchmarks. If you don't meet them, it gives you a year or two to correct the problem(s). The evergreen charter also makes it hard for authorizers, particularly school board members who may consider you competition, to say no to extending your charter. Additionally, lenders like knowing before the eleventh hour that the charter is renewed! So would your parents and students. I believe the evergreen charter is more useful than a long-term charter, since any charter can and will be revoked for reasons similar to reasons for failing to renew a charter. The idea is to put into place a framework for keeping charters out of trouble by forcing, and then rewarding, accountability.

Since the majority of charter schools that fail do so for lack of management skills, it behooves a charter school to spend significant time and energy to develop appropriate governance, leadership, and management policies and procedures. This matters whether you hired a management company to run your school (more on this later), whether you are a one- or two-person operation, or whether you are in between. Who is on your board? Do they have relevant career experience useful to the business? Useful professionals include lawyers, accountants, real estate experts, banking and finance types, and, of course, educators. A very important question is: How do you prevent conflicts of interest? When their offspring are done with the school, what kind of succession planning is in place to obtain other useful board members? Does the board provide direction, or does it try to micromanage the school? If you are the founder of a school, do you have the personality and plans to share power as your school grows?

From my days in trying to help school districts pass bond elections, we had a useful maxim for the bond campaign: if it isn't in writing, it doesn't exist! Do you have written governance, management, and financial policies and procedures? The goal is for someone to be able to quickly get a general sense of how this business is run. With respect to governance, your state (or other state's) charter school association may be a good source of policies and procedures to consider. With respect to financial controls and policies, your auditor or accountant should be willing to assist. Some considerations include who has access to the checking account, what level of expenditure requires board approval, what are the appropriate levels of reserves (including but in addition to any required by state law), and how to obtain access to working capital financing.

Like any business, you need proper access to financial expertise, especially those of you that are educators. Someone has to be responsible for watching the money and implementing the business plan, outside of the board. If you are small, these services can be contracted out to minimize the impact on your budget, but that doesn't mean the financial adviser shows up once a month at your board meeting to quickly run through the monthly interim report. This function is central to the success of your business, and he or she needs to be a part of every decision outside of the classroom.

Further, there are other subspecialties which can also be contracted: insurance consultants (P & C, business interruption, workman's comp, liability), risk assessment, business plan development, cash flow budgeting, payroll/back office, and, last but not least, facilities financial advisers (SSP alert). Often, these subspecialties are where board member experience can be useful in getting something started, but their ability to actually perform the function is usually limited by their work and family duties, not to mention potential conflicts of interest. At some point, it becomes necessary to contract out for these services, and you will do well to make use of specialized consultants as early in a particular process as possible.

What about audits? Enron and WorldCom notwithstanding, get one, whether or not required by state law. This is particularly important if your authorizer is a school district and you could also be part of their audit.

Waiting lists are another critical process to be understood. Charter schools are fortunate that they can tell a prospective student there is no room for them. If any of you operate in a growing school district, which must accept everyone that shows up, you can quickly understand how valuable this is. Use it to your advantage by requiring everyone to re-sign every year. That way you do several things: 1) you make it easier to manage any vacancies which occur, 2) your budgeting process is easier to complete, and 3) you demonstrate to potential lenders that your demand is real, and that your enrollment management procedures are sound. The second item is very important, and the timing of your process should coincide with your budgeting process to help result in a budget that actually resembles reality.

MANAGEMENT COMPANIES

Engaging an EMO (education management organization) can be a very useful way to obtain the business infrastructure necessary to run the school. There are some terrific management companies out there. But, there are also some train wrecks out there too, so make sure you get full financial disclosure and references. In any event you are well advised to consider that one day you may wish to part ways with your EMO. Different EMOs provide different services, a fact which has ramifications for the terms of your management agreement.

Some offer mainly back-office (business) services, while some offer curricula. Others provide everything involved with the school, and some go even further to provide either the facility or the financing for the facility. The services provided and the financing vehicle used impact the terms of your management agreement. In addition, for those not offering facilities, IRS regulations will also impact what an EMO's fee can be if you want to use tax-exempt financing for your facility.

In negotiating the management contract, consider where you would be if you terminated the relationship. Did the EMO upstream all leftover revenues of the school, or did you require that some would remain with the school to act as operating reserves when the romance ends? Are employees the school's or the EMO's? If they provided the facility financing, can they call in the loan if you terminate the relationship? Do you perform your own budgeting, perhaps in conjunction with the EMO, or do you leave that entirely up to the EMO? You will be happy if you considered some of these issues in negotiating the terms of your agreement. The good EMOs anticipate many such items, and will offer the corresponding terms as part of the management agreement they propose.

FACILITY EXPENSE AND YOUR BUDGET

Now that's an exciting topic, isn't it? I fell asleep just typing it! So, to keep it short, use this rule of thumb. You should be apprehensive about your facility costs exceeding 20 percent of your recurring revenues at your consistent enrollment level, whether historical or projected. If projected, is it based on a real waiting list? Remember, your school competes for students, and the amount you spend on the program impacts the desirability of the school, so maybe you can do without the brass urinals. In most cases, charter school per pupil funding is less than the traditional public school funding, and traditional public schools often have nonoperating revenues dedicated to facility debt service. If your facility expense exceeds 20 percent, you are down into the seventieth percentile of your revenues you are able to spend on the program. Many schools have facility costs in the low double digits, and some below 10 percent. Facility expense is just like interest rates: low good, high bad.

LEASING A FACILITY

There is a sailing club in Colorado called the "Why Buy Club" whose market niche takes advantage of that old saying: "A boat buyer's two favorite days are the day he buys it and the day he sells it!"

The reasons a charter school should consider leasing are many. These include especially that your school is new and unproven. They may also include your size, the lack of suitable property to purchase, or that you aren't the long-lost relative of Bill Gates, Malcolm Forbes, or Ross Perot. I would guess there are numerous folks who have forgotten more about leasing property than I know, and I reiterate to get such folks involved early. But I do want to touch upon a few key items that may relate to your ability to finance a facility later on.

The first is that your lease payments demonstrate ability to service future debt. This is a good thing, so don't lose heart if you want your own facility but find it necessary to lease. However, keep in mind the 20 percent rule of thumb in terms of its cost, and watch out for escalation clauses or other charges that could cause you to violate that rule. Put a cap on any such clauses.

Regarding the lease term, finding the right balance can be tricky. You don't want to go year-to-year and one day find yourself homeless, but neither do you want to be stuck in a long-term lease you cannot get out of if you want. At least make it so you can assign or sublet any portion of the lease freely if and when you do move on to your own facility.

One topic to understand from the very beginning of lease negotiations is the amount of tenant improvements (TI) required and who is financing those improvements. If the landlord wants your school to finance TI, know that obtaining financing for TI can be difficult unless you have other collateral to offer, because the improvements are not yours but rather the landlord's. You might need to seek such funding from nontraditional sources, discussed later.

Finally, if the facility is at least somewhat desirable as a possible long-term solution for the school, inquire about your ability to enter into a lease/

purchase (rent to own) arrangement. This could allow some of your rent to go toward reducing the purchase price you otherwise would pay in the future.

OWNING REAL ESTATE

Owning instead of leasing involves a trade-off of controlling your destiny (in terms of facility) versus the assumption of a fair degree of risk. You likely will have millions of dollars to repay, and you are locked into that location. Be sure you are ready for that, and that it is good for your school.

The next question is: build or buy? If an acceptable existing property is available, give strong consideration to purchasing versus constructing a new facility. You need a facility before you can bring in the students and their resulting state revenues, and acquiring an existing facility helps to greatly reduce or perhaps eliminate the risk of construction delays and overruns (more on that later). Some states require a list of available real estate to be published annually, so check this out if applicable.

If you have real estate and/or legal experts on your board, they can help you get started. But again, only to a point: get the paid professionals involved early.

Particularly when owning a facility, you need to think through your program and its resulting space requirements. Again, you are going to be there for a while. Remember your market and whom you are trying to serve, and factor their needs into the facility plan. More than you can fathom, things will go wrong. Whether it's in the regulatory process, the financing process, or the negotiating process, expect to have to jump over several hurdles. You are wise, if possible, to identify several site alternatives. Priorities must be set and held, in terms of desirable site attributes and other aspects.

One such priority is the overall facility budget. Keep an eye on the resulting debt burden on your operational budget, as described earlier. You can't offer a quality program if too large a portion of your budget goes toward facilities.

Also, address zoning and regulatory issues early on. The public hearing requirements can add weeks and months, versus days, to the overall process, so have these lined up well before any purchase options expire. Obtaining permits can take time.

MANAGING CONSTRUCTION RISK

Even though you have decided to own your own facility, remember: *you are not in the real estate business.* Therefore, you need to avoid taking on risks you have no business assuming. Constructing a facility is where things can go really wrong, and could jeopardize your school if they go really wrong. It happens!

A good design and construction team is a must. I strongly advise considering an owner's representative to oversee this entire construction process on your behalf, for items including contracts, bidding, permits, scheduling, and other tedious and boring stuff. This person sits only on your side of the table and represents your interests. They also free you to concentrate on the education business.

In any construction process, you will find it necessary to fund certain pre-construction services prior to closing on the financing. These include architects, engineers, surveys, appraisals, etc. If you intend to utilize tax-exempt financing, be sure to adopt a reimbursement resolution within sixty days of any checks you have written for such items. Your general counsel, bond counsel, or financial adviser can help you. This will allow you to reimburse yourself out of the financing for these items typically for up to eighteen months, and as far out as three years in some circumstances.

Some standard items you should expect to obtain for any facility financing include an appraisal (even if on an "as built" basis), a phase I environmental report, a survey, and title insurance. Try to get these lined up early in the process, particularly to deal with any exceptions in the title report.

Construction risk management also means paying close attention to the contracts involved. You should use these contracts to transfer the risks of construction to those better able to handle them. Have your attorney and owner's rep involved early. Insist on guaranteed maximum price contracts and performance bonds for subcontractors. If applicable, get liquidated damages. While all these things add to the overall cost of the project, and as a result also to the debt burden your budget must bear, this is not the place to cut corners! Don't be penny wise but dollar foolish!

FINANCING YOUR FACILITY

Well, it only took me about four thousand words to get to the point: how to obtain financing. Getting your financing is like getting a financial physical, so get ready to turn your head and cough when you enter into this process.

Sources of funding include commercial banks, bond issues, community development financial institutions (CDFIs), and other nontraditional sources. Every source has a box they call their "lending policy." They will generally try to fit you into their box in order to consummate a transaction and get paid. But sometimes that's a box you don't want to be in! Before getting into the details of each, let's make some comparisons of these in terms of regulatory oversight, the relative credit risks they are willing to take, up-front costs, length of financing, loan-to-value considerations, security and subordination, and the need to readdress in the future.

There is a relationship between the amount of regulatory oversight a lender deals with and the amount of credit risk they are willing to take. Banks are more regulated, and as a result typically won't make loans in all but the most secure situations. Institutional bond investors such as tax-exempt bond funds or insurance companies are less regulated and have full-time analysts who are supposed to be able to understand and identify credit risks, making bond issues available in many circumstances where a bank loan might not be possible. You are still being put into a box, but just one with softer walls.

CDFIs are usually the biggest risk takers, because they are trying to accomplish a higher ideal in assisting with a financing, rather than only being concerned with getting their money back. But, they are concerned about that, too. They believe they have the expertise as well as the mission to take risks others wouldn't.

Bond issues typically involve the largest up-front costs. For small transactions, these can add a substantial percentage to the financing. Banks typically charge a 1–2 percent commitment fee. CDFIs also usually have some sort of up-front fee, but their fees are usually the smaller of the alternatives.

With respect to the length of the financing, or term, these alternatives rank, from long to short, as follows: bonds, banks, and then CDFIs. Bond issues can be as long as thirty years. Bank loans are typically amortized over twenty years, but with a maturity of ten years. CDFI financings usually have a three- to seven-year term. This means that, with a bond issue, you will never need to readdress your facility financing in the future unless you want to do so. With bank loans, you will likely need another physical. CDFI loans usually are not required to be rolled over, either because they are fully amortized or because they are no longer necessary.

With respect to loan-to-value considerations, bonds and CDFIs usually will lend 100 percent of the funding necessary. Commercial banks typically look for a loan-to-value (of collateral) in the 65–80 percent range.

CDFIs and other alternative funding sources are usually the only ones willing to subordinate their interest to another lender. As such, they are useful in helping meet a bank's loan-to-value ratio, or in helping a bond issue achieve a higher credit rating than otherwise.

Lastly a quick note on personal guarantees. I have heard about some instances where charter operators have given, or were asked to give, their guarantee on a financing. *Don't do it*: this isn't life or death, just public education. It isn't worth potentially ruining your future.

COMMERCIAL BANKS

Having once worked as a commercial banker, I can relate to this joke: a banker is someone who will give you an umbrella on a sunny day. It seems they are never there when you really need them, doesn't it?

While not really true, there are usually some good reasons for this perception, relating to their friendly bank examiner. Since bank deposits are insured by the FDIC, the government wants to avoid another crisis like the S&L debacle in the late 1980s. So, the examiners scrutinize a bank's loans pretty well.

The thing to understand about bankers is they are asset-based lenders. You may have the best school ever, but that probably won't mean much to a bank. Their approach is to take less time to learn about why your school should be a going concern, and concentrate on how they will get their money back when they have to foreclose. How they do that is a thing called equity.

As mentioned above, banks want a loan-to-value in the 65–80 percent range. The way to achieve this is to either: 1) put cash into the purchase price, which is hard for a charter school to do, 2) be buying a property worth more than the purchase price (also hard to do), or 3) use subordinated debt from a CDFI or other source for the difference. It's also possible to obtain construction financing without meeting the loan-to-value if you already have a takeout in place. However, as I explained to one banker, if we had the permanent financing in place we wouldn't need their loan. In other words, thanks for the umbrella, but do you have any sunscreen? The upside of all this is that if you can meet the loan-to-value, even newer schools can possibly obtain bank financing because it's an asset-based approach more so than a "proven school" approach. The downside, versus bonds, for example, is that you will have a shorter amortization period (higher debt service) and you will have to refinance the loan at some point.

As security, banks will want a first mortgage on the property. Some will also want a "lock box" into which the payments are sent. They also may require the school to achieve certain liquidity tests, such as a current ratio (current assets divided by current liabilities) or a minimum level of working capital (current assets minus current liabilities). Try to keep furniture and fixtures, etc., out of the facility financing equation so you can use them to secure working capital financing, but if you are using their loan to acquire such items, it's likely they will be part of the security.

BOND ISSUES

Bonds are a great way to finance your facility, if you can qualify. Bond investors take much more of a "going concern" approach than do banks, so your school needs to be established and proven. Also, these financings are typically tax-exempt, as most of these investors want tax-exemption, so work on getting your nonprofit established. Finally, for bond investors, size matters, so smaller schools and transactions can be difficult on a stand-alone basis.

As mentioned earlier, bond issues have higher up-front costs, but the good news is that these are usually rolled into the bond issue so you don't need to come up with the cash. These costs are the result of the numerous professionals necessary to complete a bond issue. These include: bond counsel (gives tax opinion, prepared indenture and loan agreement), disclosure counsel (prepares offering document), borrower's counsel (gives certain opinions regarding you), a trustee, sometimes a trustee's counsel, sometimes a bond rating agency, and bond underwriter or placement agent, as well as their counsel. I would argue it should also include a financial adviser, but it is fair to say this isn't absolutely necessary. You can complete it without me, and many of you have, but it is a very good idea to have someone like me on your side of the table. (And I don't require another attorney.) Whether dealing with investment bankers, commercial bankers, or your EMO, ultimately they represent themselves rather than you because it's their money. Theirs may not be a box you want to squeeze into, no matter how badly you want a facility.

There are too many items associated with a bond issue to go into detail on each one. So, here is a synopsis.

In return for obtaining 100 percent tax-exempt financing which you will never have to refinance unless you want to, your bond issue requires certain things other types of funding do not. You will typically need to find an issuer, since most states will not confer on charter schools those items necessary to be your own issuer per IRS regulations. The issuer, typically an authority which is a political subdivision of your state, issues the bonds and lends the school, or the shell corporation, the proceeds for your project through a loan agreement.

Like commercial banks, you will provide a first mortgage on your facility. If anything goes wrong, investors will want you to feel their pain. You will also need an "intercept" mechanism, whereby all or a portion of your state aid is directed into the trust estate prior to reaching the school, because these investors will also have a first lien on your state aid. The appropriate deposits are made on a monthly basis concurrent with the state payments, and any excess is immediately returned to you. Some states have this available by statute; in other instances it is a contractual arrangement.

One feature unique to bond issues is a debt service reserve fund (DSRF). Like the up-front costs, the DSRF is also funded with bond proceeds. Investors require a DSRF for almost all revenue bond issues, even those issued by a municipality and backed by a predictable revenue source, such as sales tax. It is used to keep debt service current for a year in the event there is an interruption in the revenue stream. If it is never used, you collapse it in the final year of the debt to make your last payment. While it increases the cost of using bonds, you do get the interest earnings on the DSRF to help make bond payments.

You will typically need to covenant that you will maintain a certain level of working capital or a minimum fund balance, usually defined as a percentage of your operating expenditures.

A very important feature that should be incorporated into a bond issue is the ability to issue additional bonds. If your school wants to expand in the future for any reason, such a feature is necessary to be able to issue additional bonds on parity with the first bond issue. Typically, you should have an additional bonds test spelled out in the loan agreement that states if you meet certain debt service coverage parameters, you can issue additional parity debt. More specificity is better than less, although you don't want to make it too complicated. The balance is to give you flexibility while not giving carte blanche. Often these tests utilize the "no downgrade" approach that puts all the onus on the rating agency: you can only issue additional bonds if it won't result in a downgrade of the first bond issue. The problem with that is it leaves you at the mercy of changing rating agency criteria for a similar rating in the future. SSP or not, this is one area where a knowledgeable financial adviser can be valuable.

With any tax-exempt issue, one must take into consideration various IRS restrictions. One of the really important ones is the 2 percent on costs of issuance for nonprofit issues, which states that you can only use tax-exempt proceeds to pay for costs of issuance up to 2 percent of the par amount of the debt. Any excess is either funded with the borrower's cash, or by issuing a small "taxable tail" to pay for those costs in excess of 2 percent of par. The interest on the tail is taxable, but it's just a small portion of the issue. It is possible to avoid a taxable tail by making the issue a "governmental issue" versus a "nonprofit" issue by vesting title in the facility with a governmental body. That, however, can involve some tricky items if your authorizer is not a school district, so consult your friendly bond counsel or financial adviser in advance.

I will quickly mention a few key other IRS restrictions. You can't earn more on the investment of any bond proceeds (such as construction funds or the DSRF) than you pay on the bonds. This is called "arbitrage" and it's a no-no. You can't use any facility financed with tax-exempt proceeds for pervasively sectarian use, which impacts those schools that may be involved with a church, for example. You can only earn a small amount of "unrelated business income" from non–tax exempt entities, such as a for-profit business. Entities, such as other schools or colleges, can typically sublease space from you, and these can be important sources of revenue to support the debt. For construction projects, you must spend down the bond proceeds within a certain timeframe. No wonder the tax code is so large!

One potential disadvantage of a bond issue is the inability to pay off the debt any time you want. Typically, you can do so with a bank loan, for example. In a bond issue, there is what is called the "optional redemption feature" (call feature) which says that the investors cannot have the bonds pulled out from under them until, typically, ten years have passed. That doesn't mean you have to live with the original bond issue for ten years, but if you refinance you must borrow enough to pay back both the principal and the accrued interest to the call date. Typically, you cannot earn as high an interest rate on the escrow as you are paying on the old debt, so the amount you have to borrow to refinance may be larger than what you paid off. However, most refinancing is done to replace higher–interest rate debt with lower–interest rate debt, so debt service savings can result regardless of the higher principal amount on the new debt.

With a publicly offered bond issue, you will agree to certain continuing disclosure items to keep the bond market informed on your financial condition post-issuance. These reporting items are usually pretty tame, though, and should generally correspond to those you have with the state and your authorizer. You should ask your trustee on the bond issue to also act as your dissemination agent so you don't have to keep track of who owns your bonds. If an investor does call you to check in on you, however, it's a good idea to promptly return the call. You never know when you may be in the bond market again.

Many bond issues have a rating from a nationally recognized credit rating agency. Of the big three rating agencies, only Standard & Poor's (S & P) is currently active in the charter school world in my opinion. S & P is well regarded by investors, and their credit ratings say a lot about the financial and market position of the school. What you hope for is an "investment grade" rating, which means the risk of owning your bonds is less than non–investment grade bonds. Having said that, non–investment grade bond issues for charter schools get done, and the rating agencies themselves will tell you that the lack of an investment grade rating does NOT mean you don't have a great school. Like anyone else, rating agencies have their own boxes into which you may not fit. However, know that your interest rate will be higher if your issue is non–investment grade, because the risk is higher and there are a smaller number of potential investors. Non–investment grade issues typically have only a few investors, and they can influence the interest rate and covenants much more easily than if there are more potential investors.

A quick note about bond pools: while these can be a great way for smaller schools to spread the cost of a bond issue over a larger transaction, make sure you know whom you are getting into bed with. I think it best to participate with schools of a similar credit quality as your school. This is to avoid features to support the weaker schools that may end up costing you. In no case should you cross-collateralize or cross-default your loan with other pool participants with whom you are not affiliated in some major way.

COMMUNITY DEVELOPMENT FINANCE INSTITUTIONS

CDFIs can play an important part of your financing, as discussed earlier. Your eligibility for their funding typically is driven by whether your mission is consistent with theirs. For example, the National Council of La Raza has a CDFI, but your school needs to serve the Latino community in a substantial way, usually meaning the percentage of students at your school, to qualify for their funding. There are other CDFIs that have more generalized missions which seek to help charter schools with facility funding. It is doubtful that 100 percent of your facility financing will be through a CDFI unless you need a relatively small amount. But CDFIs can be very useful as part of the overall financing for even larger transactions. For example, they can lend on a subordinate basis to help meet loan-to-value requirements. They can also reduce the amount of first-lien debt to help increase that debt's credit rating. One advantage of working with a financial adviser without their own funding source (big SSP alert) is that they should be able to help you identify these potential sources of funding.

OTHER SOURCES OF FUNDING

Very briefly, you may be aware of the annual federal Credit Enhancement for Charter School Facilities Program (formerly the Charter School Facilities Financing Demonstration Grant program), whereby the federal government disperses funds to various entities throughout the country to help with facility financing. These funds can be used on a subordinate basis in some cases, or to act as a further DSRF to protect lenders. You can find a list of these entities on the website for the U.S. Department of Education. Those operating schools in Washington, D.C., in particular should pay attention to which entities receive an award.

Finally, some companies will build your facility for you and lease it to you, in some cases in a lease/purchase arrangement. They will find investors to fund the facility, and a portion of their return is the tax-credit they receive in addition to the imputed interest in the lease payment.

CONCLUSION

You are by now thinking "Thank God, he's finished!" Either that, or you fell asleep pages ago. The most important thing to remember is that you run a business! If you want someone else's money to build your facility, you need to demonstrate that you understand your business. If you can do that, you will be doing yourself a huge favor, whether or not you finance a facility.

18

Measurement: The Key To Charter School Marketing[1]

Brian L. Carpenter

A public school board vice president recently made the following statements to a local newspaper: "We say we're going to market, market, market this school, but we don't do it." Expressing frustration that her district continues to lose students to other schools, she also said, "We've talked about this for years, but we haven't done anything."

Ever feel that way as board member of your charter school?

The solutions to the marketing challenge at your school might not be what you think—especially if you think that money alone is the answer. The school in the example above has an annual marketing budget of $120,000, yet it is still losing students to other schools.

One reason is readily apparent: the board doesn't understand how to design and execute a marketing plan. Most revealingly, the article also stated, "district leaders said they don't have numbers on how many [XYZ] School students are leaving the district." If the board had an effective marketing plan they would have known precisely how many students had left, why they left, and where they went. In a word, an effective marketing plan should have prescribed the constant measurement of these important data. The board and administrative team should have been evaluating the results to try to win them back and keep others from leaving in the first place.

COMPETITION FOR STUDENTS

Since most schools have the goal of being friendly, nurturing, and collaborative, some people find the thought of competing with a "sister school" disdainful.

If some on your board are prone to make this mistake, you can help them understand the value of competition by pointing out that it brings out the best performance in people and helps keep the price of goods and services affordable.

Competition operates on the incentive principle. When two or more entities compete for the same customers or markets, they put forth their best efforts to win them. This incentive principle has worked throughout history. And it works in modern American schools as well, regardless of whether some on your board recognize it.

When boards fail to understand the necessity of strategically positioning the school to attract students, they will usually lose them. Complacently staking their hopes for a successful school on the "if you build it they will come" dream, the board at such a school will often witness a decline in enrollment to the point where it is not possible to continue operations. Sometimes by sheer luck, during times when the birth rate of school-age children is on the rise or the community is growing, such a school may survive for a decade or two and even increase its enrollment, but without a master marketing plan it will not likely be able to build permanent world-class facilities of its own, project a shared vision for the future, or in the end, produce sustainable excellence.

If some board members do not agree that your school needs to market itself to compete for students, your first marketing challenge is to get them on board. Failing that, get them off the board. That may sound harsh, but the fact is, if you're in the school leadership business you have a fiduciary responsibility to the school to see that it flourishes. Once every board member and administrator on your team understands the competitive nature of a successful school, then you're ready to develop a specific marketing plan.

I will explain some basic marketing principles, but a committed board will do a lot more preparation. I recommend reading all kinds of books and articles that pertain to marketing, whether the commodity being written about is soft drinks, real estate, or anything else. Most marketing principles are easily adaptable to schools. Books on marketing small businesses are exceptionally useful because in many ways most schools operate like small businesses.

DEFINING MARKETING

Let us begin by defining exactly what marketing is, drawing on an idea from an all-time best-selling book on marketing for small businesses. In his classic *Guerilla Marketing,* Jay Conrad Levinson defines marketing as "everything you do to grow your business." In the realm of competing schools, this may be easily adapted to "everything you do to recruit *and retain* students."

What are some examples of "everything a school should do to recruit and retain students?" It certainly includes advertising, but has to be a lot more. Many schools have squandered operational dollars on advertising without achieving results. The nonmarketing professional may be surprised to learn there is much more to an effective marketing plan than conventional advertising spots on billboards, radio, TV, or in the newspaper.

A FEW ESSENTIALS

Though most people don't think of maintaining buildings and grounds as part of marketing essentials, they make a good starting point. Ask yourself what impression is conveyed by the appearance of your school grounds when prospects visit. (A prospect is anyone inquiring about the possibility of enrolling a student in your school.)

Here are a few basic guidelines for thinking about the appearance of school property:

- Is the grass neatly trimmed on the school's property? Does everything have a fresh coat of paint, inside and out? Are there flowers? Are the sidewalks clean?
- Are the grounds free of litter?
- Is there adequate, friendly signage pointing the direction to the office for first-time visitors?
- Is there ample visitor parking, clearly marked and close to the building?
- Are the trash cans clean and not overflowing with trash?

In addition to the grounds being clean and inviting, of course, prospects must feel welcome by the staff. Consider the following:

- How are visitors greeted when they call or arrive? (After years of leading schools, I am still astounded at the number of schools where the front office reception staff is aloof or telephone callers are greeted by a machine!)
- Have staff members been trained to properly receive visitors?
- Do teachers know what to do when visitors are escorted into the classroom?

As simple as these points seem, they are critical elements in your overall marketing plan. You will spend a large part of your advertising budget just trying to get prospective families to visit your school so they can consider what you have to offer. Why spend all that money to get them there only to have them feel unappreciated, or that the school is unattractive?

Once you have put your house in order, you are ready to go on to more intricate marketing considerations—but not beforehand. If your school hasn't yet addressed these points above, do not dismiss them.

MEASUREMENT: THE KEY

After you've created and implemented a written plan that encompasses the basics discussed above, move on to more complex marketing issues. Serious marketing professionals would never launch an ad campaign without the next step, but schools routinely fail to do it. What is this all-important step? *Measurement.*

Measurement is the indispensable benchmark from which all marketing efforts proceed and are evaluated. Without measurement you are not marketing, regardless of how much advertising you do.

Measurement is certainly not very glamorous (perhaps one of the reasons it is often overlooked). In fact, if done well, some parts of measurement, such as data collection and entry, can be tedious. However, for the school that is serious about its marketing effort, measurement is the key to effectiveness. I describe marketing measurement as a four-step process: collection, analysis, creativity, and evaluation.

PHASE ONE—THE COLLECTION PHASE

The first step in effective measurement is accurate data collection. What kind of data should you collect and how often should you collect it? Answer: everything you can, as often as you can.

For ease of consideration let us break the previous statement into its two component parts. Collecting as much data as you can, should include all of the following at a minimum:

Family Data

- Household income
- Number of other school-age children residing in the enrolling student's household
- Ethnic origin/gender/age/grade
- Address (especially zip code)
- Parents' education, vocation, place of employment
- How far does each family drive to utilize your school?
- Do they have Internet access? Do they routinely check their e-mail?

Communication Data (data that identifies potential marketing communication "outlets")

- Radio stations that families and prospects listen to
- Local newspapers that families and prospects read
- Civic clubs to which families and prospects belong
- Private clubs to which families and prospects belong
- Churches which families and prospects attend
- Boards on which parents and prospects serve
- How often and which movie theaters are attended by families? What movies have they gone to see in the past few months?

Catchment Area Data (data that describes the area from which you draw students)

- Household income by zip codes
- Distribution of school-age children by zip code
- Information about other schools within your catchment area
- Tuition rates for private schools drawing students from the same catchment area
- Advertising information produced by other schools
- General population trends and projections for your area
- Internal data about your school performance
- Enrollment patterns (by grade, gender, teacher, etc.)
- Every student's enrolling performance on standardized tests (benchmark)
- Every student's annual performance on standardized tests (gains)
- Classroom grades compared to standardized tests results
- Reenrollment rate by teacher/building/grade level
- Student performance data on standardized tests by classroom (and teacher)
- Honor roll statistics
- Other student awards
- Student achievements outside of school (e.g., music, scouting, martial arts, etc.)
- Student community service involvement
- Teacher awards for excellence (external sources)
- School awards for excellence (external sources)
- If you have alumni, what are they doing now?

The astute reader will have noted that in all the data above, nothing was mentioned about creating clever advertising pieces. Accurate data collection is the first step in measurement, however, because it has everything to do with precise targeting of specific advertising—perhaps the most important part of successful advertising.

Measuring as often as you can requires frequent periodic data collection. As to when those periods exist depends on what kind of data you are collecting. For example, your school should collect the following data from every prospect who calls (regardless of whether they end up enrolling):

- How the prospect heard about your school
- When they first heard about your school
- Current school which they are considering leaving and why they are considering coming to your school
- Follow-up information, especially residential zip code

And you should be collecting the following data from your existing families every year:

- Overall satisfaction survey covering every area of school operations
- Why they have chosen your school
- Media outlets they listen or subscribe to
- Whether they are planning to return next year

Then there is data collection based on student performance:

- At least once a year following standardized testing

And finally, one of the most important times to collect data—when families leave the school:

- Written exit survey with any family that leaves during the year specifically asking why they are leaving
- Phone call survey to families that don't return the following year asking why they didn't return

PHASE TWO—THE ANALYSIS PHASE

You should analyze data even while collecting it. There is nothing mysterious about analysis. It is merely the process of aggregating and disaggregating the data and studying it to identify patterns or trends. One way of studying the patterns and trends is to convert the data into chart or graph format. Sometimes patterns that are not otherwise easily observable can emerge as obvious when depicted graphically.

A good example of this exercise is to take a map that covers your catchment area and stick pushpins in it marking where each family lives. Study the pattern that this creates and see if it reveals anything interesting about your school. It usually does.

The key to producing data that can be aggregated or disaggregated in ways that are useful for analysis is to record it using computer software. There are several software products—called contact managers—available off-the-shelf for a few hundred dollars that can be sufficiently configured to meet the needs of a school with up to a thousand students. If a school grows beyond that it can buy more expensive database software.

PHASE THREE—THE CREATIVITY PHASE

This third phase is what most people think of when they think of marketing. Done apart from the measurement prescriptions above, however, the creativity phase is merely advertising instead of marketing. Anyone can advertise—some even get lucky. The goal of the discipline of marketing is to reduce the luck factor so that you can target the use of your limited resources effectively.

The creative phase can be described as the process of deciding what kind of advertising to do, how to do it, where to do it, and when to do it. It should always occur in the context of the data that has been collected and analyzed for patterns and trends.

A few recommendations concerning the creativity phase:

- Don't create cheap-looking printed materials (e.g., business cards and stationery from your PC)
- Good graphic artists have creative capabilities and a knowledge of the print process that generally exceeds that of other people, so they are worth their fees
- Avoid doing too much creativity work as a committee
- Two percent of your annual budget is not an unreasonable expense for advertising
- Doing Yellow Pages® advertising is generally a no-brainer for schools because of the number of people who turn to the phone book when looking for things. Unless you run a very expensive ad, it will usually pay for itself with one or two students per year.
- Avoid typos and mistakes at all costs. There's nothing quite so contradictory and self-defeating as the words "We Strive for Academic Excellance" in your school ad.

As you develop your marketing plan, it's a good idea in the creativity phase to lay out your advertising strategy for the entire year so that the look of pieces can be coordinated or "linked." Also, knowing what advertising you are going to do in advance gives you the advantage of time when negotiating with vendors.

PHASE FOUR—THE EVALUATION PHASE

Effective advertising has one criterion: does it pull? In other words, did the specific ad or campaign achieve the intended outcome?

It really doesn't matter how much one or more board members like or dislike the artwork or colors in a particular ad. As the Latin phrase "De gustibus non est disputandum" says, "There is no disputing taste." It doesn't matter if the ad costs more money this year than it did last year. Everything costs more this year than it did last year. All that matters is, does it pull?

As a board you cannot know whether an ad pulls unless someone is collecting and reporting the kind of data previously discussed in this article, hence the importance of the collection and analysis phases of measurement.

One cautionary note: be very careful about conducting your evaluation with insufficient time for an ad to work. If you decide to run enrollment advertising on the radio, it probably will not generate a lot of inquiries after only one week. A more effective approach would be to run that kind of advertising on a regular basis throughout the course of a year and then evaluate the efficacy of the ad by the number of prospects who indicate that they heard about your school through your radio ads.

THE COST OF NOT MARKETING

The K–12 schooling market is becoming increasingly competitive. Consider the following trends:

- In the past decade, the number of students being homeschooled has quadrupled.
- Charter schools are a relatively new innovation. As they prove their worth to the American public, there will be more of them from which parents can choose.
- Independent schools continue to be popular. The advance of tuition tax credits will help make them more affordable for many parents, thereby likely increasing their enrollment.
- As conventional public schools have continued to lose students to charter schools and other choices parents have, they have increased their own marketing efforts.

All of these variables mean at least one thing for your school: It is going to be harder to recruit and retain students in the future than it is today. Although producing excellence in your school is the most indispensable element in an effective marketing plan, it is not enough. In this day and age, you must tell people about it. That requires a well-designed marketing plan in order to effectively use what are undoubtedly limited school resources. This requires the disciplines of reading, thinking, recording, and analyzing data. The cost of not properly marketing may well result in the collapse of your school.

YOU CAN DO THIS

Despite often inequitable funding provisions like stipulating that charter schools do not receive money from the state for buildings, etc., there are many charter schools succeeding across the United States. Your school can also be successful if you follow the principles outlined in this article.

There is no more worthy cause for effective marketing than the success of a school and ultimately, the success of your students.

NOTE

1. Originally published in *National Charter School Clearinghouse Review* July 2003.

19

When Charter Schools Have a Distinct Advantage Over Districts, Or, Show Me the (Grant) Money

Amy Ashley and Mike Kayes

INTRODUCTION

Whether in the earliest planning stages or upgrading existing programs and facilities, charter schools have unique but often overlooked strengths and strategic advantages that can attract grant money on both the local and national level. Though sometimes seen as limitations, a charter school's small size, its laser-focused mission or specialization, and freedom from at least some of the bureaucratic oversight that inhibits change in traditional schools, are features that may make them attractive partners to corporations and foundations. If they can also demonstrate carefully conceived plans and a commitment to improving education at the local level through methods that can be applied at the national level, charter schools will attract the attention of grant makers, both locally or nationally, who want to invest money in demonstrably improved, long-term, accountable ways of educating children.

BECOMING A CORPORATE PARTNER

Charter schools are now an integral part of the American public education landscape. They provide ubiquitous choices, opportunities, innovation, and involvement on a scale previously unknown by American students and parents. By setting challenging standards, often in underserved areas of minority and disadvantaged students, charter schools have enhanced student achievement and established themselves as responsible and accountable entities in education reform. Community and parental participation are a vital part of this success, and not only lead to greater student achievement but draw both local businesses and the public at large to the school's capacity and mission as a resource available to everyone.

Through this outreach, financial support on the local level can be nurtured through partnerships with businesses, organizations, colleges, and even the faith-based community. Support can take the form of utilizing building space that would otherwise be empty during the school day, recycling and/or donations of technological equipment the school might otherwise be unable to purchase, and volunteer services such as website design, health screening, printing services, or organizing weekend activities. Collaboration with local community groups or governments, such as the park/recreation/library board, chamber of commerce, or the YMCA, to build initiatives that will be of benefit to a wider audience than just the student body, can open the way to grants and other funding normally unavailable to an individual school. An example from Minnesota involves the partnership between a rural school and several county service agencies that raised $50,000 dollars for the school to provide space and services for family conferences, health screening, and reading tutors.

Charter schools are, on average, significantly smaller in size than district schools (by a factor of a third or even smaller). While assuming heightened accountability for student performance, they are less constrained in administrative and bureaucratic regulations, making delivery on their promise less burdensome. Grant money, in any amount, has a greater impact on these small, innovative schools since their options in utilizing the funds can be immediate, specific, and quickly adapted if necessary. The ability to respond to the changing needs of a small constituency makes charter schools ideal recipients of grants designed for specific purposes in a diverse population. Large systems are like hard to turn battleships that can easily devour cash with nary a ripple.

Some charter schools simultaneously serve as a resource for the community and as a "niche market." These schools may offer specialized instruction in a geographic area where the demand for diverse or nontraditional education is high, and consequently may have an enhanced capacity to attract corporate funding from a specific industry, manufacturer, or service provider.

Unique characteristics aside however, charter schools face several large hurdles in attracting grant money from large corporate sponsors. Inadequate length of performance history, absence of requisite teacher certification, and untested business practices make some companies wary of direct funding of charter schools. Corporate sponsors express fear that charter schools have yet to demonstrate their staying power and commitment to continuing educational programs after the initial grant money is gone. Their doubts about entering into economic partnerships with charter schools are obstacles that can be overcome with well-crafted programs that address the corporation's goals, coupled with intense efforts to build a solid working relationship over a period of time.

Even if a company won't directly fund or partner with a charter school, there may be other opportunities available that will provide a "foot in the door" for a school. Programs with open participation can facilitate introductions, foster partnerships with other schools and civic organizations, and demonstrate commitment to working within the framework of established grant making procedures. Intel, for example, annually distributes over $25,000 in Volunteer Matching Grant money to charter schools in the Phoenix area. The program encourages Intel employees to perform volunteer activities at the public school of their choice, district or charter, and in return the school will receive $200 for every twenty hours of time volunteered. Charter schools and parent volunteerism go hand in hand, making this program a natural model for communities that don't have "an Intel" present. Local businesses could be encouraged to support volunteer opportunities by "paying" for parent and community involvement in field trips, after-school activities, or chairing parent/teacher clubs and organizations. Charter schools must choose to be as entrepreneurial in their fund development programs as they are with curriculum and instruction.

In talking with the corporate giving and public affairs officers of several corporations, volunteerism emerged as an important part of the corporate funding process. Southwest Airlines makes in-kind donations to all types of school organizations. According to their manager of charitable contributions, Southwest looks for enthusiasm and organization in the attitude of the volunteers because it is always a good predictor of how successful the funding presentation and the proposed event will be.

Corporations that are not locally based, but maintain a local presence, often rely on their employees (and their recommendations) to gauge the impact and effectiveness of a community nonprofit. Schools that attract a large following of parent volunteers are receiving the equivalent of an endorsement that their programs are proving valuable and are worth the extra effort to implement. Corporations want to back winners, and a school with an active, organized, volunteer community is one way of assessing the potential success of a grant application and the school's commitment to achieving its stated goals.

Just like the saying "all politics is local," corporate giving, even by international conglomerates, often has a local emphasis at its core. Foundation grants differ slightly in this regard, if their focus is on programs implemented at the national or international level. But in some instances, such as Motorola, which has both a corporate giving program administered at the local level and a foundation administered from the corporate office, communication between both company arms is frequent and focused on remaining true to the stated goals and interests of the company.

Another way of connecting with the local population is for an international corporation to partner with a business founded and run by community interests such as in the partnership between Motorola and one of the two major Phoenix area power companies, Arizona Public Service (APS) in the Partners Advancing Student Success (PASS) Program. One of Motorola's goals is to work on policy-level issues and system change initiatives. PASS is designed to help implement the Arizona Workplace Skills Standards, an integrated effort involving parents, educators, and businesses to assure that students graduate with the ability to bring critical thinking and technology literacy to their chosen careers. Can you think of a charter high school (or twenty) in your area that could benefit?

Like all high-tech companies, Motorola hopes to open the eyes of teachers and students as to what will be expected of employees throughout their careers. Analytical problem-solving, lifelong learning in fields like chemistry, physics, and math, and being able to compete and stay focused on personal and company goals . . . this is the curriculum Intel, Motorola, and other technology giants want to sponsor. As the Arizona public affairs manager for Intel says, "We are not interested in poly-tech programs, only higher levels of learning."

The view of APS is slightly different. "Lifelong learning is important, but not everybody is made to go to college, and not everybody has to go," according to their community development consultant. APS encourages education in trades and crafts through scholarship programs, but like Motorola, they are drawn to the system change potential of the PASS program. "We like teacher professional development. By reaching 30 teachers, they can reach 3,000 students."

HOW TO MAKE FRIENDS AND RECEIVE GRANT MONEY

Salt River Project (SRP) is one of the major suppliers of water and electricity to the state of Arizona. For a quarter of a century they have supported innovative teaching strategies to improve student performance in math, science, and technology. "Our experience," according to their community outreach representative, "is that in many cases charter schools are less bureaucratic and more flexible than public district schools. It can actually be difficult to give money to public schools." For example, SRP likes marshaling some of its resources by sponsoring field trips for students, yet there are myriad schools.

Traditional district schools are also publicity shy. They usually don't compete for students or self-promote and therefore have little understanding or tolerance for public relations. A photo session involving the CEO and a group of students may be frowned on in district schools, but would not be considered nearly as exploitative in a charter school. "Part of my job is reining in their enthusiasm," says SRP's spokesperson of his charter school partners. "They love publicity as much as corporations do, making them much easier to work with . . . they don't put as many strictures on us." Instead of eschewing the publicity opportunities involved in sponsorship, charter schools are more likely to print up t-shirts with the school and sponsor logo on them, give interviews to the press proudly mentioning their liaison, and eagerly participate in public outreach events that highlight their partnership. An example is a charter high school in Phoenix. As a participant in the Solar Spectacular, SRP's solar boat competition for high schools, this school's science teacher uses the program as a way to teach mathematical and science principles to his students by making them part of his Solar Technology Team. "The real highlight for our school was that we were able to incorporate solar energy into our curriculum," he says.

Grant makers want this kind of enthusiasm. They want their names mentioned in magazines and their ideas expanded upon in class curriculum. Since having so much fun with their solar boat, this high school has built a solar car and has plans to enter it in a national cross-country car competition. And you can bet they will be receiving more grant money from SRP for that effort!

High schools within SRP's service area may apply for up to $5,000 per year in grant money for programs designed to improve instruction and scores in math and science education. The requirements are not overly restrictive, and all schools—public or private, charter or noncharter—are eligible to apply, but not all the money will be claimed. "There are literally millions of dollars of corporate grant money that goes unclaimed every year," says SRP. "SRP money not claimed for school sponsorship doesn't go back into the pot, it goes for advertising, or some other purpose. And the fact that we couldn't give away all the money we wanted to this year means we have less money for grant funding next year."

It is also a fallacy that the most needy will receive the greatest consideration in corporate giving. According to SRP and other grant makers, schools with the most resources are the most active in requesting funds and ask for the most money. They have learned that businesses misunderstand the needs of schools as badly as schools misunderstand the needs of businesses, and write grants that bridge this gap. They have learned how to ask in the language of corporations, and therefore they get what they want.

Another almost universal lament is that schools need to do better homework before submitting grants. "If I receive an application asking for $10,000.00, I know they didn't read our guidelines. The most money we give to a single school is $5,000.00 per year. SRP isn't going to make the school a counter offer, they just won't fund the proposal at all even if it is a great project . . . $5,000.00 isn't going to implement a $10,000.00 plan."

But the most successful proposals aren't just the ones who did a careful reading of the guidelines, they are the ones who picked up the phone and called. Make friends with the corporate giving department or someone else within the company willing to be an advocate for the school, and they can just about write the proposal for you. "Inside information" in this context is not only a good thing, it may be priceless and isn't that hard to get if you are willing to cultivate relationships within the company. Make as big an investment in the corporation in terms of understanding their goals and philosophy of giving as much as you are asking them to make in you.

This is not to say that unless you are golfing with the CEO every weekend your chances of getting funded are minuscule. According to the book *Fistful of Dollars*, "the strongest relationships between corporations and nonprofits begin after funding has been approved and the nonprofit starts to achieve results because of the company's support." The introduction to the company decision makers, and the resulting relationship, is built on the proposal, its potential, and ultimately the success enjoyed by both parties.

Do you lack employee contacts to smooth the introduction phase for you? Establish various advisory boards and solicit prospective members from businesses and industries. In addition to providing professional advice, these corporate leaders will become familiar with the school's objectives and strengths, and hopefully direct other volunteers, resources, and funding opportunities your way. Most major corporations and community-minded small businesses are actively looking for ways to volunteer and provide support to nonprofits in their area. The book *Successful Corporate Fundraising* says, "Many companies have launched corporate community involvement initiatives and now routinely help to match employee interests with agency needs. A very small number of companies have gone so far as to hire a director of corporate volunteerism."

Try to think of all publicity opportunities as a form of outreach to sponsors and grantors, not just prospective students. Websites with streaming video can provide a virtual tour of the campus allowing Internet users to put a picture and place next to the school name. If your school has an arts or drama program, contact the public affairs department of the local company with whom you wish to partner, tell them you are actively soliciting volunteers, and offer to make a choral, drama, or dance presentation in the company lunchroom or lobby. Volunteers and grant makers who can experience your work are more likely to commit to it.

Inviting a potential donor for an on-site visit is even better, though scheduling with an influential company representative can be difficult. However, the opportunity to show off the school's programs and facilities and physically demonstrate how important funding is to student success, is an opportunity not to be missed.

If your future sponsor does agree to a visit, treat it as a state occasion complete with photographs, student presentations, and face-to-face meetings with teachers who are well versed on the proposal and can clearly articulate how it will help their students. Have an agenda planned. Even if you don't stick to it, you will avoid wasting your visitor's time by knowing that everything you wish to show them is ready and organized. This is genuine public relations and something companies respect and to which they most favorably respond. Understand that companies not only want to become involved with a good education initiative, they want as many people as possible to know about it.

DESIGNING A WINNING EDUCATIONAL PROGRAM

In recent years, corporate giving has become decidedly proactive. Instead of waiting for grant applications to arrive and then responding to them, company officials select nonprofits with which they wish to be associated and approach them with suggestions about how the corporation can embark on sponsorship. Often their suggestions include a local representative or manager joining the board of directors. Some partnerships may concentrate on ways of incorporating social issues the nonprofit addresses with marketing initiatives for the company. The main advantage to this arrangement is that it allows the company to pick those organizations that most accurately reflect the core company values. While some would argue that the move away from pure philanthropy on the part of corporations to a more business-oriented partnership is less than charitable, corporate giving managers view it as an effective, sustainable, and scalable method of including good corporate citizenship with strategic company objectives. (It should come as no surprise that similar trends are emerging in the area of government grants.)

The ideal corporate-sponsored education initiative has a verifiable record of success, and is not so customized that it can't be duplicated in communities nationally (or internationally) where the company has a presence. It addresses those issues most in keeping with the company's view of itself and its place in the community, and offers an opportunity to contribute equipment, volunteers, technical support, training for teachers, and mentoring, in addition to funds and often refurbishment of facilities. The ideal program contributes not only to the school, but provides added benefits to the community that can be utilized or felt on a larger scale than just within the student body.

Preparation for entering the workforce is usually another key factor that must be addressed in the program, and the hiring requirements of the sponsor will determine whether that involves indoctrination into the idea of lifetime learning at the graduate level, junior college/trade school, or just the minimum requisite technological training for computer literacy. Community outreach, such as art exhibits, health screening events, or science fairs (depending on the company's business focus), are another element that schools may be asked to enthusiastically embrace and provide participation.

All corporate sponsorships demand emphasis and commitment on the part of the school to programs that foster nondiscriminatory opportunities for the underprivileged, minorities, and women (especially in engineering). Some require evidence of positive environmental impact and some require a commitment by school staff to set an example for students by volunteering for earth-friendly events and programs the company is involved in or sponsors.

So what's a school to do? How about designing a proposal that demonstrates true and thorough understanding of someone else's program priorities (providing, of course, this also fits neatly within your own mission!) and actually beginning such an initiative, even on a small and limited scale. Now go forth and display this "working model" to prove your commitment and willingness to genuinely "partner." Something like, "Okay, we've modified the curriculum, gotten seventeen parents involved in various ways, provided some teacher training, etc., *and now we're ready to take the next step!*" This alone should negate previously cited suspicions that otherwise might undermine your credibility and commitment and will allow your school to implement a doable strategic plan, with your funder's assistance, that will produce measurably improved outcomes. And here's the real catch: these changes will outlive any grant since they've been institutionalized within your mission and long-term goals.

Intel has developed the Connected to Schools Program for Phoenix area schools in underserved areas that currently have below state average test scores for the Stanford Achievement Test, ninth edition (SAT9) and have critical technology needs. It is part of the larger Innovations in Education initiative, a worldwide effort to improve science, math, engineering, and technology education. Intel Innovations in Education envisions partnerships between educators, students, and in some cases, governments, to bring the level of elementary student ability up to the point where there will be many candidates for the type of advanced education that produces highly qualified professionals ready to work in a sophisticated, technology-based economy. At the heart of the program is a two-year partnership between Intel and the school with a dedicated Intel employee to manage the relationship and recruit other employees for specific activities. Intel will provide funding for computers, computer-related equipment, and software, but beyond that they also provide:

- Mentoring and tech support between teachers and Intel volunteers.
- Earth Fest and science fair support, after-school science clubs, science camp.

- Holiday adoption of students and other celebrations.
- Literacy support, virtual reading program, and Read Across America activities.
- Accelerated and remedial math tutoring.
- School beautification projects and other refurbishment.

The school gets its own list of responsibilities, much of which sounds like the duties of a public relations professional as opposed to school administrator. The chief concern is that one individual from the school will be the primary contact with Intel and help conduct a needs assessment, then go on to develop a two-year strategic plan with specific goals, objectives, and measurable outcomes.

Another major concern is training of teachers in the classroom technology needed to make the objectives reality. (Selected schools had a 95 percent teacher participation rate in the training classes.) Additionally, the school must find innovative ways of bringing technology into the school over and above the support Intel provides, find ways of utilizing existing community services for underserved students, and provide numerous and varied mentoring and volunteer opportunities for Intel employees. Other expectations are:

- A site visit every year and presentation before the volunteer panel.
- Sharing of appropriate demographic data with Intel for evaluation purposes.
- Display a sign designating the school an Intel Connected to Schools partner.
- Appoint someone to work with the Intel Media Relations Manager to develop a marketing communication plan for the local community.
- Help develop plans for sustaining the partnership after the funding period ends.

CONCLUSION

Intel is a high-tech company and their program focus is naturally geared to creating interest in advanced science and engineering education and careers. Other corporate sponsors may emphasize arts, or reading, or earth sciences, and their manner and form of sponsorship will have a totally different set of priorities and student activities. This overview of Intel's program is presented not as a pattern to be copied, but as an impetus to view corporate grant making in a new way. When writing your own school's grant, you may not have a section dealing with science fairs and computer software, but sections of a grant that present the opportunity to talk about sustaining partnerships after the end of funding, joint community outreach efforts, and providing innovative volunteer opportunities for employees should be viewed as extremely important.

Try making up two needs statements, one for your school and one for the sponsoring corporation based on your research into their funding program. Learn to address their needs without having to be reminded that there are few grants nowadays where all the school has to provide is access for the students to the funds or equipment made possible by the grant.

Charter schools are, quite simply, more natural partners to business and industry than are their traditional district counterparts. Interviews conducted with some of the most highly respected and notable grant makers in the greater Phoenix metropolitan area confirm that they're seeking creative opportunities, coupled with a genuine commitment to generate local excitement. Charter school leaders who heed and understand this message will be well positioned to enter into serious, productive, and meaningful funding relationships and move from the perception of being stodgy institutions that are inwardly focused to true community centers that actually meet and address needs beyond their own. This is, in essence, the "gift" found within twenty-first-century philanthropy.

REFERENCES

Levy, Reynold. 1999. *Give and Take: A Candid Account of Corporate Philanthropy.* Boston: Harvard Business School Press.

Sheldon, K. Scott. 2000. *Successful Corporate Fund Raising: Effective Strategies for Today's Nonprofits.* New York: John Wiley & Sons.

Zukowski, Linda M. 1998. *Fistfuls of Dollars: Fact and Fantasy About Corporate Charitable Giving.* Redondo Beach: EarthWrites Publishing.

Thanks to the following individuals who took time to educate and inform:

- Barbara Clark
  Arizona Manager for Community Relations and Education
  Motorola
  www.motorola.com/us/arizona/learning.html
- John B. Kelly
  Arizona Public Affairs Manager
  Intel Corporation
  www.intel.com/education
  www.intel.com/community/arizona/education.htm
- Tracy Martin
  Manager, Charitable Contributions
  Southwest Airlines
  www.southwest.com

- Louise Moskowitz
  Community Development Consultant
  APS
  www.aps.com/my_community/default.html
- Darrell L. Sheppard
  Community Outreach Representative, Education and Safety
  SRP
  www.srpnet.com/community/education
  www.srpnet.com/community/education/learningcircuit.asp

Where to research corporate and foundation grant makers:

- *The Foundation Center* in New York now offers the Foundation Directory Online with profiles, contact names, and descriptions of recent grants by 74,000 grant makers administering over 250,000 grants. Subscriptions begin at $19.95 per month.
- *The Taft Group* publishes the *Foundation Reporter*, now in its thirty-sixth edition, that provides in-depth information on the decision makers, grant making policies, locations, and recent grants of the 1,000 top foundations in the country with either $10 million in assets or $500,000 in recent charitable giving.
- *Prospectors Choice* is another of their products in CD form that profiles over 10,000 grant making corporations and foundations, and also includes detailed personal information on the decision makers at these organizations. Contribution summaries and application guidelines are also included. List price approximately $650 for Foundation Reporter.
- *The National Directory of Corporate Public Affairs* lists over 2,000 companies of various sizes that have corporate giving programs. It also includes their locations, philanthropic activity, political action committee involvement, and their public affairs personnel. List price $129.
- *The Chronicle of Philanthropy* is a biweekly newspaper that reports on all aspects of charitable giving both nationally and internationally. Regular features include highlights from annual reports, featured foundations' funding interests, recent grant opportunities, and interviews with individuals in charge of corporate giving programs. A subscription costs $69.50 annually.
- *Quinlan Publishing Group* offers the *Grants for K–12 Biweekly Hotline*, an Internet newsletter, for $169 per year, and also has various special reports on funding strategies applicable to schools.
- *The Michigan State Library* has a large website devoted to nonprofit funding newsletters. Most links connect to sample issues, but subscription information can be obtained from there. www.lib.msu.edu/harris23/grants/percat2.htm.
- *National Association for the Exchange of Industrial Resources* is a not-for-profit collector of donated inventory from U.S. corporations that is then distributed to schools and other nonprofit organizations. Membership and a subscription to their 200+ page catalog (issued five times per year) is $575.
- *Gifts in Kind* is another organization devoted to product philanthropy and distributes donations made by corporations worldwide. They offer both products and services and have a registration fee of $125 for nonprofits with less than $1 million of revenue.

- *The Center for Program Resources* is the grant consulting and program development consulting firm founded by Kayes nearly a quarter century ago. It remains a most viable resource for those seeking wisdom and experience in developing a comprehensive and strategic approach to implementing school choice and education reform at a local level, not to mention simply helping schools raise LOTS of grant money! (thecenter@cox.net) We saved the shameless self-promotion for last, at least.

20

Horror Stories

Robert Maranto

Editors' Note: These horror stories are true, presented here as the charter school operators told us. We have changed certain details so as to protect the innocent and the guilty.

HORROR STORY 1: DEATH BY PROCESS; OR SPECIAL ED BLACKMAIL

Compiled by Robert Maranto and April Gresham Maranto

After fighting a principled battle and losing, these operators wised up. Special ed should be about enabling a child with disabilities to learn success-fully. Sadly, sometimes it's just about unfair preferences, parents working the system, blackmail, and kangaroo courts.

The Operator's Story

It was our second year, so we were still finding our way. A ninth grader entered in October, a little late. The student's father told us she was in special ed back in the district, and we made the mistake of believing him, so we put her in special education.

Where's the Beef?

Our suspicions began when the student and her father could name the numerous and highly varied accommodations for her disability, but not the actual disability itself. The accommodations were many, and included never disciplining her when she interrupted class, insulted teachers, or made fun of other students: her father would intervene, saying it was a violation of her IEP. Of course it goes without saying that her unnamed disability meant she could have as much time as she wanted on exams.

Perhaps most unusually, and certainly most expensively, young Jane had what we began to call, for lack of a better term, the "nine-word disability": her father claimed that she was only capable of writing nine words! She had to type everything else! Naturally, that meant that our school had to buy her a laptop on which to do all assignments and to use for note taking. This is what one might call a rather Talmudic learning disability.

Yet strangely, whenever she was sent to the office for discipline—which was often since both she and her father tended to insult people—young Jane would claim to be writing notes to prepare for her lawsuit against the school. Young Jane was really a very, very unpleasant child. The local district this kid came from had refused to classify her as special education, and she lost the hearing there. Between our psychologist and theirs, Jane had been evaluated *nine times* and never been found to have a recognized disability of any kind, except for chronic rudeness and something of a Napoleon complex.

But I digress.

We Decide to Trust the Wheels of Justice

Eventually we are tired of Jane and her father threatening to sue. We checked with some friends at her previous school district, who said that she had been found not to need special education. So finally, we hired a very expensive lawyer. He and our psychologist prepared a brief and all sorts of exhibits for the long-awaited hearing.

We had already changed the hearing date once to accommodate Jane's father, so the hearing came at the start of our Christmas break. It was 9 AM on the first day of our winter break. We longed to be out of town, anyplace warm. The hearing room was open, and in the hearing room in addition to me were the principal, our psychologist, our lawyer, and the hearing officer. The parent was . . . missing! Everyone in the room was being paid overtime by our school, so we called up the father, who explained that he couldn't come because his work was tied to the Christmas season. Presumably he was Santa Claus, so there would be no Christmas and all the little kids would miss their toys if this guy took off two hours that morning to attend a hearing he had known about for two months!

Now in a normal hearing, when this sort of thing happens, you try the case in absentia. That might work for murder, but not for special education. So instead, the hearing officer agreed to hold the hearing at 2 PM, to accommodate the father, who of course had every incentive not to show again since he was not paying for the hearing. Amazingly, he finally did show. We presented our exhibits. The hearing officer next asked our attorney to give the father our exhibits, so he could also have some exhibits. In other words, we had to give him our attorney at several hundred dollars an hour to do his preparation. Everyone on our side could not believe that now we were paying for the offense.

The next hour became even more surreal as we listened to him weep and tell sad stories about how he'd been maligned and how our school was the worst institution on the face of the earth for his child. In cross-examination, whenever our lawyer pointed out that her achievement was among the best in the school, the father argued that still, our school kept her from achieving her absolute best!

In fact, the special education laws do not guarantee excellence. If it did, then anyone who did not get a full scholarship to Harvard could sue. Rather, it guarantees adequacy. You have to be able to succeed, not to exceed. Yet the hearing officer ignored this major point, which should have told us that we had an enormous problem. After the hearing closed, the hearing officer "suggested" to us and to our attorney that it might be helpful if we had a further briefing. Another briefing meant another day for our lawyer, costing us thousands more dollars, so we were now into this case for $20,000!

It's the Process, Stupid!

We got the decision after the first of the year. We lost on every count and it was all procedural—it never went to whether this kid should be on special ed! Instead, we lost on such weighty issues as the number of days notice we gave the family (which depended on how you counted up the days). The hearing officer absolutely refused to address the central question: does this child need special ed? And we received a bill from the hearing officer for $8,000 for the privilege of having her hear our case.

Thus, we faced the awful prospect of these terrible people coming back. We could actually have lost the school because this idiot kid and her father had this piece of paper saying they could hold us up for anything, claiming that anything violates the IEP, and this hearing officer might just give it to them.

If You Pay Them, They Will Go

Finally, at this point, we had our first good idea: to pay the student and her father to go away. It turns out payment was all they wanted in the first place.

We ended up buying a computer for them, paying for credits at the junior college, and paying the father some money for his time and trouble. It cost only $5,000. So now we know just to find out what they want in advance and accede to the blackmail, because the total process cost us $30,000. We could have paid SIX blackmails for that, and otherwise we could have lost our school. We could have been forced to focus all of our resources on this one child. As it was, it cost our school a teacher's wages. It hurt all of our students.

Look At Our Case

Look at our case. This is a case where the student had lost a due process hearing before in district school, had an unknown "disability," and was one of the best students in the school. It's a strong case for the school, and a weak one for the parent. If you can't win on that case, you can't win. The question is, should we appeal? What would you do?

HORROR STORY (WITH A HAPPY ENDING): "WHAT DO YOU WANT TO WORK WITH THOSE F—IN' N—S FOR?"

George Plunkitt, as told to Robert Maranto

Any charter school needs board members who can work with the local politicians, especially if the local political leaders are not exactly outstanding public servants.

Further, charter school teachers and parents should VOTE. If you doubt this, read on. This is a true story, with all names and certain details changed to protect the innocent and guilty. George Plunkitt is a retired white businessman serving on the board of Hope City Charter School (HCC), an overwhelmingly African American school in a small industrial town not in the south. In its three years, HCC has taken 10 percent of the Hope City School District's enrollment. With a waiting list three times its size, some feel that HCC would close down the district were the state to lift its enrollment cap. See how George handles a racist city councilman trying to keep HCC from building its new campus.

There are not many towns like Hope. The voters are 60 percent black, but the city is still run mainly by whites, who get votes with jobs. Since most of the factories closed, the best jobs are with the city and the county: police, firefighters, social workers, roads, and of course, the schools. In the old days you couldn't be a teacher without joining a political party, almost like the old Soviet Union. The party machines also got votes from public housing: "if you want in, you had better vote the right way or we'll kick your butt out of here."

The problem is the parties have not been very good to the black majority, or even the white minority. Our last school superintendent, who served for a long time, a white guy, was asked back in the 1980s when he was about to retire why the district fell so far downhill when he was running it. He said right there in the school board hearing "that's all because the blacks came to town." And except for one school board member, a black Republican, nobody minded that he said that!

Since that superintendent left in 1989 we've had two state interventions and six superintendents, all but one of them black and all but two of them pretty bad, mostly looking to pad their pensions before they retired. But you can understand why the black people here will give a black superintendent the benefit of the doubt, because after all, it's like with the Indians, the white man has screwed them pretty bad in the past. But they don't always realize that a black person can screw them just as bad, and they don't have any real way to hold them accountable.

There's no city paper anymore. There's no community groups. The white folks with money—except for the political whores—left for the suburbs, and the black folks are divided between the two political parties and two dozen churches. And a lot of them are political whores too. All the mayor and the school board care about is government jobs, patronage. There's no business community to speak of anymore, just the two political parties and one teachers' union, mainly white, whose members don't think black kids can learn and want only lots of paper in their contract. Our union is really good about what they can't do, no longer hours or longer school year, but not so good about what they can do for the kids.

There are still a few folks with money here in Hope, but whether they're black or white, they're Monday Catholics. They go to whatever church on Sunday, but Monday morning they drive their kids to Catholic school. Of course one good thing about Hope public schools is that Hope pays its teachers so badly compared to the neighboring districts, and our schools are so dangerous compared to the neighboring districts, that it's no longer political patronage to get a job as a teacher. Our public schools hire anybody willing to teach in Hope, no matter how bad they are.

The old political party patronage, mainly Democratic with the city and all Republican with the county, is for consultants on the high end and cafeteria workers and bus drivers on the low end, with construction in between. You can't hire or fire a janitor in the Hope City schools without going through the city or the county party chair! The Democrats and Republicans divide it up, and the feds and the state pay for most of it. And have we got beautiful school buildings and offices! You can look at those construction contracts and see where the money's going.

Anyway, five years ago when I was on the school board Juanita Johnson, a local black leader and a caterer by trade, asked me to help her start Hope City Charter School (HCC). She saw what the Hope public schools did to her daughter, who was an addict, and she didn't want that to happen to her grandson, who she was raising. It made sense to have me on the board because as a school activist Juanita had worked with me enough to know she could trust me, but I wasn't from her world. I knew big business, I could work with the local politicians, and also I'm white. Everybody else at HCC is black and I'm white. We're pretty backward here in Hope, so there's places in this town they can go where I can't go and places I can go where they can't go. I do pretty much all the talking with business people and city officials, and they do everything with the community. I told Juanita I'm afraid to go in her neighborhood after dark because as a white guy I would stick out, but she said, "Don't worry Georgie, nobody will hurt you because they'll think you're here to buy drugs."

We opened HCC in an abandoned building in the ghetto, which we barely got up to code, but two years later when we got the grant for the new building, we took an option to refurbish an old factory on the outskirts of town, in a very nice industrial park full of trees and grass, in a white neighborhood. You'd never think it was in Hope. So I put in all the paperwork in December, the minute we got the grant, and started looking for contractors to remodel the building. Meantime, there was no action on our permit. January went by. February went by. I talked to the mayor, and he promised me he wasn't the problem, but he wouldn't tell me who was. So I started going down to the city permit office every day, and finally a little bird told me that it was Councilman Rogers who was holding us up.

Well, I knew old Dickie Rogers since back when we were kids in the projects together, and we still lived just a couple blocks from the old neighborhood. While Dickie's not one of my favorite people, we can talk, so I went down to his home that Sunday to talk it out man–to-man. He was right there on his driveway pouring black sealant. So I came up and told him the situation and that we needed this new site for the kids since the old school was overcrowded and so we wouldn't lose the grant money. I asked him how exactly we could resolve this.

The first thing he said was "Hey, what do you want to work with those f— in' n—s for? We don't want their asses up in our place. Why don't you get your f—in' ass out of there?" And I said, "You talk just like some of our kids," which made him really furious. I never take things too seriously with people like that. I figure if you let someone talk long enough you'll find out what they want and if you cut them off you'll never find out. So I let him go on for a while, and finally I said, very calmly, "Dickie, you can only push this thing so much longer and I'll have to take corrective action against you. I'll have to file a suit against you and I'll burn your ass in court just based on what you said today, you f—in' piece of s—. Now you give me my permit, and let me go on about building my building." And he said, "Get the f— off my front lawn," and I said, "I can holler this from the curb or we can talk about this like gentlemen."

Old Dickie got the black sealant from the driveway all over his shirt and his pants and he was just yelling and screaming, and I was thinking that I always knew this guy was the biggest racist around, but he must have just lost it. The city council elections are at-large, so half this guy's voters were black! Dickie was yelling and turning red and he must have weighed 280 pounds, and I was thinking that this guy was going to have a heart attack right there and then.

And so finally I said, "Look, let's calm down and discuss this. There are good reasons for you to want our school here. Not all our kids have fathers, but they have got three hundred mothers and grandmothers who can vote. I've never looked it up before, so I don't know if they do vote, but from now on I will. I know that last time around you only won by two hundred votes, and it would be something awful if next time around we encouraged our people to vote, so if our school isn't up and running by Labor Day, two months before Election Day, we're going to find some reason to get your butt outta here."

And then he said, "Are you f—in' threatening me?" and I didn't say anything. I just told him I'd see him around.

Now that was Sunday. Monday I went downtown and got the permit, and we didn't have any more problems, and both the mayor and Councilman Rogers came to our open house the first day of school and had their pictures taken at our new building, and got their pictures in the county paper, so it was a good day all around.

HORROR STORY: DO NOT TRY THIS AT HOME, OR, WHY THE ED BUSINESS IS LIKE NO BUSINESS

Robert Maranto

This story is true, though all names and places and certain details are changed to protect the innocent and guilty. A sharp entrepreneur decided to open her state's first cyber charter, taking advantage of an obscure clause in the law. The business plan worked, but the legal/political plan—or non-plan—failed. An ambitious lawyer drummed up business by encouraging districts losing students to the charter to sue, delaying payments. Envious, the solicitor for the local school board which issued the charter convinced his unsophisticated board to rescind it! And he charged the board plenty for the resulting legal work. Finally, state regulators attacked, charging paper-work failings: the chief regulator later went to work for a cyber competitor.

The only lessons are that providing a good educational service is not enough: charters also need to cultivate friendships both on the sponsoring board and among state regulators.

Though a Harvard graduate, Melissa Lebowitz was an off-the-wall and highly successful entrepreneur. At thirty, she had already built and sold two companies, earning several million dollars. She thought of education as another business. You find a niche no one else fills. You come up with a quality product consumers want. You supply the goods and then you get paid. Seems simple. Alas, it's too simple to describe education, certainly in this state.

Melissa was to learn that what works in business does not work with the public's business, a realm of egos, interests, and lawyers!

Melissa realized early on, before anyone else, that our state's charter school law had a giant loophole that would permit cyber charters. The business model was perfect. Outfit a small office, do some training, buy curricula, hire special education coordinators, and hire experienced teachers who are retired or want to work at home to take care of their kids, and then market to the homeschool crowd. Without the bricks and mortar of a usual school, without the extracurricular activities, without the swimming pools and stadia, you can both provide a quality service and make a bundle, even after giving all the kids and teachers their own laptops and paying teachers top dollar. Your revenue comes from the student's public school districts of origin, which must send 70 percent of what they spend per child. With that, you can hardly fail to make a profit.

And anyway, the school districts should welcome you since they actually come out ahead. If a district spending $10,000 per child loses a hundred kids to your school, simple economics says they should be happy since while their costs are down one million, they only have to pay your school $700,000, leaving their school $300,000 in the black. And the kids likely to head for a charter, especially a cyber charter, are often children a conventional school is glad to lose: oddballs, kids who get bullied, Goths, and just plain smart kids.

Of course, the real world is a little more complicated than simple economics. (This reminds me of the joke that an economist is a man who would marry Jennifer Lopez for her money, or a woman who would marry Tom Cruise for his.) Fixed costs like buildings mean that schools with declining student populations in fact lose money to charter schools; only growing districts gain, by avoiding or delaying new building costs.

Still more important are the egos: all those district schools who ask how dare students take *our* money and send it to a different school, especially one in another part of the state. Do they think they're better than us?

Such is the background for a cyber charter perfect storm of personalities, politics, possible conflicts of interest, and ugly, ugly lawyers.

An Auspicious Start

It all started well enough. Shortly after the state charter law passed, millionaire entrepreneur Melissa Lebowitz persuaded a small, poor, rural school district in the southern mountains to charter. The Farmville School District (FSD) had lost its main employer, an old textile mill, and desperately needed revenue for its mediocre, seven-hundred-student, two-school system. In May, FSD chartered the Sky Cyber Charter (SCC), granting permission to enroll up to 10,000 students from all over the state, in return for 2 percent per child administrative fees, an amount that could supply up to 55 percent of district revenues.

The FSD school board, two retired factory workers, an old minister, a tavern owner, and a farmer, did not really understand what they were doing. Entering into a contract they did not understand, with a young entrepreneur from the big city, they were naturally susceptible to fears of being taken for a ride.

Still, things started well enough. Sky had a good business plan, and Melissa knew how to run a start-up. By July 1, over 1,200 students had signed up for the new charter school, the state's first cyber charter. SCC billed over three dozen "sender" school districts from all over the state for its students. Before gaining the charter, Melissa had hired an office staff, website designer, and curricula coordinators, and had purchased curricula software. Now, she and her staff were working sixteen-hour days to hire and train teachers, contract for laptops to be delivered by September 1, and develop a special education plan, along with hundreds of pages of paperwork.

Then, the Sky fell in.

The Empire Strikes Back: Its Lawyers Attack

Through July, the state school boards association began receiving disturbing reports. More than three dozen school systems around the state reported that some outfit "out in the sticks" was presenting bills to educate dozens, and in one case nearly a hundred, of their students! About half the students had previously been homeschooled or had been in private schools, which made the school districts doubly angry since they had not previously paid for these kids, nor cared about them.

All of this controversy inspired the solicitor for the state school boards association, Mike Wilson. He graciously offered the district which lost the most students to Sky to contest the cyber charter in state court, for only $5,000 up front and a small contingency fee. After all, the state charter school law had not specifically noted cyber charters, so who could say whether they were legal or not? (The law did say that services could be provided by the Internet, but said nothing more.) At the very least, this gave the school district an excuse to delay payment. Wilson approached another district and another and another, and soon more than twenty districts were suing Sky in twelve separate courts all over the state! Aside from taxing Sky's legal staff, this made Mike Wilson $40,000 richer—if he won the case his total take could top $1.2 million!

Within weeks, Wilson became a hero to school boards all over the state. The dominant state teachers union gave him an award at its fall conference, and from his skillful leaking, the newspaper in the state capital called him an advocate for children. In contrast, media reports of Sky were mixed. Some newspapers emphasized Sky's glowing reports from parents, but others focused on the contested nature of the charter, something made worse when Melissa, who had better things to do, treated the media with open irritation.

A Mayberry Machiavelli

All of this publicity gave the Farmville school district solicitor an idea. In our state, the part-time (but well-paid) solicitors usually know more about their schools than the part-time (and unpaid) school board members. Solicitors get paid by the hour for their "legal work." While Sky operator Melissa Lebowitz lived far from Farmville, FSD solicitor Wayne Duffer had lived there all his life, had (barely) graduated from a nearby third-tier law school, and he wasn't going anywhere. He started to resent the acclaim Mike Wilson got for taking on Sky. He started to wonder how Sky made FSD look. And anyway, what did he really know about Melissa? Once the charter was granted, she had not set foot in Farmville. Did Melissa think she was too good for the town that sponsored her so-called school? Maybe Wayne Duffer hadn't gone to some fancy Ivy League college, but he could show Melissa Lebowitz how they did things in Farmville.

Duffer started lobbying FSD board members, and at the second school board meeting of the year persuaded them to hold hearings to yank Sky's charter, on several grounds, the chief one being that Sky had failed to pay the district its administrative fees on time—a result of Mike Wilson's lawsuits. Duffer ran the hearings, and the initial ground rules did not allow Sky representatives to speak save to directly answer questions put to them, though Sky attorneys soon got this changed. Duffer kept track of the many hours he spent investigating Sky, and by the end of the year billed the district for more than $170,000, with another $90,000 for a lawyer he contracted to do much of the actual work.

Sky itself kept going, despite the funding freeze, which cost more than 60 percent of anticipated revenues, and spending more than $500 an hour for one of the state's top law firms. Sky had distributed desktops to all students by the end of November—these were leased, though, and the vendor was threatening legal actions against the parents and the school for back payments. Sky teachers taught their courses, the twenty-four-hour-a-day online help line worked well, and the reporting systems functioned. For their part the parents, most of whom feared sending their children to their local public schools and had very low expectations, did not complain. As a Sky teacher put it, "these people were either desperate because their kids were getting beaten up at school, or else they had been homeschoolers all along and did not expect much help and just appreciated whatever they got."

State Regulators Come to the Rescue—Not

Then came the third front of the perfect storm. The state sued Sky on account of special education deficiencies. Of course, all this led to press . . . BAD press, which in turn, led to fewer students. Melissa responded by yelling at her staff, the press, FSD representatives, and state regulators. Oddly enough, this did not help. As one employee put it, "Melissa thought that if you built a better mousetrap, the world would beat a path to your door. She didn't know that mice have lawyers and lobbyists."

Still, case by case, Sky kept winning in court. Eventually, in spring, the state supreme court ruled that Wilson had no standing to sue Sky: the donor districts had to pay up. Meanwhile, the state legislature passed a new law that fully legitimized cyber charter schools and made it easier for cyber charters to receive their funding. Yet that did not stop Wilson. He kept telling school districts that nothing had changed, though now his new suits were dismissed out of hand (he billed school districts for the extra work). Regarding the special education suit, the state admitted in court that many of its alleged "deficiencies" regarded such matters as not stapling together the certified mail receipts to the official parental notification—instead they were paper clipped. Court transcripts include the following:

> *Sky Lawyer:* Does any statute state that the documents must be stapled together?
> *State Bureaucrat:* No.
> *Sky Lawyer:* Does any state regulation require that the documents be stapled together?
> *State Bureaucrat:* Yes!
> *Sky Lawyer:* Really. Is that regulation written down?
> *State Bureaucrat:* No.
> *Sky Lawyer:* Who devised this *unwritten* regulation?
> *State Bureaucrat:* I did.
> *Sky Lawyer:* Did you inform the Sky Special Education coordinator of this unwritten regulation?
> *State Bureaucrat:* No.
> *Sky Lawyer:* Why not?
> *State Bureaucrat:* It was not my responsibility to inform her.
> *Sky Lawyer:* And yet this accounts for 14 of the 22 deficiencies you identified in 46 files sampled?
> *State Bureaucrat:* Yes.

Under questioning, the state bureaucrat admitted that no special education parents had complained about services provided by Sky. Indeed, only two Sky parents had complained about anything, and the state found these complaints groundless.

All the alleged "deficiencies" were generated by the state—not by the parents.

Still, bad press and problems at the school that could not be easily fixed because of funding, led to Sky hemorrhaging students, all the while spending more and more of its resources—ultimately over two million dollars—on legal proceedings. The good news was that through the courts, the state charter school law was rewritten to allow cyber charters like Sky. The bad news was that this took a terrific toll on Sky's staff, no one more than the boss. Finally, in May, Melissa threw in the towel, announcing that Sky would close after its first academic year.

At the end, Melissa became philosophical: "I lost a quarter million on this school, which is more than tuition at Harvard, but then I also learned more than at Harvard."

Postscript: After Sky won its court cases establishing the right of charter schools to exist, an administrator in the state education department who had led the state's special education actions against Sky left the government to join a new cyber charter with a program very similar to that used by Sky. The fact that she had used state power to kill off a potential competitor was not noted in the press.

21

He Said/He Said: A Debate about Charters

Mike Kayes and Robert Maranto

Here our two coeditors square off. Has the charter movement fulfilled its promises? Mike Kayes says no, and sees charters as paving the way for dismantling the public school system. Bob Maranto counters that charter schools make public schools public, and on the whole help kids. We debate. You decide.

BEWARE THE VOUCHER MONSTER
MIKE KAYES

Our previous findings and citations notwithstanding, it appears increasingly evident to at least one of our editors (*not* the Villanova academic!), that charter schools in general and the entire education reform agenda are being carefully co-opted to form the launching pad for public support of nonpublic schools. There is no argument that charter schools are indeed public schools and that is not at issue, here or hopefully elsewhere. But as the gild begins to fall from this potential lily and charter schools suffer the death of a thousand cuts, vouchers are readily emerging as the right's next best weapon to marshal in their internecine battle for tax dollars to support a religious agenda.

One need go no further than my home state of Arizona, long standing at the cutting edge of school choice. This past session of our state legislature actually had the hubris to attempt to pass voucher legislation that would impose no means test upon intended recipients. In addition, this bill, had it passed, would have provided, by far, the greatest financial benefit of all voucher plans in the United States ($3,500 grade school, $4,500 high school).

This bill was strongly promoted by an extreme right-wing element that has seized control of both legislative houses. So the Blaine Amendment, along with common sense, decency, and educational value be damned: it's "welfare for the wealthy" time—in Arizona—and coming soon to a place near you. I believe that the concept of charter schools has simply been used by those extremists to bide their time and ultimately exploit a mood change to promote their "real" agenda: vouchers for those parents whose children voluntarily attend nonpublic schools. The argument goes like this:

"Why should we pay taxes into the public schools if our kids don't benefit, since they attend a private or parochial school (at considerable additional expense to us, of course)?" There are many roads I don't travel but that are nonetheless supported by my taxes. Faith-based groups now receive government support even though I don't belong to any. There are even wars being waged that I don't support that, regardless of my lack of support, the government uses my taxes to finance. When did education become the single, solitary function of our democratic society that no longer qualifies for broad inclusion in the commonweal of public sustenance?

It probably needs to be qualified that voucher plans such as the one that withstood judicial review in Milwaukee may be efficacious, but only in the most limited of constructs. By this I mean that when all else fails AND for those most poor and disadvantaged, there may be a need, albeit and hopefully temporary in nature, to remove children from the source of the problem and substitute something else. I will not argue against such a limited premise but I don't believe that's what the Arizona legislature has in mind and I don't think they're alone. And the roiling charter movement is, perhaps unwittingly, complicit.

Founder flounder (that disease which increasingly afflicts ongoing charter operations), coupled with simply poor business practices and sometimes unscrupulous behavior, all threaten to reduce charter schools from the status of savior to one of mere mediocrity. Further compounding these ailments is the political infighting and downright pettiness that, more often than not, confuses an action agenda at the local, state, and even national levels. In other words, there's no clear voice, no central repository of wisdom and, in fact, little agreement about what is known (versus what is felt or just desired). Amazingly, what remains in the Washington, D.C. bureaucracy is the same old system of favoritism and cronyism, with a few new players, and this is quickly fed, in sieve-like repetition, to each of the states.

So we fight about process while ignoring product. Sound the least bit familiar? All too often lately, we hear from charter operators, teachers, and even parents who proclaim, "Well, we're at least as good as the public district counterpart!" My distinct recollection is that we're supposed to be better, and considerably so, better not in affective evaluation but better in educating students, as measured objectively. That kids may feel better about their schools or parents feel better about their teachers is nice and may certainly be helpful in promoting and upholding academic achievement, but these are means to an end. How soon we forget and how convenient to do so. The "charter bargain" has always been about finding ways to provide charter schools with regulatory relief in exchange for improved student performance. It's a simple deal but when student outcomes don't justify continued support, instead of folding we simply dissemble into the same old arguments we claim to detest from others.

As our founders flounder or simply abandon their creations, as charter schools become their own battleships, hard to navigate and even more difficult to turn, as those less motivated by the sheer joy of school reform are replaced by entrepreneurs (or worse) and the charter school movement descends into the mainstream of the public education establishment, religious fanatics see a vacuum developing. And, to turn a phrase, vouchers abhor a vacuum and so it's time to clean up.

By failing to fulfill the promise and the bargain, by refusing to uphold their end of the deal, charter schools have abdicated the high ground, if not all their moral authority. Of course, there are good charter schools and excellent overall systems (like KIPP). But these are increasingly few and far between and not nearly often enough punctuated by serious efforts to close less effective offerings. How many schools have actually been closed and, of that number, how many for failure to educate their students? We focus upon financial irresponsibility, fraud, administrative snafus, etc., while the regulators, by and large, are wont to apply rigorous academic performance standards. Could it be these regulators don't really have a clue what standards to apply or how to do so? And don't the regulators now form just another tent pin in the umbrella called charter schools, needing also to protect and preserve their turf and investments? Why does all this sound so familiar and why wasn't it easier to predict ten years ago?

It is therefore my view that students and parents seeking real reform in a system that rewards and promotes choice will be hard-pressed to find viable options within the growing number of ever-weakening charter schools. We have ceded ground to the next wave: vouchers. Beware.

HOW CHARTERS PUT THE PUBLIC IN PUBLIC SCHOOLS
ROBERT MARANTO

Despite school report cards and mandates like No Child Left Behind, most public schools still treat parents like mushrooms: feed them guano and keep them in the dark.

That occurred to me when I called the principal's office at a local public elementary school. Alas, despite spending $20,000 per child annually, this "public" school could not return three phone messages left during normal business hours over a two-week period. On my fourth try I reached a live person, which was recounted in the first chapter.

It took a mere five months and twenty-two phone calls, faxes, and e-mails to the superintendent (who admitted there was a problem and thought that someone should do something about it), the school board, the principal, and various other "public servants" to allow me to visit this "public" school. Someday, I hope to watch a class.

Safety being the last refuge of scoundrels, at one point an administrator explained that public schools can't let the public in because of 9/11. They had to protect the children. Yet for some reason, local charter schools have not been targeted by Al Qaeda!

Of course "security" does not explain why public schools keep parents out—at least not in affluent suburban school districts where an armed and dangerous mommy is as likely as Bigfoot. Instead, as local school officials admit privately, they fear parents because parents might want a special deal for their kids. But why might parents want a special deal for their kids unless their kids are not being served now? Or unless the son or daughter of the school board member or state senator is *already* getting a special deal? Indeed, there are now whole books about how to get a special deal for your kid—and presumably screw everyone else's kid.

The fact is, "our" "public" schools are not small communities based on face-to-face relationships and the common equality of all citizens, but large bureaucracies based on paperwork, procedures, and connections. Our high schools are huge, but even in a typical elementary school the principal oversees five hundred students, seven hundred or so parents and guardians, and ninety or more staff, and interacts with a dynamic network of public organizations from the central office to the school board members to the teachers' union to the mental health agencies to the police departments to the zoning boards. To give more time and attention to nonconnected parents and kids would take time away from those who really matter to one's advancement. Journalist Elinor Burkett, who originally hales from my township, estimates that the typical public school principal is responsible for implementing over 400,000 regulations. After all that paperwork, who has time for kids and parents? Better to distract them with bake sales so they don't cause trouble.

Aside from the pressures of paper come the perils of politics. As a society, we cannot agree on the *purposes* of public schools, nor the *methods* to achieve those purposes. Should schools stress academic achievement or extracurriculars? Learning or self-esteem? Order or freedom? And whatever schools teach, *how* should they teach it? With traditional methods or progressive ones? And who should get the most attention? The gifted? The at-risk? The jocks? The average muddle in the middle?[1] No one agrees! So better to keep parents and others out of the schools so they will not ask embarrassing questions, or heaven forbid, come up with ideas of their own. Similarly, regarding teachers, too often schools want to hire those of mediocre talent, who are less likely to ask questions and come up with ideas. (A friend of mine complained about having to act dumb to get a local teaching job!)

Both parents and teachers come to our public schools welcomed by a banner reading, "abandon your brains, all who enter here." Lest you think I exaggerate, ask your local principal or school superintendent if he or she can name one significant change in their school which came from a parent or teacher. Most can't.

But most charters are different in at least three key, mutually reinforcing respects. First, because parents and teachers *choose* a charter, they are more likely to *agree on its purposes*. This makes for less conflict, more trust, and stronger community. People are more willing to give the benefit of the doubt to something they have chosen. Further, there really is no one best way to do education. Kids (and teachers) who will fail in one setting will soar in another. Charter schooling realizes this basic fact, and lets parents find the environment that works best for their kids, rather than drugging their kids so they fit the environment provided.

Second, most charters are *small*, less than a quarter the size of a traditional public school. Small size means that politics are face to face rather than lawyer to lawyer, and this too promotes trust and lessens conflict. Parents are more willing to accept the bad news that Brandi failed math if they are on a first-name basis with the principal and teacher. In a typical charter, the principal knows all the kids and parents. In a traditional public school, that is not the case, and it makes all the difference.

Third, charters are *funded* by parental enrollment decisions. If a charter does not please its parents, it loses money. Alienate enough parents, and the school closes. District schools, in contrast, must please politically influential local notables who set funding levels—not ordinary parents. As one insider explained to me when I asked why I could not visit a local "public" school:

> It's very unlike a private school where the amount of money they get depends on the number of kids. Here the school gets the same amount of money whether the school has a lot of kids or a few kids, but everyone is happier if they have a smaller number of kids, so it's a whole different orientation. They don't really encourage parents to attend the school.

In real life, the Golden Rule states that he who has the gold makes the rules. In charter (and private) schools parents make the rules; in "public" schools administrators and the politically powerful make the rules. This basic difference means that charter (and private) schools embrace parents as partners, even those parents who lack lawyers and political connections. Frankly, that makes for better education since parents often have good ideas, and since parents typically know more about their own kids than teachers do. Objectively, by freezing parents out, public schools are harming our children.

As detailed in the chapters above, charter schools have greater teacher and parent satisfaction, and generally produce greater test score gains[2] than traditional public schools do, even while spending significantly less money. But all of these differences come from the three basic charter features: parental choice, small size, and choice-based funding.

There's one more thing. My friend Mike fears that charter schooling is just a prelude to vouchers, and the ultimate privatization of public schools. To that, let me answer with a new definition of "public school," which I borrow from Paul Peterson, John Brandl, Paul Hill, and others. A public school is one that serves the public. It could be a charter school, a private school, or a well-managed traditional public school. Such as the one my son now attends. I don't care what you call it, so long as it helps kids. Isn't helping the public's kids what a real public school is all about?

NOTES

1. Most traditional administrators see their role as serving the average child. The "losers" and "weird kids" can be expelled, ignored, or drugged into submission.

2. Charters usually have relatively low test scores because they enroll many children who did badly in traditional public schools. After all, if your kid excels in a traditional school, you are less likely to choose a charter. Notably, studies of test score *gains*—how much a child learns in one year of schooling—usually show charter schools outperforming district schools. Charters in business for three years or longer typically have particularly good records, but in aggregate studies charter performance is pulled down by first- and second-year charter schools.

About the Contributors

Kimberly Firetag Agam is senior research associate for policy analysis at the Teacher Advancement Program Foundation. Her work focuses on a wide range of local, state, and national programs and policies aimed at improving teacher quality. Ms. Agam monitors state and federal education policy, provides her expertise to states developing teacher quality initiatives, and assists with government relations. Ms. Agam earned a BA in public policy studies from Duke University and an MA in public policy from the University of Southern California.

Heath Brown is completing his doctorate in public policy at George Washington University.

John Buck is a principal of Buck Financial Advisors LLC.

Brian L. Carpenter is director of leadership development for the Mackinac Center for Public Policy, a research and educational institute headquartered in Midland, Michigan.

Rebecca Gau is a senior research analyst at the Morrison Institute for Public Policy, Arizona State University.

Bryan C. Hassel directs Public Impact, an education consulting firm. Dr. Hassel is coauthor of *Picky Parent Guide: Choose Your Child's School with Confidence* and author of *The Charter School Challenge: Avoiding the*

Pitfalls, Fulfilling the Promises (Washington, D.C.: Brookings Institution Press, 1999).

Jeffrey R. Henig is professor of political science and education at Teachers College, and professor of political science at Columbia University.

Frederick M. Hess is director of education policy studies and resident scholar at the American Enterprise Institute, as well as executive editor of *Education Next.* Dr. Hess is author or editor of numerous books, including *Spinning Wheels, Revolution at the Margins,* and *Common Sense School Reform.* A former public high school social studies teacher in Baton Rouge, Louisiana, he holds an MEd in teaching and curriculum, and an MA and PhD in government from Harvard University.

Thomas T. Holyoke is assistant professor of political science at Hastings College. He earned his PhD in political science at George Washington University.

Myron S. ("Mike" or "M. S.") Kayes was the first and only project director of the federally-funded National Charter School Clearinghouse (NCSC) and he provided editorial oversight for the *NCSC Review,* the journal that launched this volume. Mr. Kayes obtained permanent NYS teaching, as well as administrative, certification while attending SUNY–New Paltz. For over three decades he has honed his skills as a grant-writing and development professional. He runs The Center for Program Resources (a grant-writing and program-development consulting firm) and SCHOOLS, Inc. (a non-profit education reform and research organization). Presently, Mr. Kayes is employed as the director of development for an Arizona medical center as he begins to stress over school options and alternatives for Madeline, his three-year-old granddaughter.

Natalie Lacireno-Paquet is an assistant professor in the leadership in urban schools program at the University of Massachusetts. She received her PhD in public policy from George Washington University.

Louann Bierlein Palmer is an assistant professor at Western Michigan University. She received her EdD in Educational Leadership from Northern Arizona University.

April Gresham Maranto has taught social psychology at Furman University and Lafayette College. Her scholarly work on decision-making, psychology and law, and education reform has appeared in such publications as *Family Law Quarterly, Social Behavior and Psychology,* and *Phi Delta Kap-*

pan. She coedited (with Robert Maranto) *School Choice in the Real World: Lessons from Arizona Charter Schools.* She now runs, and cleans up after, three book groups, two children, and one husband. She received her PhD in social psychology from the University of Minnesota.

Robert Maranto is associate professor of political science and public administration at Villanova University, and an associate scholar at the Goldwater Institute (Phoenix) and the Commonwealth Foundation (Harrisburg). He has done extensive research on political appointees in government, civil service reform, and school reform. In concert with others, he has written or edited books including *Beyond a Government of Strangers: How Career Executives and Political Appointees Can Turn Conflict to Cooperation.* He serves under April, Tony (b. 1999), and Maya (b. 2004). He received his PhD in political science from the University of Minnesota.

Michael Podgursky is Middlebush Professor of Economics and department chairman at the University of Missouri in Columbia. The author wishes to acknowledge research support from the Smith-Richardson Foundation. The usual disclaimers apply.

Michael B. Poliakoff is a former Pennsylvania deputy secretary of education. Dr. Poliakoff holds a BA from Yale University and a BA Hon. Class I from Oxford University, as well as a PhD in classical studies from the University of Michigan.

Lewis C. Solmon is president of Teacher Advancement Program Foundation, which focuses on improving teacher quality. From 1985 to 1991 Dr. Solmon served as dean of UCLA's graduate school of education. He was the founding president of the Milken Institute from 1991 to 1997, and executive vice president at the Milken Family Foundation from 1997 to 2005. He currently is on the boards of the Center for Education Reform and the National Council on Teacher Quality. Dr. Solmon has served on the board of trustees of four independent schools in the Los Angeles area and of BASIS charter schools in Tucson and Phoenix, Arizona. He received his bachelor's degree from the University of Toronto and his PhD from the University of Chicago, both in economics. He has served on the faculties of UCLA, CUNY, and Purdue, and currently is a professor emeritus at UCLA.

Jim Spencer is currently president of Montessori Charter School of Flagstaff, Inc., a position that he has held since 1995 when the school became the first to have its application for a charter approved by the Arizona State Board for Charter Schools. Mr. Spencer is a former Marine Corps officer (having served on active duty from 1969 until 1975) and has worked for Fluor Corporation,

Standard Oil, and British Petroleum in a number of managerial and executive positions. He holds degrees from the U.S. Naval Academy, the University of Southern California, and the Harvard Business School.

Heather Zavadsky is project director of national studies at the National Center for Educational Accountability. Dr. Zavadsky completed her contributed chapter while working at the University Charter School and Continuing and Extended Education at the University of Texas in Austin. She holds a PhD in educational policy and planning and an MEd in education administration from the University of Texas in Austin, as well as an MEd in special education from the University of Southwest Texas. Dr. Zavadsky holds superintendency, principal, special education, emotional disturbances and autism, and elementary education certifications.

Liane Zimny has been charter schools coordinator for the Oakland Unified School District (OUSD) since 2001. Ms. Zimny first gained experience with charter schools and educational reform as staff director to Mayor Jerry Brown's Commission on Education and as a consultant to Oakland's New Small Autonomous Schools Initiative. She is a master's candidate in the Leadership for Educational Entrepreneurs Program offered by Arizona State University.